SANDRA DJWA is a member of the Department of English at Simon Fraser University, Burnaby, BC, and the author of *E.J. Pratt: The Evolutionary Vision*.

Saul and Selected Poems is an original and useful introduction to the work and poetic personality of Charles Heavysege (1816-76), an important but currently neglected nineteenth-century Canadian writer. Heavysege was handicapped by a limited education and a lack of public support, yet nonetheless established himself in Great Britain and America as the 'leading intellect of [the] Dominion' in a period when native literature was scantily regarded. His struggle to express himself and to find an audience for his work mirrors the dilemma of the émigré writer of his time.

Heavysege's work is related in this volume to the early nineteenth-century English revival of poetic drama, and seen in the context of the Canadian cultural milieu of the 1860s. *Saul* is a powerful presentation of the tormented soul caught in a world of order and universal degree. Its main interest is to be found in its psychological frankness — Saul's recognition of his demon resonates with the deeper implication of the recognition of the *döppelgänger* — and in passages of sinewy verse written with a directness that anticipates E.J. Pratt.

The texts of *Saul* and 'Jezebel,' selections from *Jephthah's Daughter*, an original commentary on the major poems, a bibliography, and a review of Heavysege criticism are all included in this volume. (Literature of Canada 19)

Literature of Canada

Poetry and Prose in Reprint

Douglas Lochhead, General Editor

Saul and Selected Poems

including excerpts from *Jephthah's Daughter*
and *Jezebel: A Poem in Three Cantos*

Charles Heavysege

Introduction by Sandra Djwa

UNIVERSITY OF TORONTO PRESS
TORONTO AND BUFFALO

© University of Toronto Press 1976
Toronto and Buffalo
Reprinted in paperback 2017
ISBN 978-0-8020-2175-5 (cloth)
ISBN 978-0-8020-6262-8 (paper)

Library of Congress Cataloging in Publication Data

Heavysege, Charles, 1816-1876.
    Saul and selected poems.

    (Literature of Canada; 19)
    Bibliography: p.
    1. Title.
    PR9199.2.H4S2   1976   811'.3   76-17038
    ISBN 978-0-8020-2175-5 (bound) ISBN 978-0-8020-6262-8 (pbk.)

This book has been published with the assistance of grants from the Ontario Arts Council and the McLean Foundation.

Saul was originally published in 1857 by Henry Rose, Montreal. The second edition of 1859, published by John Lovell, Montreal, has been used for this reprint. *Jephthah's Daughter* was originally published in 1865 by Dawson Brothers, Montreal. *Jezebel: A Poem in Three Cantos* was originally published in January 1868 by the *New Dominion Monthly*, I, 4, pp 224-31.

Preface

Yes, there is a Canadian literature. It does exist. Part of the evidence to support these statements is presented in the form of reprints of the poetry and prose of the authors included in this series. Much of this literature has been long out of print. If the country's culture and traditions are to be sampled and measured, both in terms of past and present-day conditions, then the major works of both our well-known and our lesser-known writers should be available for all to buy and read. The Literature of Canada series aims to meet this need. It shares with its companion series, The Social History of Canada, the purpose of making the documents of the country's heritage accessible to an increasingly large national and international public, a public which is anxious to acquaint itself with Canadian literature – the writing itself – and also to become intimate with the times in which it grew.

DL

Contents

Introduction ix
Notes xliii
Acknowledgements xlviii
Bibliography xlix
Review of Heavysege Criticism lii
Saul 1
Jephthah's Daughter (excerpts) 329
Jezebel: A Poem in Three Cantos 337
Sonnets Reprinted from the Selection
Contained in *Jephthah's Daughter* 369

Charles Heavysege, 1816-76

Sandra Djwa

Introduction

When approaching the poetry of Charles Heavysege, we may share the apprehension of Solly Bridgetower, the fictional critic of Robertson Davies's *Leaven of Malice*. But the study of mid-nineteenth-century Canadian letters has its charms, not the least of which is Heavysege, an irrepressible creative spirit whose works reflect the literary flavour of an age. His *Saul* (1857), based on the biblical account of the tragic fall of the first king of Israel, is undeniably a curious mixture of the 'tragical-comical-historical.' A closet drama influenced by the early nineteenth-century Elizabethan revival, it shares all the excesses of the genre: the combining of the high and the low style, melodrama, archaic diction, and the regular insertion of long poetic set pieces. As Davies's satire indicates, *Paradise Lost* provides Heavysege with a cosmology and *Saul* is a stylized, but vigorous, interpretation of the debate between good and evil.[1] The demons, subject to the many arts of sinking, provide some of the most disarmingly amusing interludes of the play.

What Davies overlooks, however, is the fact that *Saul* is effective closet tragedy, that it developed from a highly unpromising literary climate and that Heavysege in 1860 was a major North American dramatist. Heavysege, whose gift was minor but genuine, was handicapped by a limited education and by public indifference; nonetheless he established himself in Great Britain and America as the 'leading intellect of [the] Dominion'[2] during a period when native literature was scantily regarded. Writing in 1870, George Stewart, editor of *Stewart's Quarterly* (1867-72), commented caustically that if the poet laureate of England should take up residence in Canada intending to make a living from poetry, he could expect a diet of salt water and gaspereaux:

> The provinces have been but poor fields hitherto for men of letters. ... The strong and deep-rooted apathy evinced by the public towards books of Canadian origin is not only very wrong, but pernicious to the country.[3]

In Heavysege's struggle to express himself and to find an audience for his work, we see mirrored the dilemma of the nineteenth-century émigré writer whose literary terms of reference remained basically English even when his place of residence had changed to that of the Canadian colony; a colony which, in turn, encouraged such loyalty by giving its primary allegiance to British traditions and British literature long after it had become a Dominion in name. This attitude is clearly present in an 'Alumni Oration: The Beginnings of a Canadian Literature' given by Charles G.D. Roberts at Fredericton in 1883: 'Now it must be remembered that the whole heritage of English Song is ours and that it is *not* ours to found a *new* literature.'[4]

Despite lapses, *Saul* is effective closet tragedy in the early nineteenth-century English tradition. It portrays powerfully the predicament of the tormented soul in a world of order and universal degree, a world governed, as it was to the Elizabethans, by the Old Testament God. When Saul, like Prometheus, rejects this order, he takes on the attributes of the Romantic hero. Ultimately, however, Heavysege views Saul's offence as Shakespeare did that of Macbeth, as an offence against degree. The eloquence of the drama develops from Saul's questioning of the moral order (a questioning suggestive of Byron's Lucifer from

Cain, 1821) and from the tragic spectacle of Saul's fall into destruction. As suggested by Coventry Patmore's favourable unsigned review, 'The Modern British Drama,' the implications of Saul's fall from grace and its relation to dramatic structure were more easily understood by the Victorians. Patmore's article, published in the influential *North British Review* (August 1858), was to establish Heavysege as a Canadian dramatist of some substance and *Saul* as 'indubitably one of the most remarkable English poems ever written out of Great Britain.'

> There are two things ... which [Heavysege] proves that he knows, namely, the Bible and human nature; and a poet cannot be said to be really uneducated who knows these well. Shakespeare he also knows far better than most men know him; for he has discerned and adopted his method as no other dramatist has done. He takes not virtue and morality, and their opposites *generally*, as other dramatists do, but these under the single aspect of their dependence upon spiritual influences. ... Like most of Shakespeare's plays, this drama has the appearance of being strangely chaotic. There are hundreds of passages for the existence of which we cannot account, until the moral clue is found, and it would never be found by a careless and unreflecting reader; for the work is exceedingly artistic.

Saul's tragedy is that of spiritual pride: 'Faith lacking, all his works fell short.' It is this 'moral clue' of the Luciferean sin of disobedience and its punishment, which, as Patmore justly observes, unites the disparate sections of the drama.

The attempt to place the Romantic rebel within the traditional religious cosmos, in effect justifying the ways of God to man, was undoubtedly a reflection of Heavysege's early training. Born in Huddersfield, Yorkshire,[5] in 1816 to a family of reduced means, he worked from the age of nine, for ten to thirteen hours daily. In response to a letter from the American writer, Charles Lanman, who was preparing an article on his work, Heavysege wrote:

> I was what is usually styled religiously brought up, and, though my works are dramatic, taught to consider not only the theatre itself, but dramatic literature, even in its best examples, as forbidden things. Hence, when a boy, it was only by dint of great persuasion that I covertly obtained from my mother some few pence weekly for a cheap edition of Shakespeare that was then being issued in parts.[6]

Some years later, he requested Lanman not to make reference to any family 'narrowness of circumstances' claiming that his father had been heir 'to a patrimony which, from a romantic idea of justice, he, on coming of age, sold, and divided the proceeds amongst his relatives.' In addition, his maternal grandfather had 'wasted a small fortune in the indulgence of a too gay and hospitable disposition, which eventually brought him to end his days in an inferior position.'[7]

Heavysege became an apprentice woodcarver and eventually established his own business in Liverpool, employing several men. But, in the words of a contemporary journalist. having 'neither that tact nor business faculty necessary to compete successfully with the world,'[8] he emigrated to Canada, ten years after his marriage to Mary Ann Oddy in 1843. In Montreal, he initially worked as a journeyman carver for the firm of J. and H. Hilton, cabinetmakers and upholsterers. The American critic, Bayard

Taylor, recalled meeting him in 1860, possibly at the Grand Trunk workshops:[9]

> Here, amid the noise of hammers, saws, and rasps, in a great grimy hall smelling of oil and iron-dust, we found the poet at his work-bench. A small, slender man, with a thin, sensitive face, bright blonde hair, and eyes of that peculiar blue which burns warm, instead of cold, under excitement...[10]

Later that year, Heavysege became a reporter for the Montreal *Transcript* and eventually joined the staff of the Montreal *Daily Witness*. His sixteen years in newspaper journalism were interrupted only by a brief return to woodcarving, during which time he wrote *Jephthah's Daughter*.[11] While his decision to work as a journalist might have been made in the hopes of better providing for his wife and large family, it was considered unwise by at least one of his contemporaries, the poet John Reade: 'I never saw him spending his intellectual strength in that way without feeling how lamentable his choice had been.'[12] Heavysege had been in the habit of composing while working at his woodcarving bench; the close relationship between the subjects of his verse and his woodcarving is reflected in a granddaughter's memories of an ornately carved living room table 'covered with most grotesque gargoyle heads – devils, etc.'[13] But in Victorian Canada, newspaper work was considered 'genteel' and the manual labour of woodworking was not. Heavysege was later to regret his concessions to necessity and gentility; he wrote to Lanman: 'You will know that to be the reporter and local editor of a daily newspaper does not permit of the seizing of those inspired moods, which come we know not how, and leave us we know not wherefore.'

As the awkward circumlocution of the last sentence and occasional lapses of grammar and syntax in *Saul* might indicate, Heavysege was a self-taught man. The Reverend A.M. Dawson, addressing the French Canadian Literary Institute of Ottawa on 'The Poets of Canada' (1868), observed: 'His success is all the more wonderful that his educational advantages were very limited,' and ascribed his poetic gift to 'assiduous self-culture.'[14] Dawson was echoing Bayard Taylor's 'The Author Of Saul,' published in the *Atlantic Monthly* (October 1865). Taylor's article, together with Patmore's review, was to establish Heavysege as the major poet of the Dominion. The *Atlantic Monthly* review also provides additional information on the poet's early literary interests:

> Milton seems to have been the first author which made a profound impression upon his mind; but it is also reported that the schoolmaster once indignantly snatched Gray's 'Elegy' from his hand, because he so frequently selected that poem for his reading lesson. Somewhat later, he saw 'Macbeth' performed, and was immediately seized with the ambition to become an actor.

Macbeth, Milton, and Gray's *Elegy* (with its reference to the rural 'mute, inglorious Milton'), combined within a basically moral framework to shape Heavysege's poetic; indeed, much of his verse can be accommodated by the three-tiered cosmology of the Bible and *Paradise Lost*. As his father disapproved of drama, it is not surprising that his first literary attempt was *The Revolt of Tartarus* (1852), a religious epic in the manner of *Paradise Lost*. But the young man who attended the public theatres and who once wanted to become an actor had absorbed the prevailing

Romantic spirit. Within the carefully orthodox Miltonic cosmology of *The Revolt of Tartarus* as within the biblical narratives of *Saul* (1859) and *Jephthah's Daughter* (1865), we find strong assertions of Romantic individualism and concomitant religious doubt. Externally, especially in *Saul* and *Count Filippo* (1860), Heavysege is writing the pseudo-Shakespearian drama of the early nineteenth-century revival; internally, especially in his depiction of Saul and Jephthah's daughter, he is moving towards the modern psychological study, that reversal of Aristotle's categories described by Robert Browning in his preface to *Strafford* (1837) as 'Action in Character rather than Character in Action.' The existence of both strains — particularly the new Romantic subjectivity within the old dramatic form — is characteristic of the drama of the 1820s, especially of Byron's *Cain*.

At the start of the nineteenth century, the popular English stage was dominated by melodrama and burletta; as a result, many serious writers abandoned the stage in favour of the closet, believing that the only hope for a renewal of serious drama lay in the medium of poetry. Turning back to the golden age of English drama, playwrights such as Thomas Beddoes revived the poetry and diction of the seventeenth century. But when playwright turns poet to write for the closet, objectivity, brevity, and dramatic speech are disregarded in favour of subjectivity, prolixity, and 'poetic' effect. These defects, reflected in Heavysege's work, were integral to the dramatic tradition he inherited. He would have attended the English theatre in the late 1830s and throughout the 40s when the Romantic revival of heroic drama drew from the continental tradition, from Shakespeare, and from the Bible. Byron's interest in the biblical character, first manifested in the slight poems 'Saul' and 'Jephthah's Daughter' of

Hebrew Melodies (1814), culminated in *Cain* and *Heaven and Earth* (1821). Heavysege knew *Cain* well and at least one of the *Hebrew Melodies*; 'The Destruction of Sennacherib' underlies two fine extended passages in *Saul* (I.i.8). The continental tradition was largely represented by the Italianate revenge tragedy, from which Shelley's *The Cenci* (1819) is derived. Byron wrote *Cain* and *The Two Foscari* (1821) in emulation of the Italian dramatist Vittorio Alfieri, then generally considered one of the most impressive of the continental dramatists. The plays of Alfieri, including *Filippo, Saul,* and *Antigone* had been translated by Charles Lloyd and enjoyed a wide reception when published in England in 1815.[15] By 1820, then, Alfieri had become a significant factor in the English revival of heroic drama.

There are two versions of Heavysege's first dramatic poem, *The Revolt of Tartarus*, a six-book epic in blank verse. The first version, bearing his name, was published in London and Liverpool in 1852; the second, considerably edited, appeared anonymously in Montreal in 1855.[16] This poem prefigures much of Heavysege's subsequent verse as the character of the poem's protagonist, the rebellious Satan, draws from the Satan of Milton's *Paradise Lost* and from the Lucifer of Byron's *Cain*. The initial impulse for the poem is found in Books One and Two of *Paradise Lost*, in particular, the characterization of the fallen angels at the 'great consult' and the description of the infernal games. Heavysege's adaptation, however, is a sequel to *Paradise Lost* as Satan has already caused the downfall of the first Adam and Eve. Punished by God and seeking revenge, Satan journeys through the upper galaxies in search of new Edens to conquer. The description of his flight through space draws heavily on Milton and also on Byron's description of the flight of Lucifer and Cain. But although *The*

Revolt of Tartarus does present the Romantic Promethean rebel, Heavysege does not carry to full tragic intensity Byron's assertion of a capricious God functioning in a Manichean universe. The claim of Heavysege's Satan that evil holds equal power with God is recognized as a transparent fiction, even by those new Adams whom he tempts to disobedience. Heavysege describes Satan grotesquely attempting the sexual temptation of Eve as 'harlot-like, rubb[ing] in / The glory of the morn upon his cheek.' The gigantic rebel of Shelley and Byron becomes here a lesser being, a palpable sinner. Because Heavysege's conventional morality lessens his characterization of evil, and in fact caricatures it, its possible dramatic power is lost; there can be no real conflict between the Old Testament God and Heavysege's Satan. The latter's reinstatement as ruler of Hades at the end of the narrative, thematically significant as a justification of the ways of God to man, is in dramatic terms a crudely managed *deus ex machina*. Heavysege, who begins this epic with the Romantic assertion that he will sing the fate of the fallen angels, is, in fact, affirming his own faith in Christian obedience and a political hierarchy.

This paradigm is consistent throughout Heavysege's work. His protagonists, somewhat in the manner of the nineteenth-century dramatist, Joanna Baillie, are presented as ruled by a dominant passion: Saul is overly proud, Jephthah is rash, Jezebel is concupiscent. These Romantic rebels are placed, however, within the old Shakespearian world of order and universal degree. As might be expected, the dramatic action cracks under the strain as two opposite views of the position of the individual in the universe are contrasted. Although Heavysege presents the new hero, because his allegiance is ultimately with the old order his successive protagonists (Satan, Saul, Hylas, and Volina of *Count Filippo*, Jephthah, Jezebel, and the advocate of the novel of the same name) are ultimately reduced to a common fundamentalist denominator — that of sinner. This bald morality would be distasteful to contemporary readers were it not for the general truth of his psychological portraits, for the flashes of genuine poetry and for the interest of the imaginative processes which his works reveal.

Although *The Revolt of Tartarus* focuses on Satan's attempt at revenge upon God through the temptation of man, one of the curiosities of the narrative is the way in which the discussion of the problem of evil is extended into the secondary action. Satan's flight to the new Eden of the upper worlds is framed by an account of a revolt taking place in Tartarus during his absence. Heavysege reveals his essential conservatism in his description of this revolt. There are suggestions that the uprising is to be seen as a desire for individual liberty and freedom culminating in the deposing of Satan, the rightfully appointed King of Hades. The subsequent 'holiday' proclaimed on the election of a new government has analogies with the fourth of July holiday of the American Revolution or the Bastille Day of the French. The satanic individualism which led to Lucifer's rebellion against God in Heaven finds its political parallel in this expression of republicanism in Tartarus. It is not surprising that Heavysege elected to emigrate to Canada rather than to the United States shortly after completing the poem.

The primary source of Heavysege's major work, the drama *Saul*, is the biblical account of the rise of Saul, his disobedience of God's commands and the subsequent anointing of David (1 Samuel 8). Drawing again on Byron's Lucifer, Heavysege provides the familiar Romantic justification, the cruel Jehovah, for Saul's spiritual rebellion. Saul's rebellion is further mitigated by the secondary theme of the political conflict of king and priest, an interpretation of biblical history consistent with nineteenth-century thought[17] and also found in Alfieri's *Saul*. By providing two rationales for Saul's rebellion, Heavysege presents him as the 'noble villain' of Romantic heroic tragedy, yet in dramatic context both justifications are undercut. Politically, it is demonstrated that the fabric of society falls apart when the king disobeys God; spiritually, Saul's revolt is categorized as Luciferean. As we saw in *The Revolt of Tartarus*, in this depiction of a hierarchical society Heavysege reflects not only his British conservatism but also the values of Victorian Canada. The reworking of the text of *Saul* became one of Heavysege's main preoccupations and he published three versions of the drama;[18] the second and best edition is reprinted here.

In his introduction to *Saul*, Heavysege refers to the 'heroic qualities' of Saul and the 'picturesque grandeur' of his descent: 'How are the mighty fallen!' This view of Saul as the tragic hero of a biblical drama demands the elevated style, and it is to *Macbeth* that Heavysege turns for an initial portrait of the great but not good man who falls inevitably into evil. The dramatic action of *Saul* frequently parallels that of *Macbeth*. Saul, leaving to massacre the Amalekites, is described in terms reminiscent of Macbeth before the killing of Duncan; Saul's vision of the phantom of David, crowned, telescopes Macbeth's vision of the ghost of Banquo and the line of Banquo's issue; similarly, the demons and the Witch of Endor of *Saul* perform the same supernatural function as the three witches of *Macbeth*. The following passage in which Saul calls upon the spirits of the air is typical of such adaptations:

Ye punishing ministers,
Ye dark, invisible demons that do fly
And do heaven's judgments ... (I.i.5)

More interesting than such parallels are those occasions when a differentiation is made between the characters of Saul and Macbeth. Saul, unlike Macbeth, is full of spiritual pride. Macbeth, overhearing the grooms of the murdered Duncan talk in their sleep, regrets he could not say 'Amen'; Saul, hearing in David's song a request for God's grace reacts angrily: 'What have I done deserved the loss of grace? / I cannot say "amen".'

Further details of *Saul*, especially the characterization of Michal, David's brave and passionate wife, and an excessive use of the clumsy 'sacerdotal' (for 'priestly'), indicate that Heavysege was indebted to Charles Lloyd's translation of Alfieri's *Saul*. In Alfieri's drama, Saul's general, Abner, is the symbolic embodiment of his 'evil spirit,' a function here served by Malzah. But whereas Alfieri had preserved the unities by compressing the whole action of *Saul* into the final battle scene, Heavysege adopted the more sprawling Shakespearian style. Following the biblical chronicle, he was able to develop the alteration in Saul's character over an extended period of time.

To illustrate Heavysege's narrative technique and indicate his characteristic sensibility, a comparison can be made between the biblical account of the killing of Agag (1 Samuel 15:32) and that described in *Saul* (I.iv.6). Faithfully reproduced is the fury of the biblical Samuel as contrasted with the figure of Agag, the enemy king, stepping forth 'delicately' to remark: 'Surely the bitterness of death is passed.' But the whole passage is climaxed by Heavysege with a vigorous depiction of the mutilated corpse of Agag:

> Listen how
> The ground, after the soaking draught of blood,
> Smacks its brown lips. It seems to like royal wine
> Beyond small-beer leaking from beggar's veins. (IV.vi.6)

In the gusto of this and following passages, as in the clearly sexual references of *Count Filippo*, we find a sensibility frankly at odds with the elevated subjects and the mannered confines of the closet drama. But it is precisely this jarring combination of the sacred and the boisterously crude that characterizes Heavysege's poetic sensibility.

In *The Revolt of Tartarus*, Heavysege was grappling rather clumsily with the problem of evil, characterizing it as Luciferean pride, willful disobedience, and lechery; he returns to this subject in a much more interesting fashion in *Saul*, approaching George Meredith's position in *Modern Love* that a man's tragedy is determined by individual psychology and mutual wrong. Ostensibly, *Saul* retains the old Miltonic panoply of which Malzah, the Evil Spirit from the Lord, was especially admired by Heavysege's Victorian readers. It seems clear that Heavysege originally intended Malzah, an improbable Puck-Ariel-Caliban, to embody good and evil and to function as the agent of both God and Demon. Consequently, Malzah is made to regret his initially self-imposed, later God-ordained task of tormenting Saul: he confesses it 'unfiends' him. Despite such comic lapses, various details of the play do coalesce to suggest that Malzah is more a projection of Saul's own evil than an external agent: 'He struck at David, and said 'twas I,' laughs Malzah (II.iii.2). Furthermore, the garden scene in which the maddened Saul first recognizes his demon resonates with the deeper psychological implications of the recognition of the *doppelgänger* (II.iii.4). In this context, Malzah and the other demons come to represent that 'latent treachery in us all,' which Saul, after witnessing the massacre of the Amalekites, recognizes as an essential part of much human nature:

> ...the broad multitude know nought of judgment.
> Revenge, with them, was at the bottom of it;
> Whilst sensuality rose to the top like scum.
> Revenge is hunger of the mind, and hunger
> Makes all things cruel; — yet the wolf not sports with,
> But rends his victim, and his sharp head plunges
> At once into its bowels. Oh, 'twas foul
> Behaviour! — but I fear that most of men,
> If they were licensed by divine decree,
> Would change to demons, and for aught be ready. (I.iv.6)

Despite inversion and archaism, the cumulative effect of this passage is powerful. The striking image of the 'natural' wolf (to be preferred to human duplicity) and the masculine argumentative tone of the passage is not to be found again in Canadian poetry until E.J. Pratt's *Brébeuf and His Brethren* (1940). This vigorous tone sharply distinguishes Heavysege's verse from much of the vague Romanticism of his contemporaries as found in Charles Sangster's *The St Lawrence and the Saguenay* (1856) and Charles Mair's *Dreamland and Other Poems* (1868). Although Heavysege's poetic style is basically rhetorical, it is a rhetoric infused with psychological insight which can sometimes move towards the flexibility of plain speech — Saul's 'Revenge is hunger of the mind, and hunger / Makes all things cruel' — or the shrewd analysis of Saul's position immediately after he has been anointed by Samuel – 'Fitness always / Knows whether it be worthy, though it knows / Not whether 'twill be chosen' (I.1.4). It is quite possible that it was this combination of direct speech and psychological insight which led Nathaniel Hawthorne, then United States Consul at Liverpool, to commend *Saul* to Coventry Patmore, the British poet and critic.

The first scene of *Saul*, although prolix, is dramatically effective; it provides a supernatural framework, introduces the main characters, and establishes the dominant theme: the struggle between good and evil. The play opens with a group of demons dancing on the Hill of the Lord. When Saul enters with the Prophets, the songs and prayers of the Israelites are effectively juxtaposed with the shouts and laughter of the demons:

> Mocketh all things the Creator,
> Mocketh his whole realm of nature;
> Think not sons of earth he'll spare,
> Who smote the nobler things of air. (I.i.1)

This doctrine, spoken by the demons, is suggestive of Byron's *Cain*; furthermore, the supernatural framework invokes *Macbeth* by way of the 'All Hails' of the opening scene from *Cain*. By juxtaposing Israelite and demon, Heavysege introduces the two contrasting motifs of the drama: the first, the tyrannical omnipotent God, a view presented by the demons and later to be echoed by Saul, and the second, the Old Testament God, stern, slow to action, but ultimately just, the view held by the Prophets and by David.

Saul's character is developed to indicate a growing *hubris* which ultimately becomes satanic. When told that God is displeased with the Israelites for choosing a king, his reaction is an echo of the biblical Cain's response when God rejects his offering (Genesis 4:5.6). Saul early admits his own 'proud imagination ... rash impatience,' and it is these Cain-like qualities that precipitate his first impiety when he usurps the function of the priest Samuel and offers the sacrifice at Gilgah:

> 'Tis not the sacrificer but the victim;
> 'Tis not the hand, but 'tis the heart God looks at. (I.ii.7)

Saul's justification of his action recalls Byron's *Cain*: 'Evil and good are things in their own essence, / And not made good or evil by the giver' (II.ii). A sentiment similar to both passages is expressed in Milton's *Comus*: 'None / But such as are good men can give good gifts' (702-3). We may assume that both references and their satanic implications would be recognized by Heavysege's educated readers. Significantly, Saul again verges on Lucifer's position after the slaughter of the Amalekites when he attempts to stifle words 'as would appall the reverent ear of men, / And make me seem, even what I fear I am, / The Omnipotent's accuser' (I.iv.3). Finally, cast off by God and maddened by demon possession, Heavysege's Saul speaks as Byron's Lucifer.

ABNER
Jehovah's ways are dark.
SAUL
If they be just, I care not.
I can endure till death relieve me, — ay,
And not complain; but doubt enfeebles me,
And my strong heart, that gladdeth to endure,
Falters 'neath its misgivings, and, vexed, beats

> Into the speed of fever, when it thinks
> That the Almighty greater is than good.
> > ABNER
> Beware how thou dost charge Him who hath made thee! (II.ii.3)

The doctrine of Byron's Lucifer is clearly present here:

> Souls who dare look the Omnipotent tyrant in
> His everlasting face, and tell him that
> His evil is not good! (*Cain*, I.i)

However, as Abner's speech indicates, this doctrine, in the context of the play, is contained and thereby controlled by the Christian argument.

Consequently, it is difficult to accept fully T.R. Dale's contention that Saul is Heavysege's spokesman and that the drama is blasphemous: 'a potentially dangerous and explosive work' in its view that 'the Jehovah of the Old Testament historical books is an unmerciful tyrant.'[19] As we have seen, Saul is eloquently rebellious in the key scenes of the play, but as his arguments are specifically identified as Lucifer's and imbedded within a Christian matrix, the play as a whole (especially the justification of David) refutes Byron's concept of the malignant God. Certainly Heavysege's contemporaries interpreted *Saul* in this manner; we find among the literary essays of Andrew J. Ramsay (*One Quiet Day*, 1873) the following capsule description: 'Original and alone in style: untrammelled in imagination, and bold as Byron's "Cain" without Cain's blasphemy and deepening cloud of doubt.'[20] This point is worth stressing because much contemporary criticism of Heavysege builds on T.R. Dale's arguments;

Dale's contention that *Saul* could not be acted and his thesis that 'Heavysege was really ... on the side of the devils,'[21] seems to underlie Robertson Davies's satire while Northrop Frye's subsequent analysis of *Jephthah's Daughter* appears to develop some aspects of Dale's concept of the cruel Jehovah as summarized in the latter's article in the *University of Toronto Quarterly* (October 1952).

As in much closet tragedy, the dramatic action of *Saul* is too slight for the expanded form; Part One, describing the rise of Saul, is well-paced; but Part Two, chronicling David's rise and Saul's corresponding decline, is padded; and Part Three, detailing a series of confrontations between the two, drags interminably, except for the climactic scene in which Saul consults the Witch of Endor. Interestingly, an adaptation of *Saul* prepared in 1973 for the Canadian Broadcasting Corporation by Peter Haworth reverses this curve; it is the last two-thirds of the drama depicting Saul's growing madness and his frantic search for David that compel the listener's attention. Stripped of poetic baggage and reduced to a functional two-hour performance, the play not only succeeds dramatically but has an undeniable rhetorical power.

The romance, lightness of tone, and verbal wit (especially the overt eroticism of puns and sustained conceits), which characterize *Count Filippo; or, The Unequal Marriage* (1860) are a departure from the martial rhetoric of *Saul*. This extreme shift in style may have had a bearing on the play's reception in the highly moralistic 1860s; the *Athenaeum* considered it of no importance, and Bayard Taylor criticized it on historical principles: 'We know there never was a Duke of Pereza in Italy.'[22] Later critics were not more generous; in fact, there was no generally favourable reading of the drama until A.J.M. Smith's re-evaluation in his important anthology, *The Book of Canadian Poetry* (1943).

Count Filippo is immediately recognizable as the stuff of Shakespearian drama: the framing structure of ducal justice suggestive of *Measure for Measure*; the role of the courtier, Gallantio, as Iago-Pander; the freshness of the Romeo and Juliet romance of Hylas and Volina; and the concluding justice scene in which Gallantio, like Iago, is condemned to torture and death. The skillful *double entendres* of the first third of the play are reminiscent of the plays of Beaumont and Fletcher that were so fashionable in the 1830s and 40s. However, unlike *Saul* and *Jephthah's Daughter*, the narrative source of this Italianate tale is not immediately apparent; it would appear that it is derived not from English drama but from Alfieri's *Filippo*. Alfieri's version includes Filippo, a Spanish tyrant, Carlos, his hapless son, Isabella, Filippo's young wife and two courtiers: Gomez, an intriguer, who is Filippo's agent, and Perez, a genuinely good man who attempts to assist young Carlos and Isabella, the representatives of innocent love, individual freedom, and political justice. As is typical of the dénouement of Italianate revenge tragedy, Perez is murdered and Carlos and Isabella kill themselves.

In Heavysege's adaptation, the setting is transferred from Spain to Italy where there is a merging of the good courtier, Perez, with the aged ducal figure, this producing the 'unhistoric' Duke of Pereza. Filippo, his good and faithful courtier, has married the virtuous but restless young Volina. Hylas is the only son of Perez; Gallantio is a cynical rake of the court and Paphania is his mistress. When Filippo departs for the dukedom of Arno to arrange a marriage for the unwilling Hylas, Gallantio, holding a grudge against Filippo, urges Hylas to seduce Volina. The very witty sexual comedy of the first third of the play abruptly turns to tragedy when Volina reciprocates Hylas's affection only to recognize that both have fallen irreparably from God's grace.

Throughout the play, there is a constant linking of sexuality with a loss of grace. Hylas's rebuff of Gallantio states this clearly:

> Urge us no more to evil: we'll not hear on't;
> For we should fear our soul were banned from heaven
> Did we accomplish now your full desire. (IV.2)

This theme is reinforced by Volina's penitent journey to the confessional where Filippo is disguised as a priest:

> FILIPPO
> Speak, daughter: God is love; none need despair. —
> You keep the primal virtue, chastity?
> VOLINA
> I ought; but, oh, who do that which they ought?
> FILIPPO
> Few: yet remember, if you have offended,
> There was forgiveness even for Magdalen.
> VOLINA
> May Heaven forgive me, too, for I do need it. (V.ii)

Terse but eloquent, this scene is moving in context. Through Heavysege's presentation of the aged Filippo as a basically good man who recognizes the validity of Volina's defence and the legitimate claims of young Hylas upon her affection, and through his use of the framing structure of Christian atonement, Heavysege is able to transform Alfieri's revenge tragedy into Christian drama. Nonetheless, there is a certain moralistic excess in the concluding action when Filippo, Hylas, and Volina, all equally repentant, are dispatched by the author to a cloister.

Despite this eminently moral conclusion, *Count Filippo* was not well received when it was first published; very probably it was too frank for the tastes of Victorian Canada. Judging from Heavysege's extensive revisions of the play, revisions discovered in his personal papers and possibly undertaken just before his death in 1876, it was the moral tone that he wished to improve.[23] Pencilled changes on the title-page show that he hoped to publish a second edition. The drama, already concise, was shortened by approximately one-third; in addition to the correction of minor errors, Heavysege abbreviated passages, deleted archaisms, and removed much of the Paphania-Gallantio subplot. A comparison of the following passages illustrates the nature of his editing:

> It is man,
> Not horse, you want, — a lover in a husband.
> Wherefore does yours not squire you through the glades?
> Pleasure is doubled when the donor's pleased:
> But for a double pleasure where were th' world?
> That is renewed in mutual delight. (II.i)

The revision reads:

> 'Tis your husband
> Should squire you through the glades.
> Fie on the Count! (II.i)

It is tempting to speculate on the extent to which the spectre of the Canadian Mrs Grundy shaped these and similar recantations.

In his long narrative poem *Jephthah's Daughter* (1865), Heavysege returns to a theme similar to that of the earlier *Saul*; the struggle of a great but rash Israelite leader at odds with his God. In general, the narrative is based on the biblical account of

Jephthah (Judges 11:31): 'whatsoever cometh forth of the doors of my house to meet me, when I return in peace from the children of Ammon, shall surely be the Lord's, and I will offer it up for a burnt offering.' Jephthah achieves his final victory; but when to his horror his daughter comes out to greet him, the distraught father cannot revoke his oath. Heavysege makes several dramatically effective changes to this account. The young girl does not readily accede to her fate but, Iphigenia-like, struggles against death. Furthermore, Jephthah's vow is specifically characterized as 'rash,' an interpretation also present in an earlier Canadian poem, 'Jephtha's Daughter' by J.S., published in *The Literary Garland* in 1841.[24] Finally, Jephthah pleads with God and, like Agamemnon, makes inquiries of his priests in an attempt to circumvent the required sacrifice. Heavysege, who had been lent a copy of Euripides' *Iphigenia* by John Reade in 1858,[25] points to the parallelism of the Greek and Hebrew stories in the opening passage of his own poem, but he asserts that the tale of Jephthah's daughter is the sadder of the two; it is 'more fraught with ... grim fate' and evokes 'a wail more desolately wild,' presumably a reference to the lament described in Judges 11:40, a lament analogous to the wailing for Tammuz.

The symbolic characterization of the young girl is quite effective. Initially described as a joyous, vital spirit, she becomes horror-stricken with the recognition that she is to be a human sacrifice. Her first apprehension of her fate and her mother's unsuccessful attempt at comfort, in particular, are finely drawn. The dramatic device of presenting the young girl as emotionally frozen –

> And still he calls, still she unchanged abides;
> As one, whom polar cold has numbed to death,
> Abides unchanging in the wintry air; –

provides a powerful correlative for that emotional withdrawal from life which leads to the acceptance of death. Because the initial image is that of frozen grief, Heavysege is able to modulate the girl's state from trance to reverie, and finally from reverie to transcendent dream. In her dream, Jephthah's daughter, like Milton's Eve, becomes reconciled to the part she must take in the history of her people, seeing herself crowned in Paradise: 'I dreamed that I was walking in blest meads, / With great Manasseh, patriarch of our tribe.' Her final request, 'give me leave to knock at death's pale gate,' is simple and eloquent.

Because the girl remains in the forefront of the poem, yet apart from the immediate action, Heavysege can focus on the confrontation between husband and wife. The passage in which the mother accuses Jephthah of a lack of common humanity ('Fathers, like beasts, seek to devour their young') is particularly moving, as is her cry, ironic in context, that she will denounce Jephthah to Heaven. Heavysege clearly perceives the Romantic, and for that matter, human argument against the cruel Jehovah who demands sacrifice. Nonetheless, the arguments of the wife are not allowed to be dramatically convincing, primarily because Heavysege permits maternal lamentation to lapse into vituperation. Nor is the character of Jephthah convincingly drawn in the middle scenes. His emotional response to the forfeit of his vow is particularly inept: 'Oh, fool, fool, fool. / Rash fool, base knave, to pledge her! swindler I / Dishonourable gamester, an embezzling boy...' The rhetoric that served so well in the martial *Saul* is entirely out of place in *Jephthah's Daughter*, a fact soon noted by the contemporary reviewers of the poem: 'We have rhetoric — rhetoric at times embellished by delicate fancy — but scarcely ever nature.'[26]

In contrast, Jephthah's explication of the events leading to the vow and the central scene in the glen in which he asks God to release him by supplying, as He did for Abraham, a 'ram,' are psychologically convincing. This scene reveals Jephthah's character and, in effect, justifies the ways of the Old Testament God to man. Waiting for a sign from heaven, Jephthah hears:

> The hill-wolf howling on the neighbouring height,
> And bittern booming in the pool below.
> Some drops of rain fell from the passing cloud,
> That sudden hides the wanly shining moon,
> And from the scabbard instant dropped his sword,
> And, with long, living leaps and rock-struck clang,
> From side to side, and slope to sounding slope,
> In gleaming whirls swept down the dim ravine
> (Ill omen!): and, mute trembling, as he stood
> Helmless (to his astonished view), his daughter,
> All in sad disarray, appeared.

Northrop Frye cites the first two lines of this passage and finds in this scene a central example of the tendency in Canadian poetry to present a nature from which God has withdrawn his face:

> It is clear that what Jephthah is really sacrificing his daughter to is nature, nature as a mystery of mindless power, with

endless resources for killing man but with nothing to respond
to his moral or intellectual feelings.[27]

However, this reading is not supported by the immediate
context of the passage which suggests that God does reply,
although not as Jephthah wishes. Then too, the landscape of
this poem is not a specifically Canadian nature but rather a
landscape derived from literature, in this case Tennyson's *Morte
d'Arthur*. The alliteration of the passage, the sustained vowel
sounds, the bleakness of the landscape and the description of
Jephthah's sword all echo Tennyson's poem. The sword 'whirls'
as does Excalibur; it clangs on the sloping rocks as does Sir
Bedivere's mail; and it is associated with omen. These similarities are more than fortuitous. Like Sir Bedivere, Jephthah is
described as a character unwilling to keep his oath; he must be
rebuked until he performs the required sacrifice: 'No ransom
may there be, no compromise.' The omen of the falling sword
followed by the sudden manifestation of his daughter (an ironic
reversal of the Abraham story and the 'ram' which Jephthah
had arrogantly demanded) suggest that from Heavysege's point
of view, Jephthah is not, in fact, offering up his daughter to
Frye's 'mindless nature' but rather to the stern Old Testament
God of Judgement manifested in a Victorian poetic landscape.
It is likely, however, that Canadian aspects of the poem are to
be found in the conjunction of polar metaphors and a
Darwinian nature. After the loss of Sir John Franklin at the
North Pole was confirmed in 1853 and again in 1857, and after
the publication of Darwin's *Origin of Species* in 1859, much
Canadian Romantic poetry was infused with a particularly
'northern' strain of Darwinism.

Although Jephthah does seriously question the severity of the Old Testament God, he nonetheless regards him as a just God, as his earlier acknowledgement of guilt indicates:

> Who shall go scatheless and not suffer loss
> That dare attempt to stipulate with Heaven,
> And bribe Jehovah to bestow success?

This essential distinction also underlies the metaphoric descriptions of Jephthah and his daughter. Jephthah is insistently characterized as 'a rash, imperfect man' whose vows are 'rashly made and violently kept.' His position is summarized by the priests who serve the function of chorus in the concluding scene of the poem: 'Thou mayest not go back from thy rash vow, /Nor palter with the Holiest in an oath.'[28]

In this context, Jephthah's continuous vows and prayers may be seen as the attempt to make a better bargain with God. Offering himself and his household in exchange for the promised sacrifice of his daughter, 'Say what ransom thou / Demands, what price?' he is still exhibiting the same *hubris* which led to his initial disastrous vow. In contrast, his daughter is characterized as an innocent lamb, ultimately the perfect sacrifice. She is the 'lone lamb, / That hither came, gay skipping from the fold,' a 'lamb without a blemish!' As the fairest of the Hebrew maidens, she is the most fit for sacrifice:

> Nothing, once dedicate to Heaven, returns;
> Nought, so to Heaven devoted, is withdrawn,
> However costly, or however dear; —
> Much less when, as in thy estate, not only
> Hath Heaven, by its proper part performed,

> The stubborn compact ratified and sealed,
> But when of the possessions 'tis the prime,
> The fairest, choicest, nearest of them all.

The metaphoric significance of these two characterizations effectively deepens into symbol in the central dramatic scene at the wooded glen where Jephthah, rashly demanding from heaven a 'ram,' is answered by the sudden appearance of his daughter – the required 'lamb.' Any suggestion here of the mutilation of the body, which Northrop Frye also finds characteristic of the view of nature expressed in *Jephthah's Daughter*, is primarily a reflection of the essential biblical connection between the religious beliefs of the Old Testament Hebrews and the fertility myths of their neighbours.

In addition to long biblical narratives, Heavysege wrote a number of shorter poems, many of which are now unavailable. Copies of his *Sonnets* published in Montreal by H. and G.M. Rose in 1865, 'The Owl,' a poem of twenty-five stanzas, and the 'Ode' read at the Shakespeare Tercentenary in Montreal on 23 April 1864, have not been found.[29] From what we can judge, they were highly uneven in quality. The *New Dominion Monthly* of September 1876 reprinted an undistinguished excerpt from the Shakespearian 'Ode' of which the following couplet is representative: 'We claim thee as our joy, our pride, / Our benefactor, friend and guide.' Judging from sonnets quoted by early reviewers and those reprinted in *Jephthah's Daughter* it seems apparent that several were reworkings of material edited out of the first edition of *The Revolt of Tartarus*. 'The Dark Huntsman,' a conventional set piece on the approach of death,[30] was published in the *Canadian Monthly and National Review* (September 1876) with the mistaken assertion that the poem had been written just before the poet's death. An earlier version had actually been published by the Witness Press of Montreal in 1864 and was found in Heavysege's personal papers. 'Jezebel' (*New Dominion Monthly*, January 1868) is a dramatization of the biblical account of the infamous queen who contrives against God and his priests. Heavysege is particularly successful in depicting the confrontations between Ahab and Jezebel and the description of the death of Jezebel, her bones licked by dogs, has a macabre vitality.

Heavysege also published a novel, *The Advocate* (1865). A potboiler of unassimilated Gothic elements, it marshals an improbable euphuistic style under chapter headings culled from Shakespeare. Lamentably unsuccessful in conception and execution, it suggests that Heavysege was attempting to cater to the popular taste for melodrama. The hero, the advocate, is presented as a man dominated alternately by good and evil instincts. He seduces a virtuous young woman, Mona Macdonald, by whom he has a child, Amanda, his 'good genius.' The 'evil genius,' a 'dwarfish, swarthy creature, half-oaf, half-imp,' is Narcisse, his son by his French-Canadian housekeeper. As Malzah had earlier destroyed Saul, so Narcisse, literally as well as symbolically, becomes the instrument of the old man's destruction: in both cases evil is characterized as self-engendered. The romantic interest of this melodrama is provided by the love affair of young Amanda and the noble Claude Montigny, a happier version of Volina and Hylas. The hackneyed but sprightly quality of *The Advocate* and its relation to Heavysege's earlier verse may be demonstrated by this excerpt from the first chapter.

'Mona Macdonald, I am neither selfish nor sensual, though women call me so; not prone to be provoked to marriage; though Satan in your shape has for so many years tempted me thereto, I have still remained in the bachelors' Eden, in spite of you and the Serpent. Marry you! Do I look in the humour for mischief? ... Marry you! To marry is to commit two souls to the prison of one body; to put two pigs into one poke; two legs into one boot, two arms into one sleeve, two heads into one hat, two necks into one noose, two corpses into one coffin, and this into a wet grave, for marriage is a perennial spring of tears.'

As shown by the innocence of these rhetorical flourishes, Heavysege was always reluctant to strangle his literary darlings. His critical attitude is best summarized by Samuel Dawson, who edited and published *Jephthah's Daughter*: 'He had a high opinion of his own work, and was obstinate about having anything cut out by his friends. Being a man without general culture he could not well distinguish in his own work between what was good and what was bad. He knew what cost him a long time to do, and he was apt to overvalue that.'[31] However, as prolixity and melodrama dominated Heavysege's theatrical experience, it is not surprising that he was unable to counteract these qualities in his own work. There was no indigenous theatre in Montreal between 1850 and 1880 although Montrealers did patronize the offerings of visiting players. Murray D. Edwards reports that William Charles Macready played scenes from Bulwer-Lytton's *Richelieu* and Byron's *Werner ou L'Héritage* at the Theatre Royal in 1844, but he adds that the possibly more typical melodrama which followed was *Six Degrees of Crime*, or *Wine, Women, Gambling, Theft, Murder and the Scaffold*.[32] Except for one abortive attempt in which he prepared an acting script of *Saul* for the American actress Charlotte Cushman,[33] Heavysege's closest experience with the stage came in March 1862 when he gave a public reading of *Saul*, probably at his own expense, in Nordheimer Hall in Montreal.[34]

Heavysege's personal papers indicate that literature in Canada in the 1860s did not pay even if the author was considered the leading poet of the period. From receipts saved by Heavysege, it is apparent that he financed personally the publication of the third edition of *Saul* with Fields, Osgood and Company of Boston. The record of his efforts to pay his debts both to the publishers and his friend George Martin, who had advanced him money,[35] is one of dogged persistence based on an unshaken belief in his own poetic talents. There was little real support for literature following Confederation,[36] as is demonstrated by a succession of literary magazines between 1869 and 1880 — a chronicle of initial high hopes followed by inevitable failure occasioned by lack of national support. Despite the brave attempt of the *Canadian Monthly and National Review* (1872-82), English and American literary magazines continued to dominate the Canadian tea-table just as Byron, Emerson, Tennyson, and Longfellow decorated the Sunday parlour. G. Mercer Adam, editor of the *Canada Bookseller*, wrote angrily in June 1870: 'The prevalent habit among the people of speaking contemptuously of our native literature is a bad and senseless one.'[37] A review of Heavysege criticism, included here as an appendix, shows that he was not recognized in Canada until praised in England and the United States. This review is an account of the vagaries of the development of Canadian criticism. Heavysege was not fully accepted in the 1880s partly because any literary Canadian was automatically considered second-rate. During the wave of nationalism that developed in the 1920s, it was considered that as an émigré writer he was not a Canadian and dismissed on that account. It was not until the re-evaluation of the literature in the 1940s by Ralph Gustafson, A.J.M. Smith, and Northrop Frye that there begins to emerge a critical consideration of Heavysege's works.

Heavysege was limited, then, not only by defects in taste occasioned by temperament and by a constricted intellectual background, but also by the absence of a supportive cultural milieu. He did have occasional literary friends, notably the poet George Martin, and was invited to become an honorary member of the Montreal Literary Club, a short-lived association sparked by D'Arcy McGee whose members included J.W. Dawson, Pierre J.D. Chauveau, Sir William Logan, and Henry J. Morgan, but, on the whole, his literary contacts were scanty. Somewhat retiring in person, Heavysege spent much of his life in literary isolation. His inspiration came from his limited reading, from nature, and from music. A daughter recalled:

> He loved Canada's beautiful maple trees, her gorgeous autumn leaves, her silent country, and the snow. Often did he climb Mount Royal to see the sun rise from its summit. ... The elements in commotion, a storm brewing or breaking, the starry heavens, all called forth words of rapture. ... He had a violin ... a sort of safety valve for pent-up feeling. His love for music is shown in 'Saul.' He would join our little family concerts for a few moments, throwing in his rich, deep voice in

rolling abandon, then would slip away again to his writings and proof-sheets.[38]

After an arduous day at the *Montreal Witness*, which would not have ended until eight or nine o'clock, it was his habit to work until late into the night: 'Mother used to fear for his health, but he said he would rather shorten his life than not write.'[39] The figure of Heavysege in his later life is a bleak one: ill, struggling to pay off debts incurred by the third edition of *Saul*, bowlderizing *Count Filippo*, and burning what remained of his unpublished manuscripts, as he could not afford the postage required to send them out to publishers. His death in 1876 was attributed to 'nervous exhaustion.'[40]

Feeling increasingly unappreciated by his adopted country, he had conveyed his unhappiness in a letter to Charles Lanman in 1865:

> Canada has not a large cultivated class, and what of such there is amongst us not only misdoubts its own judgment, but has generally no literary faith in sons of the soil, native or adopted. I often think that if fortune had guided my steps towards the States, say Boston, when I left England, the literary course of my life would have been influenced for the better.

There is some wishful thinking in this account. Heavysege overvalued his poetic gift, the 'fire promethean'; such faith was required if he was to continue as a poet against considerable odds. For, as a co-worker on the *Witness* reminds us: '*Saul* was published in Montreal where it received a somewhat cold reception and much criticism.'[41] What little encouragement he received came largely through the efforts of the New England writers: through Hawthorne who recommended *Saul* to Patmore, through Emerson and Longfellow who commended his work and attempted to assist with the publication of American editions,[42] through Taylor and Lanman who wrote appreciative critical articles. Given a strong support for North American literature in the United States at this period, Heavysege would have found more satisfactory literary employment in Boston than was possible in Montreal. Bliss Carman and Charles G.D. Roberts, it might be recalled, took up residence in the United States some fifteen years later for much the same reason; in a piece of doggerel 'The Poet is Bidden to Manhattan Island,' Roberts explained half-humorously, half-seriously, that he would henceforth 'Pipe for them that pay the piper.'

In the largest sense, there is a strong connection between a nation's political maturity and its willingness to support a national literature: the fact that Canada continued to be culturally colonial until well into the 1920s mitigated against Heavysege and against the poets of the Confederation; as a consequence, it impeded the development of an indigenous literature. However, this lack of support for a national literature and the concurrent absence of a literary milieu, although contributing factors, do not excuse Heavysege, who was writing closet drama some thirty years after the main impulse had passed. His third edition of *Saul* did not sell, as the letters from Fields, Osgood indicate, because even in Boston there was no market for 'dramatic compositions' in the 1860s.

In retrospect, however, it is precisely in the areas in which Heavysege stands apart from his age – either behind it or in advance of it – that his work is most interesting. Despite frequent borrowing from early nineteenth-century drama, Heavysege is in many ways a primitive. He accommodates character and action to a basically seventeenth-century morality in which man's *hubris* is met by divine retribution. Yet within the moral structure, an irrepressible spontaneity — vital, naïve, often vulgar — erupts, thus producing strikingly dual portraits of human nature. In this psychological frankness, he anticipates writers nurtured on Freud. And, as adaptations of *Saul* and *Count Filippo* have shown, Heavysege's characters in action are dramatically effective. Then too, in the presentation of nature in *Jephthah's Daughter*, he anticipates that Darwinian view of Canadian nature that is to dominate in the poetry of the 1880s and 90s.

Undeniably, Heavysege was a highly uneven craftsman; his range of expression, although sometimes rising to considerable heights in *Saul*, could often plummet disastrously. A.J.M. Smith has aptly remarked upon the curious 'mixture of the grand and the grandiose, of the magnificent and the ridiculous' in *Saul*.[43] In comparison with the polished and eloquent poetic dramas of Tennyson and Browning, his work is recognizably homespun; to this extent Robertson Davies is justified in his satire. Nonetheless, compared with the lesser but substantial figures of the earlier English Romantic revival, with Thomas Beddoes or Joanna Baillie or Charles Wells or, for that matter, with any other dramatist writing in North America in the 1850s, Heavysege is a major figure and it is in this context that we must judge him. Handicapped by limitations in his own literary background and by the lack of a supportive Canadian culture, his considerable achievements in *Saul* and *Jephthah's Daughter* are all the more impressive.

NOTES

1 Heavysege considered Saul's tormentor, the evil spirit Malzah, his chief poetical creation. Lawrence J. Burpee, 'Charles Heavysege,' *Transactions of the Royal Society of Canada*, 2nd series, VII (1901) section ii, 30
2 Charles Lanman, 'Charles Heavysege,' *Haphazard Personalities* (Boston: Lee and Shepard 1886) 271
3 George Stewart, 'Canadian Literature,' *Stewart's Literary Quarterly Magazine* (January 1870) 345
4 *University Monthly*, Fredericton (June 1883) 64
5 Heavysege's birthplace is given variously as Liverpool, 'near Liverpool,' and Yorkshire. Heavysege, in letters to Charles Lanman, claims only that his 'ancestors on the paternal side' were from Yorkshire and that Bayard Taylor's article in the *Atlantic Monthly* (October 1865), which gives Liverpool as his birthplace, was 'generally correct.' The first identification of Huddersfield is found in *A Treasury of Canadian Verse*, Theodore H. Rand, ed. (Toronto: William Briggs 1900).
6 Heavysege to Charles Lanman, 12 October 1860. This reference, and the following ones, to his correspondence with Lanman are found in Charles Lanman, *Haphazard Personalities* 273-7 and in Burpee, *TRSC* 53-5.
7 In a letter to her niece, Mrs Clara Groves Gould (13 July 1933), Mrs Harriet Pettigrew, daughter of Charles Heavysege, recalled 'talk about my Father's Mother being a descendant of nobility, or almost royalty.' Thomas R. Dale, the author of an unpublished doctoral dissertation on Heavysege (University of Chicago 1951) determined that there was no record of a land-owning Heavysege family in England.
8 *Northern Messenger*, Montreal and New York (15 September 1876) 1
9 Daniel Clark, in an unpublished lecture on 'Canadian Poets and Poetry,' reported in the *Hamilton Evening Times*, undated newspaper clipping
10 Bayard Taylor, 'The Author of *Saul*,' *Atlantic Monthly* (October 1865) 414
11 Heavysege to Charles Lanman, 2 October 1865

12 Burpee, *TRSC* 21
13 Mrs James G. Rogerson, granddaughter of Jane Heavysege, to Miss Clara W.H. Gould, 12 May 1970
14 Aeneas MacDonell Dawson, *Our Strength and Their Strength: The North West Territory and Other Papers Chiefly Relating to the Dominion of Canada* (Ottawa: The Times 1870) 154
15 Charles Lloyd, *The Tragedies of Vittorio Alfieri: Translated from the Italian* (London: Longman, Hurst, Rees, Orme and Brown 1815)
16 Most readers will have access to the latter version, published by H. and G.M. Rose, in which Heavysege omits the introduction to the poem. He has also edited prefatory comments to each of the six books in the second edition. However, Heavysege did not omit the following pedestrian passage introducing Book Five:

> Let posterity
> Declare (or this generation) whether I bore
> The fire promethean, or a worthless flash,
> Whose dull report I took for distant fame.

Other changes include a limiting of the temptation scenes and the deletion of a wholly unpoetic passage describing Lucifer's fall through space. Most effective are changes made to the last lines of the poem where the emphasis is shifted from Satan and his three henchmen to focus on Satan alone — 'And Satan raised his head in grisly joy, / At such triumph, and his rule secured.'

17 'The poet ... gives us glimpses of another interpretation held by many critics of Hebrew history, in which the tragic fate of the great first King is ascribed to the rage and revenge of the priesthood when he rebelled against their tyranny.' Louisa Murray, 'Heavysege's "Saul",' *Canadian Monthly and National Review* (September 1876) 250-1. This secondary political interpretation may also reflect the king-priest confrontation of George Darley's heroic drama *Thomas à Becket* (1840). A psychological study of character, Darley's drama also presents the impish Dwerga, possibly a model for Malzah.

18 There are three editions of *Saul*. The first, published in Montreal by Henry Rose in 1857, contains many extraneous low-life passages. The

second edition, published in London by Sampson Low and in Montreal by John Lovell in 1859, omits many of these passages, such as: 'The foaming yeast of my spirits / Falls at this muggish weather' and 'the sun's abed. / And has cursed black nightcap on his head.' In addition, the colourful Fly, Tiptoe, Grab, Clutch, and Taken are submerged into the generic 'demons.' The third edition was published by Fields, Osgood and Company of Boston in 1869 and financed by Heavysege. It was reprinted by John Lovell of Rouse's Point, New York, in 1876, the year of Heavysege's death.

19 T.R. Dale, 'Our Greatest Poet — A Century Ago,' *Canadian Forum* (February 1958) 245-6. See also his 'The Life and Work of Charles Heavysege, 1816-1876,' (PhD diss., University of Chicago 1951).
20 J.R. Ramsay [pseud.], *One Quiet Day: A Book of Prose and Poetry* (Hamilton, Ont.: Lancefield Bros 1873) 33-4
21 T.R. Dale, 'The Life and Work of Charles Heavysege' 91
22 Taylor, *Atlantic Monthly* 417
23 A copy of the book, heavily edited in pencil, is now in the possession of Miss Clara W. Heavysege Gould of Vancouver, a great-granddaughter of the poet.
24 *The Literary Garland* (September 1841) 446-7. The poet stresses, as does Heavysege, the physical beauty of the young woman ('Father, am I doomed to die, / Now in my youth and loveliness') and introduces a scene of 'rugged rock and slippr'y steep' analogous to the rocky steep of Heavysege's wooded glen.
25 Burpee, *TRSC* 22
26 *Athenaeum* (25 February 1865) 272
27 Northrop Frye, 'Preface to an Uncollected Anthology' (1956), reprinted in *Contexts of Canadian Criticism*, Eli Mandel, ed. (Chicago: University of Chicago Press 1971) 189
28 This insistence on Jephthah's rashness is not part of the biblical account in Judges. Heavysege may have developed it from the earlier version of 'Jephtha's Daughter' in the *Literary Garland* or, more likely, it is analogous with Eve's 'rash' act in *Paradise Lost*, 'her rash hand in evil hour / Forth reaching to the Fruit, she pluck'd, she eat' (IX, 780ff.). The Montreal *Witness* of 15 July 1876, reporting Heavysege's

death of the previous day, erroneously described him as the author of 'Jephtha's Rash Vow.'

29 'The Owl' is listed in Charles C. James, *A Bibliography of Canadian Poetry (English)* (Toronto: William Briggs 1899). As early as 1901, Lawrence J. Burpee noted that he was unable to find the *Sonnets*.

30 Felicia Hemans published a similar poem, 'The Wild Huntsman,' (*The Poetical Works of Felicia Hemans*, London: Ward, Lock, nd, p 95), which drew on a popular German myth of the passage of the wild huntsman as a presage of war; the *New Dominion Monthly* of February 1868 published a poem similarly titled, noting that it was translated from the German of Buerger. All of these versions may have been spurred by Sir Walter Scott's well-known translation of the same poem.

31 Burpee, *TRSC* 20

32 Murray D. Edwards, *A Stage in Our Past* (Toronto: University of Toronto 1968) 87

33 According to William Boyd, Miss Cushman intended to play the part of Malzah, but 'her death, shortly after the completion of the play, unfortunately killed the production.' Burpee, *TRSC* 91. Heavysege refers to his 'acting play for a New York manager' in a letter to Charles Lanman in 1860. Miss Cushman's death, however, did not occur until 1876.

34 Burpee, *TRSC* 22

35 Burpee reports that Martin lent Heavysege a sum set aside for the publication of his own book of verse, but when Heavysege found himself in financial difficulties, Martin 'took the note and tore it into pieces, and it was never again mentioned between them.' Burpee, *TRSC* 24. Heavysege's personal papers reveal that under the arrangement made by Heavysege with Ticknor and Fields (later Fields, Osgood) of Boston in November 1868, the poet undertook the payment of the cost of 'manufacturing' ($600), the firm retaining 10 per cent on the sale of retail copies. The first small edition of 280 copies (150 of which were sent to Heavysege) was soon exhausted and Heavysege contracted for a further printing for which there was little sale. He remained indebted to the publishers for the sum of $190.26 up to April 1875. Promissory notes to George Martin, contained in the Heavysege papers and dated

between 1868 and 1871, show that they were repaid with interest up to July 1871. The remaining note for $156.94 is receipted with payment of $10.92, indicating that Heavysege was attempting to pay off the debt.

36 Alfred G. Bailey, 'Literature and Nationalism after Confederation,' *University of Toronto Quarterly* 25 (1956) 409-24
37 *Canada Bookseller* (June 1870) 5
38 Burpee, *TRSC* 52
39 Mrs Harriet Pettigrew to Mrs Clara Groves Gould, 13 July 1933
40 Mrs Edith Freeman, granddaughter of Charles Heavysege, to Miss Clara W.H. Gould, 11 May 1970
41 Letter to the editor of the Montreal *Witness*, signed 'Admirer.' Burpee identifies the writer as George H. Flint (*TRSC* 23). An undated newspaper clipping of the letter in its entirety is included with the Heavysege papers.
42 Burpee, *TRSC* 55-7
43 A.J.M. Smith, *The Oxford Book of Canadian Verse* (Toronto 1960) xxvi

Acknowledgements

I would like to thank Anne Yandle, Head, Special Collections Division of the University of British Columbia Library, for her continued assistance in locating nineteenth-century material. Clara W. Heavysege Gould of Vancouver kindly provided access to her collection of Heavysege papers, and Peter Haworth and Norman Newton of the Canadian Broadcasting Corporation, Vancouver, supplied copies of radio dramatizations of *Saul* and *Count Filippo*. In addition, the President's Research Grant Committee of Simon Fraser University provided a research grant for the summer of 1973. I am greatly indebted to Marilyn G. Flitton, who prepared the supplementary list of Heavysege criticism and assisted with the preparation of the manuscript.

Bibliography

POEMS BY HEAVYSEGE

The Revolt of Tartarus: A Poem London: Simpkin, Marshall & Co.; Liverpool: D. Marples [1852]

The Revolt of Tartarus; A Poem Montreal: H. & G.M. Rose 1855

Sonnets by the Author of 'The Revolt of Tartarus' Montreal: H. & G.M. Rose 1855

The Dark Huntsman (A Dream) Montreal: 'Witness' Steam Printing House [1864]

'The Dark Huntsman' *Canadian Monthly and National Review* X (August 1876) 134-51

The Dark Huntsman Ottawa: Golden Dog Press 1973

'Ode' read at Shakespeare Tercentenary, Montreal, 23 April 1864

The Owl 1864 (details of publication unknown) C.C. James, *A Bibliography of Canadian Poetry (English)*

Jephthah's Daughter Montreal: Dawson Brothers; London: Sampson Low, Son, and Marston 1865

'Jezebel, A Poem in Three Cantos' *New Dominion Monthly* I (January 1868) 224-31

Jezebel, A Poem in Three Cantos Montreal: Golden Dog Press 1972

DRAMAS BY HEAVYSEGE

Saul: A Drama, in Three Parts Montreal: Henry Rose 1857

Saul: A Drama, in Three Parts 2nd edition, carefully revised and emended. Montreal: John Lovell 1859

Saul: A Drama, in Three Parts 2nd edition, carefully revised and emended. London: Sampson Low, Son & Co. 1859

Saul: A Drama, in Three Parts 2nd edition, carefully revised and emended. London: Sampson Low, Son, and Marston; Montreal: John Lovell 1859

Saul: A Drama, in Three Parts A new and revised edition. Boston: Fields Osgood and Co. 1869

Saul: A Drama, in Three Parts. A new and revised edition. New York: Lovell Printing and Publishing 1876

'Saul, a Drama in Three Parts' Unpublished radio adaptation by Peter Haworth for the CBC produced by Norman Newton 1973

Count Filippo; or, The Unequal Marriage. A Drama in Five Acts Montreal: The Author 1860

Count Filippo; or, The Unequal Marriage. A Drama in Five Acts Montreal: E. Dawson & Son; Toronto: R. & A. Miller 1860

'Count Filippo, or The Unequal Marriage' Unpublished radio adaptation by Peter Haworth for the CBC produced by Norman Newton 1968

Count Filippo Toronto: Toronto Reprint Library, University of Toronto Press 1973

OTHER WORKS BY HEAVYSEGE

The Advocate, A Novel Montreal: Richard Worthington 1865, 1866

The Advocate Toronto: Toronto Reprint Library, University of Toronto Press 1973

PAPERS

A collection of Heavysege material in the possession of Miss Clara Walters Heavysege Gould of Vancouver. Miss Gould is the granddaughter of Jane H. Walsh, Heavysege's eldest daughter. The collection is comprised of material, largely letters, contracts, and clippings, gathered by Dr Charles Heavysege Walsh and Mrs Clara Groves Gould from their mother, Mrs Jane H. Walsh; from Mrs Annie D. Elliott, daughter of Harriet H. Pettigrew, and from Mrs Edith Freeman, daughter of Mrs Kate H. Fowler.

Review of Heavysege Criticism

Some of the earliest periodical and newspaper criticism have proved unobtainable but are here included as cited in Lawrence J. Burpee's compilation of Heavysege material, 'Charles Heavysege,' *Transactions of the Royal Society of Canada*, 2nd ser., VII (1901), section ii. 19-60.

George Murray. Review of *Saul.* Montreal 1857
   Cited by Burpee (pp 26, 42). 'In *Saul* we found a certain power of expression and wealth of imagery spoiled by defective versification, by anachronisms, and prolixity.'
[Coventry Patmore] 'The Modern British Drama,' *North British Review* LVII (August 1858) 78-80
   A copy of *Saul* was given to Patmore by Nathaniel Hawthorne, then American consul at Liverpool, with his recommendation. Patmore describes the work as 'indubitably one of the most remarkable poems ever written out of Great Britain.' His article is the source of much of the later criticism.
'A Canadian Dramatist,' *The Saturday Review* VIII (10 September 1859) 312-13
   'a writer who displays a vein of dramatic genius more original and vigorous than any modern playwright we can call to mind'
Review of *Count Filippo* 'New Books' *Albion*, New York (21 July 1860) 345
   'the author does not show in wise or philosophical views of life the fruits of profound knowledge or instinctive comprehension of its relations.' Yet, 'if it be the work of a young man, and he

has the genius to create a style of his own, he may become the first dramatic poet of the age.'

George Murray. Review of *The Advocate* Montreal 1865

Burpee finds this review the most satisfactory of those appearing in Canadian papers. 'Outside periodicals would not condescend to mention it, and indeed it deserved no better treatment. ... [Murray] treated it adequately, and very severely' (p 49)

Review of *Jephthah's Daughter* in *The Athenaeum* no. 1948 (25 February 1865) 271-2

The reviewer considers the work to be the only one of importance by Heavysege since *Saul* for its language, skillful gradations of feeling and careful design in structure. A loss of vigour and inspiration is also noted.

Allid (pseud.) 'Canadian Literature, or What Has Been Done in It,' *The Saturday Reader*, Montreal (16 September 1865) 20

A brief reference to *Saul* and *Jephthah's Daughter*. 'Heavysege is but little read. ... His language ... is inclined to be quaint and crabbed ... yet some passages are true Catholic poetry.'

Bayard Taylor 'The Author of *Saul*,' *Atlantic Monthly* XVI (October 1865) 412-18

A sympathetic account of the author and his work, stressing the theme of the solitary, neglected genius. Taylor gives Liverpool as Heavysege's birthplace and describes his meeting with the poet in a 'machine-shop' in Montreal. Discusses the *Sonnets, Saul, Count Filippo* (which 'added nothing to his reputation'), the Shakespearian 'Ode,' and *Jephthah's Daughter*

Henry J. Morgan 'Charles Heavysege,' *Bibliotheca Canadensis* (Ottawa: Desbarats 1867) 181

Biographical reference, including excerpts of reviews in the *North British Review*, *Albion*, and *Athenaeum*

Charles Lanman 'Charles Heavysege,' *Washington Weekly Chronicle* (28 November 1868). Reprinted in *Haphazard Personalities* by Charles Lanman (Boston: Lee and Shepard 1886) 259-77

Discusses *Saul*, cites several of the sonnets, mentions *The Revolt of Tartarus* ('a juvenile effort ... long ago disappeared from public view'), the 'Ode on Shakespeare,' and *Jephthah's Daughter*. Contains Heavysege's letters to Lanman (12 October 1860, 11 February 1861, and 2 October 1865). 'While filling their papers with fulsome praise of snobby lordlings from England, [the press of Canada] have not, for the most part, had time to recognize the fact that the woodcarver of Montreal was the leading intellect of their Dominion.'

'Jezebel – A Poem in Three Cantos, by the Author of *Saul*,' undated newspaper clipping, Charles Heavysege Papers [1868]

Questions Heavysege's choice of subject for the spirit and purpose of poetry: 'notwithstanding all the inherent repulsiveness of his heroine, who reminds us of Lady Macbeth, the writer has given us a fresh proof of his peculiar power. ... His music is not that of birds or of rippling waters; but rather the reverberation of thunder, the sound of a distant cataract, or the deep bass voice of a tempest careering through a forest of pines.'

Notice of the 3rd edition of *Saul*. *Harper's New Monthly Magazine* XXXVIII (March 1869) 563-4

Describes *Saul* as a poem of 436 pages, reproduced in Boston in a handsome volume of tinted paper. 'Those who look to such works ... for the isolated passages of thought or suggestion, will find some reward for their search, although we are not inclined to class Mr Heavysege with Shakespeare, as the *North British Review* has done.'

Charles Sangster 'Charles Heavysege and the New Edition of "Saul",' *Stewart's Quarterly Magazine* III (April 1869) 88-105
Contains a brief discussion of the *Sonnets* (1855) and a long descriptive analysis of *Saul*, in an attempt to draw the attention of the 'too-apathetic Canadian people, ever painfully lukewarm in all matters pertaining to true poetry' to the new, revised edition of the drama. Views Heavysege as a Canadian 'who has already reflected no little honour on his adopted land' and who 'stands intellectually a full head and shoulders above all others of the poetic race in the Dominion of Canada.'

Richard Grant White. Review of *Saul* in 'Literature and Art,' *Galaxy* VII (May 1869) 763-5
Comments on the remarkable phenomenon of the little acceptance *Saul*, 'a strong and singular work,' received since its publication

Review of *Saul* in the Boston *Commonwealth*, 1869. Publisher's publicity sheet, CHP
'It must rank above every dramatic poem written in the English language during the present century. ... His blank verse is brilliantly expressive, and his imagination has capacities shown by no other in our day.'

Aeneas MacDonell Dawson 'The Poets of Canada,' *Our Strength and Their Strength, The North West Territory and other Papers chiefly relating to the Dominion of Canada* (Ottawa: The Times 1870) 154-6
Classes Heavysege as a Canadian poet: 'his works of greatest note having been written and published since he came to settle

permanently in Canada. ... The Muses may well take pride in the care they have bestowed on his initiation, and no Eleusinian or other Mysteries were ever more creditably mastered.'

Andrew John R. Ramsay 'Some Canadian Books,' *One Quiet Day: a Book of Prose and Poetry* (Hamilton: Lancefield Bros 1873) 32-8

Criticizes a reviewer who advised Heavysege to omit the scene from *Saul* where the evil spirit, Malzah, shirks his work. Cites *Saul* and mentions *Jephthah's Daughter* ('also a gem')

James Douglas, Jr 'The Present State of Literature in Canada, and the Intellectual Progress of its People during the last 50 years,' *Canadian Monthly and National Review* VII (June 1875) 465-76

'A good poem is the product of an age, and it is, therefore, no disgrace if Canada has not been the fortunate home of its author. The only work of importance which has issued from the Canadian press is Heavyside's [sic] "Saul" a dramatic poem, which, despite the dowdy dress in which it appeared, called forth loud praises from the organs of criticism in England.'

Daniel Clark 'The Poetry of Charles Heavysege,' *Canadian Monthly and National Review* X (August 1876) 127-34

Commemorates Heavysege's death on 14 July 1876. Biographical information based on Taylor's article. Discussion of work limited to the *Sonnets, Saul,* and *Jephthah's Daughter*

'The Life and Poems of Charles Heavysege,' *New Dominion Monthly* (September 1876) 281-6

Notice following Heavysege's death with biographical details and an account of the reception of his work. 'Montreal, at the present time, is not the best place in the world, nor even in Canada, for a new literary work first to see the light, and in 1857 it could hardly have been expected that such a work as "Saul" would meet with a hearty reception. Take the beautiful binding and gilt edges off even the best of our poets, and the most read now-a-days, and it will perhaps be found that before very long they may be banished from the very great majority of drawing-room tables, and have given them inside positions on book shelves, and to be placed there means neglect. "Saul" had nothing typographically to recommend it, and books are too often judged by their print and covers; but it hid rich gems, which were afterwards to be brought to notice. "Saul, a Drama," was not a name to attract attention, and the author's was unknown; the subject was not a national one, and the book had nothing in it to especially attract the attention of Canadians...'

'Charles Heavysege,' *Northern Messenger* XI (15 September 1876) (with portrait)

   A biographical sketch commemorating Heavysege's death

Louisa Murray. 'Heavysege's "Saul",' *Canadian Monthly and National Review* X (September 1876) 250-4

   An appreciative, descriptive analysis of *Saul*

John Reade 'Charles Heavysege' A poem *Rose-Belford's Canadian Monthly and National Review* II (March 1879) 301

John G. Bourinot 'The Intellectual Development of the Canadian People,' *Rose-Belford's Canadian Monthly and National Review* VI (March 1881) 225-6

   ' "Saul" like Milton's great epic, now-a-days, is only admired by a few, and never read by the many.'

George Martin 'Charles Heavysege' A poem *Marguerite or the Isle of Demons and Other Poems* (Montreal: Dawson Bros 1887) 219-21

George M. Rose. 'Charles Heavysege,' *A Cyclopedia of Canadian Biography* II (Toronto: Rose Publishing Co. 1888) 32-3
Biographical information based on Taylor's article. 'To Art Heavysege, so his critics say, owed little. ... but he owed much to Nature. ... what might he not have done for himself and his adopted country, had he been favoured by circumstances as he was by Nature.'

William Douw Lighthall, ed. *Songs of the Great Dominion* (London: Walter Scott 1889) xxix
'He died in 1869 [sic] ... Canadians do not read him; but they claim him as perhaps their greatest, most original writer, if they could weigh him aright and appreciate him ... he will probably always command their awe, and refuse to be forgotten.'

'Charles Heavysege,' *The Dominion Illustrated* II (27 April 1889) 263, 266
Account of a paper read before the Society of Canadian Literature in March 1889 by G.H. Flint of the Montreal *Witness*, based on Lanman. 'A statue in one of our squares or other evidence that he has not been forgotten would be a graceful act...'

William Sharp, ed. *American Sonnets* (London: Walter Scott 1889) xxx, 288
Cites Heavysege an an exemplar of the chief offenders against the true sonnet form, but also as having the 'potentiality of becoming one of the greatest sonnet-writers on either side of the Atlantic.'

A.B. DeMille 'A Sketch of Canadian Poetry,' *Canada; An Encyclopedia of the Country* V, ed. J. Castell Hopkins (Toronto: Linscott 1899) 164

'For years his claim to be a poet of high rank was denied by those to whom he submitted it.' States that his work never became popular and his reputation rests on *Jephthah's Daughter* and some of the 'irregular sonnets.'

Theodore H. Rand, ed. *A Treasury of Canadian Verse* (Toronto: William Briggs 1900) 393

Biographical note giving Huddersfield as Heavysege's birthplace and the date of his death as 14 July 1879

Lawrence J. Burpee 'Charles Heavysege,' *Transactions of the Royal Society of Canada* 2nd ser., VII (1901), section ii, 19-60

The most extensive account of Heavysege's life and works, well documented with sources, personal reminiscences, extracts of criticism, and reprinted letters from Longfellow, Lanman, Emerson, Taylor, John A. Macdonald. A critical discussion of all the published works, including *The Owl* and 'The Dark Huntsman.'

Thomas O'Hagan *Canadian Essays: Critical and Historical* (Toronto: William Briggs 1901) 13

A brief reference to Heavysege repeating the claim that Longfellow considered *Saul* to be 'the best tragedy written since the days of Shakespeare.'

Archibald MacMurchy *Handbook of Canadian Literature* (Toronto: William Briggs 1906) 43-8

Paraphrases earlier reviews. 'It is much to be regretted that Heavysege failed to observe the dignity and power of the brevity of the Bible record [of Saul], and that he did not more closely follow in the footsteps of the incomparable Shakespeare, whom he prized so highly.'

E.B. Greenshields 'A Forgotten Poet' *University Magazine* VII (October 1908) 343-59

The description of *Saul* leads to a discussion and analysis of the biblical Saul. Includes references to *Jephthah's Daughter* and the *Sonnets*

Mrs C.M. Whyte-Edgar *A Wreath of Canadian Song* (Toronto: William Briggs 1910) 35-8

'The most remarkable figure in ... the whole realm of Canadian literature, is that of Charles Heavysege, the man who, amid the occupations of the workshop, dreamed his weird dreams and wove his strange imaginings into the most ambitious poetry then essayed in this young land.'

Thomas Guthrie Marquis *English-Canadian Literature* (Toronto: Glasgow, Brook 1913) 571

'*Saul* was as much apart from other Canadian literary efforts as was Saul in Israel from the men of his time. It had a vigour, an intensity, a dramatic excellence that no other Canadian poem before its time, or indeed until the closing years of the 19th century, approaches. ... It is probable that it took shape in Heavysege's mind early in life and that the poem was composed before he left England.'

R.P. Baker *A History of English-Canadian Literature to the Confederation* (Cambridge: Harvard University Press 1920) 168-76

A review of Heavysege's life, based on earlier accounts, and a criticism of his works which Baker finds to be greatly overestimated. 'Proof of his lack of literary skill is to be found in *The Advocate* ... the worst of the notoriously bad novels written in the Dominion.' Claims Heavysege remained singularly unappreciative of the sympathy and favours of associates – 'a lack of taste ... reflected in his verse ... its chief weakness'

Archibald MacMechan. *Headwaters of Canadian Literature* (Toronto: McClelland and Stewart 1924) 101

Rejects Heavysege as a Canadian writer. 'Heavysege's overrated *Saul* ... might have been written anywhere; it is not nearly as "Canadian," as Byron's *Beppo*, written in Italy, is Italian.'

J.D. Logan and D.G. French *Highways of Canadian Literature* (Toronto: McClelland and Stewart 1924) 48

A brief reference: 'The accident of his having remained in Canada and of having published at Montreal his *Saul*, which had been conceived in England, does not give him as much right, if any at all, to be considered a Canadian émigré poet as attaches to Kidd or Mrs Moodie.'

Lorne Pierce 'Charles Heavysege (1816-1879),' *An Outline of Canadian Literature* (Toronto: Ryerson 1927) 63-4

A brief account of his life and work, critical in tone ('the endless dialogue is wearisome'). 'There is nothing Canadian about [his] work; the effect of his poetry on subsequent Canadian literature has been nil.'

M. Joan Montgomery 'Charles Heavysege,' *A Standard Dictionary of Canadian Biography*, eds. C.G.D. Roberts and A.L. Tunnell (Toronto: Trans-Canada Press 1938) 198-201

A sympathetic evaluation of all his published works and circumstances, based on Burpee, but with some additional biographical data. Concludes: 'In the final analysis, Heavysege's reputation will probably rest on passages from *Saul, Jephthah's Daughter* ... and the *Sonnets*

A.J.M. Smith 'Our Poets,' *University of Toronto Quarterly* XII (October 1942) 79-80

'[The sonnets] reveal in little the strength and originality that make *Saul* so significant an interpretation of the moral world'

— ed. *The Book of Canadian Poetry* (Chicago: University of Chicago Press 1943) 10-12, 73-5

Comments on the grudging recognition of Heavysege in Canadian handbooks of literature. His own review, citing Patmore, suggests that in *Saul*, 'the magnificence of the finest passages. ... commands the highest admiration' and that *Count Filippo* is 'a brilliantly written and well-constructed problem play.'

Ralph Gustafson 'Anthology and Revaluation' (a review of A.J.M. Smith's *The Book of Canadian Poetry* [1943]), *University of Toronto Quarterly* XIII (January 1944) 232-3

'There is nothing comparable in the range of Canadian literature to Heavysege's creation, in *Saul*, of the character Malzah. ... That Heavysege could have been lost sight of, is cause for conclusions of substantial significance.'

Northrop Frye 'The Narrative Tradition in English Canadian Poetry' (1946), *The Bush Garden: Essays in the Canadian Imagination* (Toronto: Anansi 1971) 150-1

Observes that *Jephthah's Daughter* is 'the real commencement of a distinctively Canadian form of the narrative poem'

Desmond Pacey *Creative Writing in Canada* (Toronto: Ryerson 1952) 24-5

'Although he had almost nothing to say of Canada in his writings, something in the Canadian environment seems to have stimulated him to increased literary activity. ... The best that can be said for Heavysege and his works is that they are literary curiosities.'

Thomas Randall Dale 'The Life and Work of Charles Heavysege,' PhD dissertation, University of Chicago 1951

Comprises an exhaustive analysis of Heavysege's work with chapters on his life, *The Revolt of Tartarus*, the *Sonnets*, *Saul*, *Count Filippo*, *Jephthah's Daughter*, *The Advocate*, the minor poems and on the published criticism, as well as appendixes on Heavysege's vocabulary, allusions, and possible sources, and his inclusion in anthologies

'The Revolt of Charles Heavysege' *University of Toronto Quarterly* XXII (October 1952) 35-43

Maintains that Heavysege's dominant theme, the rebellion against a tyrannical deity, is based not on legend or his own imagination but on the Bible itself, an interpretation overlooked by Victorian reviewers

Robertson Davies *Leaven of Malice* (Toronto: Clarke Irwin 1954) 195-7, 212-17

A novelist's gentle gibe at academic sophistry and the developing enthusiasm for North American literature (Amcan)

Northrop Frye 'Preface to an Uncollected Anthology' (1956), *The Bush Garden: Essays in the Canadian Imagination* (Toronto: Anansi 1971) 171

Describes *Saul* and *Count Filippo* as 'Victorian dinosaurs in the usual idiom: *Count Filippo*, in particular, like the Albert Memorial, achieves a curious perverted beauty by the integrity of its ugliness.' With *Jephthah's Daughter*, Heavysege is described as 'the first poet to come to grips with the central tragic theme in Canada — the indifference of nature to human values.'

Wilfrid Eggleston *The Frontier and Canadian Letters* (Toronto: Ryerson 1957) 8

Heavysege does not qualify as a Canadian author for he was 'essentially an Englishman writing in Canada on Biblical themes.'

R.E. Rashley *Poetry in Canada: The First Three Steps* (Toronto: Ryerson Press 1958) 12-17

'The occasional excellence of imagery, the impression of brooding power in *Saul*, the liveliness of the characterization of Malzah, the occasional force of the sonnets show that Heavysege was potentially a poet of some reach and scope. None of these things is entirely original in him, however, and none can be separated from the mass of inept, confused, derivative material which is the bulk of his work. ... It seems scarcely possible that anyone could breathe so little of the cultural climate of his environs. ... He is not a contemporary poet at all; he is a stranger to his own times, a good illustration of the immigrants' irrelevance to the new world.'

Ralph Gustafson, ed. *Penguin Book of Canadian Verse* (Harmondsworth, Middlesex: Penguin Books 1958) 21

Describes Heavysege as one of the 'Three Charleses,' along with Sangster and Mair, who made a 'substantial beginning' in Canadian poetry. Although *Saul* is 'without the conditions for tragedy' and 'much of the writing is transcription,' occasionally Heavysege 'touches mastery.' *Count Filippo* is inclined to be 'moral, but for sheer exuberance, liveliness, and linguistics, North America has little to equal it.'

Thomas R. Dale 'Our Greatest Poet: A Century Ago' *Canadian Forum* XXXVII (February 1959) 245-6

Considers *Saul* to have been 'a potentially dangerous and explosive work' in its view that 'the Jehovah of the Old Testament historical books is an unmerciful tyrant.' Expresses surprise that there was 'no uproar' at this blasphemy at the time of its publication, but rather 'more praise than any book from Canada had received since Haliburton's *Sam Slick* books twenty years earlier.'

A.J.M. Smith, ed. *The Oxford Book of Canadian Verse* (Toronto: Oxford University Press 1960) xxvii
'There perhaps has never been in the poetry of the English-speaking peoples anywhere so curious a mixture of the grand and grandiose, of the magnificent and the ridiculous as *Saul*.'

John P. Matthews *Tradition in Exile* (Toronto: University of Toronto Press 1962) 56
Brief reference to Heavysege's position in the central parent tradition, unaffected by native influences. 'But, as Bailey's *Festus*, which had seemed to Tennyson one of the supreme achievements of English poetry, sank to obscurity within ten years of its appearance, Heavysege's *Saul* did not outlast its author.'

Michael Tait 'Playwrights in a Vacuum: English Canadian Drama in the 19th Century,' *Canadian Literature* 16 (Spring 1963) 5-18. Reprinted in *Dramatists in Canada: Selected Essays*, ed. William H. New (Vancouver: University of British Columbia Press 1972) 13-26
Outlines Heavysege's background and some of the formal and stylistic inadequacies of *Saul* and comments on the limitations of his circumstances and environment. 'He had about him something of the eccentric evangelist whose inner illumination

fortifies him in the teeth of the world's disdain. If the light Heavysege followed was three parts false, to some incalculable extent the reason was the darkness of the society about him.'

Carl F. Klinck 'Literary Activity in Canada, East and West, 1841-1880,' *Literary History of Canada*, ed. Carl F. Klinck (Toronto: University of Toronto Press 1965) 147-9

Draws on Thomas R. Dale's unpublished thesis on Heavysege (Chicago, 1951) and points indirectly to the unavailability of much of Heavysege's work for readers' assessments

Murray D. Edwards *A Stage in Our Past* (Toronto: University of Toronto Press 1968) 88-94

A discussion of Heavysege's poetic dramas, suggesting that the early critics' considerable interest in *Saul* and their rejection of *Count Filippo* was prompted largely by moral considerations of their themes

Norman Newton 'Classical Canadian Poetry and the Public Muse,' *Canadian Literature* 51 (Winter 1972) 40-3

As producer of a radio adaptation of *Count Filippo* (prepared by Peter Haworth), Newton discovered that the play 'worked' in performance – 'Here was a live mammoth.' Considers Heavysege to be a true Jacobean, transplanted whole into the nineteenth century. '*Saul* ... is indeed an astonishing work, a work that seems, when one enters into it without reservation, to display something like genius.'

J.C. Stockdale 'Charles Heavysege,' *Dictionary of Canadian Biography* V, Marc La Terreur, ed. (Toronto: University of Toronto Press 1972) 346-8

A compilation of most of the published material on Heavysege. Concludes that he is 'one of those mysterious figures [who] leave behind works to be examined anxiously for possible literary values, and to be claimed loudly as Canadian if any value, no matter how small, be found.'

Kenneth J. Hughes 'Heavysege's *The Advocate:* The Art of Failure,' *Journal of Canadian Fiction* II (Summer 1973) 95-8 Finds parallel elements in *The Advocate* and Shakespeare's *The Tempest.* Written in the language of a Jacobean, the novel is adapted to the socio-economic and political environment of Quebec society between 1760 and 1860.

Saul

INTRODUCTION.

THE reader of the history of Saul must have been struck by its picturesque grandeur, its sadness and tragic issue. First of the Hebrew Kings, his reign far surpasses in dramatic interest every other in the long line of his successors, whether upon the throne of Judah or of Israel. We see him taken from humble life and elevated to the government of his nation, up to that hour a pure theocracy. For having in an emergency assumed the priestly office, we see him deposed by God. Having failed to execute full judgment on Amalek, we find his deposition confirmed, and himself in the terrible possession of a demon. Under this influence, strengthened by jealousy, we behold him attempting, first in person and afterwards by means of Israel's enemies, the life of his benefactor, David; next imbruing his hands in the blood of the priests of God; and, after persisting in a series of persecutions of David,—now become his son-in-law and victorious general,—in his old age going to a battle-field, that he had been supernaturally assured should be fatal to himself and his elder sons, whereon, after witnessing the defeat of his army, he falls by his own hand.

Such, in brief, is the story of a man whose heroic qualities are celebrated in that matchless elegy beginning " How are the mighty fallen !"—such the career which the author of this volume has ventured to make the subject of its pages.

SAUL.

FIRST PART.

PERSONS REPRESENTED.

SAUL, *King of Israel.*
JONATHAN, *his Eldest Son.*
ABNER, *a relative of Saul, and a General in his Army.*
SAMUEL, *High Priest of Israel.*
JEHOIADAH, *a Priest.*
AHIAH, *a Priest.*
DAVID, *a young Shepherd, and subsequently King of Israel.*
JESSE, *father of David.*
AHINOAM, *Queen of Israel.*
GLORIEL, *Chief of the Celestial Spirits.*
ZOE, *Saul's Guardian-Angel.*
ZELEHTHA, *an Angel.*
ZAPH, *Chief of the Evil Spirits.*
MALZAH, *the " Evil Spirit from the Lord."*
ZEPHO, *Zaph's Messenger.*
PEYONA.
PROPHETS, ELDERS, MESSENGERS *from Jabesh Gilead,* OFFICERS, SOLDIERS, *a* COURTIER, *a* LEVITE, *a* PEASANT, *Saul's* ARMOUR-BEARER, *Jonathan's* ARMOUR-BEARER, *a* PHYSICIAN, DOMESTICS *of the Palace,* &c.

SAUL

ACT I.

SCENE I.

The Hill of God, with the Philistine garrison adjacent. A number of DEMONS *dancing;* ZAPH, *their chief, observing them, and* ZEPHO *gazing intently in an opposite direction.*

ZAPH.

Gently; this is sacred ground:
Foot it in a quiet round.
Zepho, keep a keen look-out,
So that none disturb the bout.

What now behold'st thou?

ZEPHO.

A great rabble.

ZAPH.

Of what composed?

ZEPHO.

Of prophets mostly.
With solemn sound they stalk quite ghostly;
And, 'midst them, one whose height and port
Declare him of superior sort.

ZAPH.

Dost thou know him?

SAUL.

ZEPHO.
                Methinks I do.
ZAPH.
Strain through the air thy lynx-like view
           [*Aside.*
With such, oft angels come and danger.

ZEPHO.
Yes, now I know the towering stranger:
His name is Saul, one Kish's son.
His father's asses lost, he'd gone
To seek them; but a diadem
Has found instead of finding them:
And they now found, he home doth steer,
'Midst plaintive sound approaching here.
Which news I learned as late in Ramah,
Unseen, I walked; and this small drama
There viewed myself,—upon Saul's head
A phial-full of oil saw shed
By Samuel; who then hailed as king
This Saul, and kissed him, promising
That signs should happen to him three,
The last of which you soon shall see:
Two are already.

ZAPH.
                Spirits all,
A stranger comes whose name is Saul.
He has lately been, I hear,
By Samuel, the authentic seer,
Anointed to hold future reign
Within this now priest-ruled domain.
With him come prophets, chanting loud,
And others, a miscellaneous crowd.

FIRST DEMON.
Then dancing's over!—It is ever so!—
I'll e'en about my business go.

####### SECOND DEMON.
Prythee defer awhile adieu :
They are near, and rather noisy too.

####### ZAPH.
Watch their motions :
Methinks they're coming to devotions.

####### THIRD DEMON.
Here they are, each like a zany,
And braying loud, "Jehovah!" many.

Enter SAUL *and a company of* PROPHETS *and* SPECTATORS, *the* PROPHETS *chanting.*

####### PROPHETS.
Jehovah! Jehovah! O Israel's God,
In pity look from thine abode
Upon us low.
Thou who once brought our fathers up
From Egypt, and didst cause to stoop
Proud Pharaoh, and his host o'erthrew,
Do thou now for us interpose ;
Oh, look again on Jacob's woes!

####### THIRD DEMON.
This is doleful.

####### FOURTH DEMON.
     I'm in tears.

####### SECOND DEMON.
Dry your eyes, and ope your ears.

####### ZAPH.
Keep your countenances ; be decorous :
There seems a pretty farce before us.

####### SAUL (*recitative*).
On Jacob thou hast looked, O Lord,
According to thine ancient word.

####### FIFTH DEMON.
He knows not that.

12   SAUL.

ZAPH.

Your tongues restrain:
The prophets are going to howl again.

PROPHETS (*in chorus*).

Thou, who from bondage brought us forth,
Us saved from Moab's and Ammon's wrath;
From Amalek and Edom saved
Thy people, though they misbehaved;
And gave them manna from the skies,
And from the rock bade waters rise;
And led them to this promised land,
Across Arabia's burning sand,
With cloud by day and fire by night,
An awful yet celestial light,—
Jehovah, hear, and let thy spear
Of vengeance terrify our foes!
O God, attend; thine ear down bend:
Oh, let the time of sorrow close
This access of thine Israel's woes!

THIRD DEMON.

Were this not better than the last,
I now from hence had fled aghast.

ZAPH.

Hist:
Let not a syllable be missed.

SAUL.

The Lord, at length, hath looked upon
His heritage: your cry hath gone
Even unto his holy hill.
God shall your ardent wish fulfil.

PROPHETS.

How long, how long, how long, O Lord,
Shall Israel mourn!

SAUL.

From sorrow turn.

PROPHETS.

Say, Lord, how long the land shall be
In shadow of an enemy:
How long shall violence us meet,
And wrong possess the judgment-seat?

SAUL.

I heard the Lord arise and swear
Jeshurun was his special care.

DEMONS (*shouting in chorus*).

Ha, ha! ha, ha! beware, beware;
Such was once *our* special fare:
Mocketh all things the Creator,
Mocketh his whole realm of nature;
Think not sons of earth he'll spare,
Who smote the nobler things of air.

PROPHETS.

O God, give ear, Jehovah, hear:
Is Israel not still to thee dear?
Did'st thou not once, for Abraham's sake,
Them thy peculiar people make?
O God, arise, and Ammon shake!
Jehovah!

DEMONS.

Ha, ha! ha, ha!

PROPHETS.

Jehovah!

DEMONS.

Ha, ha! ha, ha!

PROPHETS.

Jehovah!

DEMONS.

Ha, ha! ha, ha!

PROPHETS.

Almighty one!

DEMONS.

He'll hear anon:
Ha, ha! ha, ha! pray on, pray on.

PROPHETS.

Oh, heal our hurt.

DEMONS.

'Tis princely sport
To hear them sue in such a sort.

ZAPH.

Grow not too loud and insolent;
Who can turn God from his intent?
Haply He indeed hath meant
Good, quick coming and spread wide,
Over Israel's mourning pride.
Cease your laughter; it may come after.

FIFTH DEMON.

Master, it is many a day
Since we were allowed be gay;
Let us laugh, then, while we may.

ZAPH.

Peace; Saul sings.

SAUL (*air*).

I.

O Canaan fair, my country dear,
Lo, thy deliverance draws near;
The spear is raised, bent is the bow
That shall thine enemies o'erthrow.

II.

Thy grief is passed, thy mourning done;
Put now bright hope's clean garments on:
The Lord regards thee from the skies;
He bids thee from the dust arise.

III.

Fair Land of Promise, clothe in smiles
Thy landscapes, thy neglected piles;
For thou shalt be redeemed ere long
From foreign foe, domestic wrong.

IV.

O land that worship'st the true God,
Behold on high his outstretched rod:
Rise, bid the alien from thee flee;
The Lord, the Lord is yet with thee.

FIRST DEMON.

This seems the true prophetic vein.

THIRD DEMON.

I'd like to hear that song again.

FOURTH DEMON.

He is deceived.

FIFTH DEMON.

Yet who deceived him?

ZAPH.

There hath none
With a lie unto him gone.

SECOND DEMON.

'Tis the confidence of his nature.

ZAPH.

Rather it is his Creator
Who this hour him works upon.

SIXTH DEMON.

'Tis tedious here.

ZAPH.

Hence let us hie;
I hear, though faint yet clear,
Spirits coming down the sky.

(*The* DEMONS *vanish, and a company of* ANGELS, *conducted by* GLORIEL, *descend.*)

GLORIEL.

I heard the sound of spirits in haste departing.

FIRST ANGEL.

Yonder o'er the hills they are darting.

GLORIEL.

If my sentiment be true,
They who lately hence withdrew
Belong unto the fallen crew.
Let Saul be guarded :—
Zoe, to thee that task's awarded :
Fare thee well.

[*Exeunt* ANGELS, ZOE *remaining.*

A PROPHET.

Tall stranger, whosoe'er thou art, we see
That God is with thee; therefore come with us.

SAUL.

I'll follow you. [*Aside.*] Three signs were promised me,
Which have in kind and number come to pass.
Soon as I Samuel left my heart was changed;
And now I feel that which I cannot name :
Solemnity and courage fill my soul,
That, war intending, yet sits throned in peace.

[*Exeunt* SAUL *and the* PROPHETS.

ZOE.

I must attend him whom to me is given
To guard from hell and to assist towards heaven.

[Exit ZOE.

FIRST SPECTATOR.

Know ye the name of yon gigantic figure,
That, eminent o'er all, with haughty port,
Enrapt stood prophecying, and now stalks
Like some great purpose, hence ?

SECOND SPECTATOR.

'Tis Saul ; and, lo,
The burden of his words was hope for Israel.

THIRD SPECTATOR.

Is Saul amongst the prophets ?

FIRST SPECTATOR.

To free the land,
Shangar and Sampson were not likelier.

FOURTH SPECTATOR.

Speak low. Let us separate ; we know not whether
There be not here some spy of the Philistines.

[Exeunt.

SCENE II.

Country near Gibeah. Cattle grazing at a distance. SAUL, *after being anointed king by Samuel, has returned home to Gibeah, and is there occupied as formerly.*

SAUL, *musing.*

How tame now seems to me this herdsman life !
Unprofitable too : I naught do here,
Naught that can serve good purpose : I am like
A taper that is left to burn to waste
Within an empty house. Why do I stay ?

Others could tend these herds as well as I,—
And haply better, for my thoughts are far
From meads and kine, and all the servile round
Of household duties, same from year to year,—
Alike far from the rural dull routine,
And traffic of the town, when I it visit
To exchange my herds and corn for silver shekels.
Yet I will wait my time:—and yet the steer
Puts forth his horns when his due months arrive,
And pushes with them though they be but tender;
The blade starts through the clod in spring; the leaf
Then on the bough sits in its pride of green:
The blossom, punctual to its season, comes,
Milk-white or ruddy; and the perfect fruit
Appears with autumn; nor the snow doth fail
The hoary winter. Doth the snake not shed
Its slough? the fledging leave its natal nest?
Twice what I once was now I feel to be!
Down, proud imagination; quiet keep,
Thou rash impatience:—and yet Samuel said,
" Now God is with thee, act as thou seest fit."
What should I do? Deem this less zeal than pride,
And here in all tranquillity abide.

[*Exit.*

SCENE III.

Contiguous to a Hamlet.
Enter three HEBREWS *and an* ELDER.

FIRST HEBREW.

We are to assemble, sayest thou, to-morrow at Mizpeh?

ELDER.

Yes, to receive a king from God and Samuel:
Loudly, with others, you demanded one.

FIRST HEBREW.

We did and do demand one; and with reason,
For Samuel is aged and his sons corrupt.

SECOND HEBREW.

And yet 'tis said that Samuel was displeased
At the idea, and gave, at first, no answer.

ELDER.

He did from us—(for I was one of those
Who were deputed by you to convey
To him your wish)—he did from us retire,
As we supposed to ponder your request
Alone, and lay it before the Lord; but soon
Returned, and in such sad and solemn style
Foretold the issues of our granted wish,
That, for a season, we stood wavering;
Even as the headstrong wind, when, having blown
Strongly out of one quarter, on a sudden,
As if uncertain of its next direction,
It restless veers, travelling nor east nor west,
Nor north nor south; so we, surprised,
Perplexed, revolving, and not knowing whether
To retain this evil or to accept of that.

FIRST HEBREW.

What said he to you?

ELDER.

That our king should be
Exacting and despotic; that, indeed,
The nation no immunity should have
Beneath his rule, naught sacred from his grasp;
Our sons, our daughters, lands, our labour, skill,—
In fine, our all, should yield to him subscription.

SECOND HEBREW.

Already a tenth the Levites are endowed with.

ELDER.

He said our king would tithe the remainder.

FIRST HEBREW.

And
To that your answer?

THIRD HEBREW.
Did you not remonstrate?
ELDER.
We said as we had been told to do,—" Give us a king."
SECOND HEBREW.
But did you not make stipulations, nor
Propose abatement of those hard prerogatives?
ELDER.
No; for how could we, since they to us were rather
Foretold by the grieved prophet, than ordained;
As though the king should don them with his crown,
And wear them as his true and natural garment.
THIRD HEBREW.
I wish that I had but been of your number!
I would have spoken boldly for the nation.
What, were you not our representatives?
ELDER.
What could we, save reiterate our instruction?—
" Let us be governed like to other peoples;
Let a king rule us in the days of peace,
And lead us to battle in the hour of war."
THIRD HEBREW.
Here's a dilemma!
FIRST HEBREW.
Well, I will repair
To Mizpeh to-morrow, and behold the man
Who shall hereafter in the name of king
Cause us to tremble. Will he dream to-night
Of his approaching fortune? If the choice
Should fall on me, woe falls on you, good gentlemen.
ELDER.
Approach this crisis in a proper spirit;
For it will be the Lord to-morrow at Mizpeh,
And by his grace shall reign whom then is chosen.

THIRD HEBREW.

'Twixt King and Levite little will be left us.—
I shall not go to Mizpeh.

ELDER.

Thither go,
At the grave summons.

SECOND HEBREW.

Grave it is for all;
But most for those who have fair wives and daughters.

FIRST HEBREW.

Would the King take our wives?

THIRD HEBREW.

Would he'd take mine!

SECOND HEBREW.

He would take our sons if strong.

FIRST HEBREW.

Ourselves if skilful.

SECOND HEBREW.

Our property, our lands.—'Tis rather harsh.—
I know not whether I shall go or not.

FIRST HEBREW.

What have we done in our dim discontent!

THIRD HEBREW.

None than yourselves have been more loud for change.

SECOND HEBREW.

Yes, for a change from bad to better;—but this
Were to exchange pale twilight for black darkness.
Beshrew our folly! there's worse state than Priestdom.—
Still, let's prepare to start betimes to-morrow.

[*Exeunt the three* HEBREWS.

ELDER.

Thus are we ever stricken with dismay
When Heaven has granted our inordinate wishes.—
These men aghast are at their answered prayer,
And wear but ill their countenance of courage.

                                                          [*Exit.*

SCENE IV.

Mizpeh.

Sound of a multitude at a distance. Enter HEBREWS, *meeting.*

FIRST HEBREW.

Have you seen the King?

SECOND HEBREW.

                        We have.

THIRD HEBREW.

How seems he to you?

FOURTH HEBREW.

A lion, and a tiger, and a man,
Agreed to dwell in one magnificent den.

FIRST HEBREW.

If his spirit answers to his form,—and I
Believe it does,—he is the very being
For our occasion; that has grown so foul,
It needs the very devil to scour it fair;
And I suppose, from your description, sir,
He is that gentleman.

FOURTH HEBREW.

                      I do not jest.

FIRST HEBREW.

Nor I.

FOURTH HEBREW.
Have you not seen him?
FIRST HEBREW.
Yes, indeed:
T' avoid it would have been most difficult.
Taller by th' shoulders and upwards than the crowd,
He moved; and loftier bore his head above it,
Than bears a swimmer his above the waves.
From every point he was conspicuous.
SECOND HEBREW.
He's of strong passions doubtless.
THIRD HEBREW.
I observed,
When Samuel told us that we had rejected
God's rule in asking for ourselves a·king,
His countenance fell, surprised: and I remarked
He bit his lips, and symptoms of displeasure
Spread o'er his face; but they soon passed away,
And left him as before.
FOURTH HEBREW.
Had he a prescience
That he should be selected?
FIRST HEBREW.
Fitness always
Knows whether it be worthy, though it knows
Not whether 'twill be chosen: and although
Incompetency oft mistakes its meed,
Ability ne'er does so. 'Tis a foolish
Saying, " The wise know not their wisdom, nor
The fair their beauty."
FOURTH HEBREW.
Then, 'twas surely strange
He should conceal himself amongst the baggage.

THIRD HEBREW.

But when they found him, marked you not his mien?
Thence slowly he came, and seemed to know his worth:—
And once I fancied that he looked too proud;
Contemplating with a disdainful look
The myriads around him.—Hark! they shout.

      [*Shouts of " God save the King !"*
Let's join the throng.
              [*Exeunt.*
  [*Enter* SAUL, *and a band of* HEBREWS *following him.*

SAUL.

You will accompany me, you say. So be it.—
If prompted, follow me and be the ball,
Tiny at first, that shall, like one of snow,
Gather in rolling.

A HEBREW.

       We will follow thee
Wherever thou shalt lead.

SAUL.

      To Gibeah, then;
And you shall soon have scope to prove you men.
            [*Exeunt omnes.*

SCENE V.

The country near Gibeah. SAUL, *returning from the field, observes the people weeping.*

SAUL.

Why are the people weeping?

A HEBREW.

      Oh, sorrow, sorrow!
Thou too wilt weep when thou hast learnt the reason.

Nahash the king of Ammon has besieged
Jabesh Gilead, which has promised to surrender
To him in seven days, if none relieve it;
And on this sore condition, that the wretch
Shall thrust out the right eye of every man
Within the place, that with the hideous deed
He may reproach, hereafter, every Hebrew.

SAUL.

Hear me, O God!
So be it done to me and unto all
To me belonging, yea, and tenfold more,—
If more can be by living man endured,—
If I shall fail to drive this monster back.
Ye punishing ministers,
Ye dark, invisible demons that do fly
And do heaven's judgments, turn your course towards him.
Go, send them hither who have brought the news.

[*Exit* HEBREW.

Now, every motive that can my resolve
Strengthen, come double to my heart: hear me
Again, O God.
If I should not perform more than my vow,
May I and all in Israel be disfigured;
Woman, youth and maiden, child and infant, all
Be brought to *total* darkness. Dusky fiend,
Who would come on us, bringing demi-night,
And quench forever half our light of day!

The HEBREW, *re-entering with the* MESSENGERS.

Behold those here who can thine anger raise.

SAUL, *to the Messengers.*

Go tell the men of Jabesh Gilead,
To fear not that foul Whelp of Twilight, Nahash:
They shall have help.

A MESSENGER.

Seven days he has given us,
And, if we be not in that time relieved,
We must e'en submit unto his pitiless terms.

SAUL.

Away, fear not.

[*Exeunt the* HEBREW *and* MESSENGERS.

No further words; let deeds
Come next.   Now, herds and flocks, a last adieu :
Men are, henceforth, my flock, my pasture Canaan :
I will forthwith to Bezek, and there raise
My standard, and woe unto them who follow
Not Saul and Samuel.

SCENE VI.

Near Bezek.   The gathering of the Hebrews.   Time, evening.
SAUL *standing upon an eminence.*

SAUL.

The ground is hidden with men; the heights appear
Like to huge ant-hills, and the valleys swarm
With moving life.   Where will these numbers be
In fifty summers? even in thirty years
Half of these multitudes will be in the grave:
In twenty more a miserable remnant
(Drained of the vigor, if not of the courage,
That brings them here to-day) will sole remain
To tell deeds yet undone :—in fifty summers
To morrow's yet all uncommenced feat
Shall be a hoary tale; yon thronging actors—
Each now impatient to perform his part—
Shall almost all be quiet in the grave:
Even as the snowdrifts left on Lebanon
In the hot days of June, few, few they'll be.

[*Enter* MESSENGERS *of the inhabitants of Jabesh Gilead.*

Haste on to Jabesh Gilead, lest should fail
The hearts of its inhabitants, and they surrender
Themselves precipitately to the Dog,
In the fond hope thereby to soften him:
To-morrow, by the time the sun is hot,
They shall have help: quick, get you over Jordan.

FIRST MESSENGER.

If ever blessing fell on man, mayest thou
Receive one, our deliverer that shall be;
For is not Samuel with thee, and with him
Is not the Lord, as once, at Eben-ezer!

SAUL.

Go; I will succour you.

SECOND MESSENGER.

      The winds of heaven
Behind thee blow; and on our enemies' eyes
May the sun smite to-morrow, and blind them for thee;
But, O Saul, do not fail us.

SAUL.

     Fail ye!
Let the morn fail to break; I will not break
My word. Haste, or I'm there before you. Fail!
Let the morn fail the east; I'll not fail you,
But, swift and silent as the streaming wind,
Unseen approach, then, gathering up my force
At dawning, sweep on Ammon, as Night's blast
Sweeps down from Carmel on the dusky sea.
Our march is through the darkness. Now begone;
We'll hear no further till our task be done.

      [*Exeunt* MESSENGERS.

If gratitude and earnest prayer, from them
Who have the greatest cause for both, be earnest
Of answering victory, we shall to-morrow
Have given to the idolaters such a wound
As all the balm of Gilead, which they claim,
Shall not suffice to heal:—a wound so deep,
That they shall think that Jephthah lives again:
Or that the old Zamzummim giants, whom
Their sires destroyed, have sent from hades a spirit,
Who comes incarnate, leading Israel's ire;
So dearly shall this arrogant siege yet cost them.

Our forces are beginning the swift march,
Which must throughout the coming night continue:
I will descend and lead them as is fit.
                                              [*Exit.*

SCENE VII.

The vicinity of Jabesh Gilead.   Time, dawn.

SAUL, *pacing to and fro.*

SAUL.

The day breaks calmly, howso'er it end;
And nature shows no great consent with man,
Curtailing not the slumber of the clouds,
Nor rising with the clarion of the wind
To blow his signals.   I hear the enemy
Arousing hastily his sleepy legions:
Ammon perceives us.   Wherefore comes not Abner?

ABNER, *entering.*

We are ready to assault.

SAUL.

                          And so am I.
Thy force lead as I bade thee.   Jonathan
His orders has: like thee, he'll quit him well.
Prompt let us be, and not more prompt than fell.
                                          [*Exit* ABNER.
Each moment to the foe is worth an hour: why comes
Not with my arms the youth who bears them!   Boy!
                          [*Calling on his Armour-Bearer.*
"Prompt" is the word upon the tongue of time,
From day to day on echoing through the years,
That glide away into eternity,
Whispering the same unceasing syllable.
Boy, bring my arms!—not now we'll moralize,
Although to fight it needs that some must fall.
When this day's work is done, and serious night
Disposes to reflection and gives leisure,

We will review the hours of the past slaughter;
And, while around to heaven ascends a dew
Distilled from blood now throbbing through its veins,
Sorrow for whom we must.   Till then we'll act:
Survive who may, retain who shall his breath,
We'll now assault and start the work of death.
     [*Enter a youth bringing the shield of* SAUL.
Why loiteredst thou? quick, give to me my shield;
Now quit thee well on this thy virgin field.
           [*Exeunt.*

A sound of trumpets heard, and an increasing noise of the onset. At length Ammonitish soldiers are seen fleeing across the hills, and Hebrew soldiers pursuing them.

SCENE VIII.

Another part of the Country.

Enter SAUL *and a* TRUMPETER, OFFICERS *and* SOLDIERS.

SAUL.

Now let the trumpet sound the call to halt,
For two of the enemy are not left together;
And all have thrown away their arms: indeed,
So quick a thaw I never knew before,
Nor vapor melted faster into naught.

FIRST OFFICER.

They have gone much faster than they came, and left
Behind them baggage and rich trophies many.

SAUL.

They will remember this day long as they
Shall keep a calendar.
     [*The* TRUMPETER *blows the recall.*
But let us sheathe these trenchent ministers;
For, by the souls for whom they have hewn a passage
Unto some far, mysterious gehenna,
Or to the troubled sepulchre of the air,

They have well done. Behold of plain and hill,
They, aided by the bow and spear, have made
A very shambles with the enemy's slain,
That lie in heaps before the walls of Jabesh,
And thence to this grow fewer, like the drops
Of blood sore oozing from the savage beast,
As it flees before the hunter till 'tis drained.
We have drained this day the pride of Ammon. Lo!
As when October strews the land with leaves,
So hath our fury larded it with dead.
And yet I pity them, poor breathless wretches,
And would revive them if I could do so,
Would not the exasperating memory
Of those dire terms provoke me to rekill them.
How fares it with thee?   [*Enter* JONATHAN.

JONATHAN.

How fares it with you, father?

SAUL.

Well, as it ought, so ill faring with our foes.

JONATHAN.

They 'll rue the day wherein they crossed our borders.

SECOND OFFICER.

But few of them remain to retraverse them.

JONATHAN.

Ere the recall's far-pealing note had reached us,
Our soldiers were disputing for the victims,
They had so far diminished.

THIRD OFFICER.

Is 't possible,
That we so soon have reaped so rank a field,
And scuffle for the gleanings! Nahash has
Escaped us.

FOURTH OFFICER.

Greater curse yet overtake him!
May lightnings sear his sight, and may nor sun
Nor the sweet stars again by him be seen.

FIRST OFFICER.

Thou Moon, rise not to him; nor break again
On him, thou Dawn.
SECOND OFFICER.

       Ye hearth, ye altar fires,
Expire when he looks on you.
THIRD OFFICER.

        Ye women's eyes,
Unto his gaze seem bleared with sudden age,
Or shew but horror.
JONATHAN.

      Amen. Is my father
Angry or sorrowful?
FIRST OFFICER.

        He has not yet
Appeased his vengeance' hunger, yet with its food
Is surfeited.
JONATHAN.

      He is given to reverie:
I'll speak to him. Father, but yesterday
These Ammonites at Israel scoffed secure;
To-day, they are destroyed.
SAUL.

       Like waving ears
Of lusty corn, upright we are to-day;
To-morrow we are laid low by the sickle
Of something unforeseen.
JONATHAN.

      Now Jabesh Gilead
May point in safety the living finger of scorn
At the cold heaps of dead around her walls;
And boys and women, yea, and tottering hags,
Go pull them by the beard, or, with their nails,
Extract, unchecked, pale corses' eye-balls, angling
Unhurt within those reservoirs of tears:
Yea, out of dead men's mouths may pluck the tongues
That yesterday at this hour bullied them.

SAUL.

Let us return, and leave it for the vulture,
Smelling the odour of mortality,
To hasten here and batten. Boy, blow again,
And louder, the recall.
    [*The recall is again sounded, and* SAMUEL *enters followed by a crowd.*
Hail, holy seer; hail, men of Israel!
Ye men of Israel, thank the Lord to day;
For 'tis his power that hath before you driven
Nahash and all the Ammonitish crew.
All did I say? how little now their all!
You have destroyed them in their arrogance;
You have dissolved them with the wand of change.
Last evening they lay down amidst their camp,
That gleamed in starlight; but no more shall they
See stars nor morning, for their eyelids down
Are sealed by frosty death. Where now is Nahash?
Fallen, fallen is the cruel pride of Ammon!
Its warriors strew for many a league our land,
And the wild beasts devour them: they no grave
Shall have except the fox's maw, and belly
Of unclean beasts; nor with their sires shall lie
Many fugitives, for, still as with their flight
The dust-cloud rose, we laid it in their blood.
Dearly they've paid for their grim proposition!
Let them return for their slain, unless tears blind
Those who, with bloody deeds, had this day thought
To have blinded others. Let Nahash gnash his teeth;
Now let him howl at home, and ask his gods
Wherefore they thus forsook him. Joy, O joy!
The God of Israel is above all gods!
    [*Acclamation of the multitude.*

ONE *of the multitude.*

Let those who said "Shall Saul reign over us!"
Be put to death!

ANOTHER.

Yes, let them die.

MANY *at once.*
                    They shall.
             SAUL.
To-day no man shall suffer death, for God
To-day hath saved and gladdened Israel.
Further acclamation, and cries of " *God save the King!* " " *God save King*
                    SAUL!"
             SAMUEL.
Now let us go to Gilgal and there crown him.
       [*Exeunt all amidst acclamations and flourishing of trumpets*

SCENE IX.

The Country. Enter HEBREWS.

             FIRST HEBREW.
Pray which of you were at the coronation?
             SECOND HEBREW.
I.
             FIRST HEBREW.
                    And how went it?
             SECOND HEBREW.
                    Well, mixed up with ill.
             FIRST HEBREW.
What happened? did the people change their minds?
             SECOND HEBREW.
No, but we had committed a great sin
In asking for a king; so Samuel told us,
And, to confirm his saying, called on God
To send down rain and thunder, though 'twas harvest.
             FIRST HEBREW.
Ah, then your revelry was changed to sorrow.
             SECOND HEBREW.
'Twas, for a while; but Samuel re-assured us;
Showing us, that as in the past Jehovah

Had saved us by Jerubaal, Bedan, Jephthah,
So He would now—if we were faithful to Him—
By our anointed king. Yet was it fearful
To see the sky fast darken, and to hear
The thunder-growl approaching, until one
Wide flash of lightning quivered from the clouds,
And hung above us, glaring like the eye
Of God looking down upon us in his wrath.
All trembled, all stood mute, excepting some
Who, motionless, low muttered deprecation.
Few dared uplift their eyes; and the hurled deluge,
Smoking upon the ground, that shook with din
Beneath us, seemed to speak intense displeasure.

FIRST HEBREW.

How then looked Samuel?

SECOND HEBREW.

Rapt.

FIRST HEBREW.

And Saul?

SECOND HEBREW.

I saw him stand, methought, half frowning; but
Terror so shook me and confused my sight,
That scarcely I knew what was and what was not.

THIRD HEBREW.

This augurs ill.

SECOND HEBREW.

The worst is past, and all
Depends, 'twould seem, on us and our behaviour.

FOURTH HEBREW.

Did Samuel say aught else deserving mention?

SECOND HEBREW.

Much, much before this climax; but 'twas chiefly
In his own vindication; challenging us
To prove injustice 'gainst him in his rule,
And, in the event of it, offering restitution.

FIFTH HEBREW.
Referred he to his sons' flagitious doings?
SECOND HEBREW.
No.
FOURTH HEBREW.
    Let their evil in his good be lost;
Even as the filthy and defiling smoke
Is lost in the pure air.
FIFTH HEBREW.
                    Yet recollections
Will stick like smuts upon one's memory:
And Samuel's whiteness, though it may reflect
A light on his sons' blackness, but thereby
Doth show it forth more ugly than we thought it;
And they unfitter seen, or now to aid him
Or to succeed hereafter; their demerits
By his worthiness shewing greater than first fancied;
Even as the dusty atmosphere of a room
When bars of sunshine are projected through it,
Shews more polluted than we first believed it.
But let that pass: what more declared the prophet?
SECOND HEBREW.
He shewed us that the priestly government
Had come from God by Moses and by Aaron.
FIFTH HEBREW.
His order, yes, the spirit of his order,
Gave utterance there: all power it had before,
Which now must be divided with another.
The old man, doubtlessly, is stung at seeming
To be by us cast off in his old age:
But what is done is done, and for the best;
Huzzah, then, for the King!
THE OTHERS.
        Huzzah for King and Priest!
                          [*Exeunt omnes.*
END OF THE FIRST ACT.

ACT II.

SCENE I.

Michmash. A handsome Apartment.
Enter SAUL *and* JEHOIADAH, *a priest.*

SAUL.

I know that tempest and a foul disease
Discomfited and humbled the Philistines;
But nor the weather nor painful emerods
Are always at your bidding; nor is Samuel
Immortal, that he should have power to pray
Ever for you, and raise up new Eben-ezers;
And when he's gone, what's Levi! Ye will say,
The Lord will raise new Samuels up in Israel.
Hath not the Lord raised me? caused mine anointing?
God is our helper, our deliverer, sayest thou?
God now shall help us in another way:
He shall assist me to transform the Hebrews
Into men, they who, till recently, were children,
Unstable, offending him by fresh relapses;
Yet, in the hour of danger, crying to Him,
As babes, when smitten, halloo for their mothers;
Or spendthrifts, clutched by angry creditors,
Beg from their sires fresh sums to purchase pleasures.
All this is changed, for none again awhoring
After strange gods shall go, as erst they did;
Nor demons nor the stars consult shall any.
Henceforward war and agriculture shall
Be ours, as war and commerce are our foes',
Whose discipline with discipline we'll meet.

Nor from henceforth, with raw and instant levies,
I cope with the trained armies that Philistia
Persists to send against us: I more men
Must have, and more of Israel's substance ere
I open the campaign, which shall not close
Until the land is cleared of aliens;
Then must I turn within and look for foes
Intestine, they who wear friend's faces
Yet are masked traitors, and, with envy filled,
Go about carping at us. Nahash's ruin
Was but the beginning of the rude purgation
That I intend for Israel; her at length
No enemy shall ravage, nor shall any
Of hers malign her king without a cause.
I have too patient been of opposition ;
Hence my scant force, whose numbers are no more
Than, say, two thousand here and at Mount Bethel,
And Jonathan's one thousand men at Gibeah.
[JEHOIADAH *remains silent*.
Why ponderest thou? Might they be stationed better?

JEHOIADAH.

The people murmur that your majesty
Hath taken these men by force, whom they regard
As being the superexcellence of the nation.

SAUL.

The people have instigators, whom, if I
Discover, I will cut off! Tell me, dost thou,
When needing for the altar a new victim,
Not still require a beast without a blemish?
And shall I then lay hands on the offscouring?
Can work be without means? and if a king,
Shall I forego the pomp and state wherewith
A king is ever surrounded? Let beware
All idle tongues, or I will pluck them out,
And haply, in my exasperation, throw them
Into their owners' faces.
[*Enter a* COURIER.
Say what news:

That news thou bring'st thy way-worn plight declares,
And good should be its burthen by thine eye:—
Comest thou from Jonathan?

COURIER.

From him I come,
Your majesty, and bring you joyful tidings:
I all the night have hurried on to bring
You glorious day:—his highness, Jonathan,
Hath overthrown the Philistine garrison
At Geba.

SAUL.

My brave son! how happened it?
What provocation, other than their presence,
Incited him to assail them?—or were they
Our son's assailants?

COURIER.

Them the prince assailed;
And for he would, and gave no reason save
He could and would.

SAUL.

Now we shall stink i'th' nostrils
Of proud Philistia, who will all her war
Soon launch against us:—Well, so let it be.—
At Gilgal we must rapidly assemble.
I will reward thee, welcome messenger.
Follow me, Jehoiadah.

[*Exit* SAUL.

COURIER.

You scarcely seem
To relish my news, good father.

JEHOIADAH.

Sirrah, check
Your tongue. Would'st thou have me rush into the street
And there cry "Hallelujah!"

[*Exit* JEHOIADAH.

COURIER.

Didst "sirrah" me,
Lean Levite? 'Tis well that thou art gone,

Or, by my soul, thou sour, disdainful priest,
This hand had else profaned thee. All the tribe
Of Levi have been cankered from the hour
That we obtained a king. Why, let them fret,
And fall away like watered lime; their pride
Long time has needed humbling.
                                              [*Exit.*

SCENE II.

The Country near Gibeah.

Enter, in haste, four HEBREWS *from different quarters.*

FIRST HEBREW.

The Philistines are coming like their sea,
And lashed to fury by the gale from Geba.
" To Gilgal, unto Gilgal!" is the cry:—
The king is gone and with him the three thousand.

SECOND HEBREW.

I heard the tocsin bellow in the night.
The king is prompt.

THIRD HEBREW.

                    Ay, let us after him;
For Samuel is to join with him at Gilgal.
What is thy weapon?

SECOND HEBREW.

            The sword: what thine?

THIRD HEBREW.

            The spear.

Fellow, what thine?

FOURTH HEBREW.

            A cudgel.

THIRD HEBREW.

            Let's along;
And if we fight not, we shall swell the throng.
                                              [*Exeunt.*

SCENE III.

Near Michmash.

SAUL *and* JEHOIADAH *reconnoitering the Philistine encampment.*

SAUL.

Would that that host were mine, or that mine were
Accoutred like it and for war appointed!
But we must meet it with such as we have:
And Samuel's presence, and the strong belief
That Heaven has ordained for us victory,
Shall help us wrest one from the iron palms
Of yonder military, that appear
More than the burning stars in number, and
With arms and armour making the dull earth
More shining than the heavens! How like a bivouac
Of bright, descended angels they appear,
As thus the sun illumes their brazen mail,
And silver-sembling arms of glittering steel!
They are tall fellows; chariots too I see
That fly on wheels, as angels fly on wings.

JEHOIADAH.

Why did prince Jonathan rashly fall on Geba!
Unless God interpose, we are unable
To meet the anger of enraged Philistia.

SAUL.

I prythee peace.

JEHOIADAH.

                'Twas premature, your majesty:
The set-time of Jehovah had not come.
He had not been enquired of, but headily
This struggle was begun: 'twas ill advised
To vex the enemy without permission.
We cannot withstand, much less o'erthrow, yon **armament**,
With which compared we are but a rabble rout.

SAUL.

Thou lately thought'st a rabble as good as soldiers.

JEHOIADAH.

Thou hast no chariots, thy cavalry are weak :
Thy followers are many, but the enemy's horse
Count twice the number of thy chosen men :
In vain will be our uttermost resistance.

SAUL.

How often have our ancestors driven back
The bold begetters of that mail-clad host !

JEHOIADAH.

Jonathan is brave, but was too forward at Geba.

SAUL.

Would'st thou hold the prince's virtue as a vice ?
Let Samuel come and thou shalt see what thou
Hast only heard of, Jonathan's bravery :
We wait the prophet's coming to sacrifice ;
But had he not enjoined me to await him,
I would at once to the foe have battle given,
Expecting Heaven's assistance.—But he's right ;
The vulgar to whom courage is not native,
And who have not acquired, by proud traditions,
The fear of shame and dainty sense of honor,
Must by religion's rites obtain the valor
Which best is carried ready in the heart.

JEHOIADAH.

If Samuel come, and if the Lord be willing,
Doubtless our army shall have victory.

SAUL.

We are not serving other gods ; His altars
Attend you, and I with death do punish those
Who still resort to demons instead of Urim ;
Then wherefore downcast hangest thou thine eyes,
Even as if Dagon, Seignior of the Sea,
Could cope with Him who rules both land and main ?

D

JEHOIADAH.

If Samuel come not—

SAUL.

    Come not! He has promised.

JEHOIADAH.

Our army is as water, theirs as fire.

SAUL.

This is the most detractive spirit I have known. [*Aside.*
              [*Exit.* SAUL.

JEHOIADAH.

      Samuel loves him,
But I detest him, and should any king
Detest, for kings must overshadow our order.
          [*Exit* JEHOIADAH.

SCENE IV.

In the Hebrew's camp, at Gilgal.
Enter SAUL.

SAUL.

Come! Samuel, come! wherefore is Samuel lingering?
Age ought to prize the present, so brief its future.
May all the blest fortuities combine
To hasten him hither.   [*Enter* ABNER.
    Well, what cheer?

ABNER.

      Not well;
Our army is by far too faint of heart.

SAUL.

So I suspected.

ABNER.

      Nay, they shame me; for
They are appalled even by the mere report
Of the foe's mien, as he lies couched at Michmash.

SAUL.

I knew it; yet thy words do half unman me,
And strengthen in me uneasy apprehension
Of evil threatened by Samuel's delay ;
For should we be attacked ere he arrive,
What were all generalship, all zeal and courage,—
The bravery of a few conjoined with cowards ?
I never deemed them heroes, but so soon
To fall a-trembling doth indeed enrage me.
Go whisper them the Seer's expected hourly.
         [Exit. ABNER.
A gently-floating rumour will assure them
More than a confident blast: Come! Samuel, come!
         [Exit SAUL.

SCENE V.

Another part of the camp. Time, the following day.
Enter three Hebrew OFFICERS, *meeting.*

FIRST OFFICER.

What news?

SECOND OFFICER.

     The king has issued an injunction
To kill all found deserting.

THIRD OFFICER.

       Then he'll kill us
As fast as the Philistines could desire him:
Oh shame, oh shame! I am ashamed to own
The craven herd to be my countrymen.
How the foe must be scoffing if they know it!
Even as the countenance of the sun dispels
Hoarfrost, so has the enemy's mere presence
Made vanish half our army, which now hides,
Even by whole companies, in caves and thickets,
In clefts of rocks, on mountains and in pits;

Some have e'en over Jordan beat retreat
To Gad and Gilead, and the remainder
Tremble like women.

SECOND OFFICER.

Lo, the king comes hither.

[Exeunt.

Enter SAUL, ABNER, *and Saul's* ARMOUR-BEARER, *a youth.*

SAUL.

He who retreats from the Philistine's eyes
Now runs directly into death's black jaws;
None can escape, I have the camp surrounded
With those who will not spare: if more choose flight,
Let them dig downwards for it to the grave.

ABNER.

Ay, let them dig to hell; for they no outlet
Above the ground shall find to pass our lines.

SAUL.

Had but our pack of mongrel hounds kept heart,
Our lines had been a leash from which they had sprung
At the enemy's throat, so soon as I had slipped them;
Nay, at the very worst of death and defeat,
These fields, to the perished, might have been the gates
And earthly entrance into heavenly meads.

ARMOUR-BEARER.

'Tis said that all who fall in righteous battle
Go instant thither.

ABNER.

Yes, whither else?

SAUL.

My boy,
All patriots are angels after death:
The soul that, in its country's cause, has staked
And lost its sum of future days, can never
Visit Gehenna, or darkle down perdition.—
Go furbish now my armour for to-morrow.

[Exit ARMOUR-BEARER.

ABNER.

'Tis but a dreary day, but it may brighten;—
Here comes our friend the Levite.

SAUL.

No friend of mine!
[*Enter* JEHOIADAH.

So, hie thee home: I have thee in such love,
I cannot let thee risk thy life here longer.
[*Exit* JEHOIADAH.

A hundred Philistines in the camp were better
Than that man pacing it with that villainous look.

ABNER.

What different spirits animate mankind!
How different his from thy young armour bearer's.

SAUL.

My armour-bearer! were all such as he,
Samuel's absence would but little trouble me.
[*Exeunt.*

SCENE VI.

A part of the Hebrew camp. Time, night-fall of the sixth day.
Enter SAUL *and* ABNER.

SAUL.

To-morrow's the seventh day: let messengers
Be sent to hasten Samuel should they meet him.

ABNER.

I have sent some already to that end.

SAUL.

Abner, Abner, if all go well to-morrow
(As it is possible, even yet, it may),
And if, indeed, we be not forced to flee
Then, or before, from the Philistine horde,
I will in peace raise all the means for war ;

As doth the husbandman in summer raise
The crops that are to be his food for winter.
I will have soldiers plenty, ready made;—
No rabble from their fields and city crafts,
Running in haste, with various, uncouth arms
To the rendezvous, and running home when seeing
A grimmer foe than they had reckoned on.
This has been my intention since the day
On which I routed Nahash; as thou knowest,
And knowest how greed and sloth have it retarded.

ABNER.

Our nation is unwarlike, and the Philistine
Is the perfection of a well-trained soldier.

SAUL.

Knowing that, I am surprised that they should linger
Yonder in Michmash. Have they harlots, think'st thou?
Or do they drench in wine, or chew the drug
Of lazy satisfaction, that their ships
Bring from the furthest corner of the East?
Or, as we wait for Samuel and Jehovah,
Do they now wait the special aid of Dagon,
Who now, down revelling in his waters green,
Or, lulled in the embrace of some sea-goddess,
Forgets Philistia's legions.

ABNER.

       'Tis most strange:—
Surely 'tis Heaven that restrains them from us.

SAUL.

I do believe that most of our pale remnant
Would flee at the first sound of the foe's bugles,
Blown by him to the tune of an advance.

ABNER.

I know that numbers to-night will slink away,
Snake-like, upon their bellies.

SAUL.

I think the guards are trusty.

ABNER.
So think I,—
And yet I'm doubtful.

SAUL.
Would that there were no night,
For half the world abuse it.   Let them go ;
Although it is ungrateful as 'tis cowardly
Thus to desert me coldly by degrees,
As breath from off a mirror.   Set the watch ;
I'll to my tent, albeit not to sleep.

[*Exeunt.*

SCENE VII.

The camp.   Time, the morrow.
Enter ZOE, *as if fleeing from something.*

ZOE.
Oh, blinding hastiness ! he will not listen
Whilst I dissuade him from impiety :
I will not see the deed.

Exit, and enter SAUL, ABNER, OFFICERS, *and* SOLDIERS.

SAUL.
Attempt not to dissuade me, Abner : no,
Seven days we have waited and he is not come.
Bring the burnt-offering and peace-offering to me :
'Tis not the sacrificer but the victim ;
'Tis not the hand, but 'tis the heart God looks at.

SAUL *offers, and, having finished,* SAMUEL *enters.*

SAMUEL.
What hast thou done !

SAUL.
Chide me not, only listen :
Seven days I have seen my forces wasting from me,
And thou camest not within the time appointed ;
Then I said unto myself, " The enemy

Will yet attack us ere we shall have made
Our supplication," so I forced myself,
And have this moment finished offering.

SAMUEL.

Thou hast done wrong, thou hast been disobedient:
Unhappy man! for now thy dynasty
Upon the throne was to have been confirmed
For ever, and the sceptre finally given
To thy posterity, that now no crown
Shall ever wear, they by thyself discrowned,
Dethroned, thy throne now given unto another
Whom God hath chosen, a man after his own heart,
To be the Captain over Israel,
Instead of thee, presumptuous and daring.

[*Exit* SAMUEL.

SAUL.

Why, let him go:—how little it requires
To expose a man when taken by surprise!
We know the cause of this denunciation:
He fears I would be priest as well as king.
Not I.—Indeed, we live and see strange things.
Is it true? can he, so old and wise, have been
So snatched away by anger?—wrath with me too;—
Am I not higher than he? He cannot have
Such strange and foul suspicion:—kingly cares
Alone are surely a sufficient burden
For one man's spirit to carry! Ah, when last
We parted here 'twas in a different mode.—
He said my throne was given unto another;
By me were my posterity discrowned;
I had done wrong, been disobedient.—
I may have erred, but how been disobedient?
Seven days I waited, ay, till the skirts of the term
Had disappeared, and with it—oh, foul shame!—
Near all my army. Oh, fond Saul, fond fool,
To agree to any such monstrous proposition

As a week's waiting for him ! Why should slow age
Chain the swift wheels of manhood ? But for his
Most stupid interdiction, I had urged
At once my road-stained car of battle down
On the Philistines. Weak-willed Saul ! considerate
Of a proud dotard's reeling authority :
Now mine reels too. Philistines now approach :
Saul is no longer able to oppose you,—
Saul, that advanced upon you wet with speed,
And would have cast against you such a tempest
But for the o'erblowing of this old man's week,
That the whole world hereafter should have doubted
When told of the horrid mischief.

ABNER.

My good cousin,
My high, undaunted, and anointed sovereign,
Cease raging thus in public.

SAUL.

It is false ;
Not changed towards me is God's purpose, only Samuel's.
I will not fear : though men desert me, God
Is not among the faithless :—yet how can I hope,
With such an army all composed of mist,
Such dastard wretches, such predestined bondsmen,—
How can I hope to quell the enraged Philistines ?
Oh, that I had myself been a Philistine !
For on the unwarlike Hebrews scorn I fling,
And rue that I was ever made their king.

[*Exit* SAUL.

ABNER.

I'll after him ; I know not what he'll do
In his violence.

[*Exit* ABNER, *the rest retiring in silence.*

SCENE VIII.

Near Gilgal.
Enter Saul *and* Jonathan.

SAUL.

All's over here;—let us withdraw and weep
Down in the red recesses of our hearts,
Or, in our spirits, silent, curse the cravens
Whom uttered execrations too much honor.
Home, home, let us, dishonored,—home, if there
Be yet for us a home, and the Philistines
Drive us not forth to miserable exile.
Will they allow us, like to a breathed hare,
Spent, to return and repossess our form?
Will they endure us in Gibeah? or must we
Discover some dark den on Lebanon,
And dwell with lions? or must we with foxes
Burrow, and depend on cunning for our food?
Better with lions and with foxes mating,
Than be companions of the brood of Israel;
Yea, better with the hill-wolf famishing,
Than battening with the drove that forms the world.

JONATHAN.

Alas, my sisters,—

SAUL.

      Alas, thy mother;—she
The silent critic on my life. Thy mother
And sisters may be forced, ere long, to dwell
In some dank cave, or o'er the borders flee
With us, and seek in some strange realm asylum.
Why, let it be so; we can live 'midst strangers.
Of all the myriads who followed us hither,
How many are left us?

JONATHAN.

     A poor six-hundred.

SAUL.

Ay, is my picked three thousand dwindled so!
What next, what next? There is no virtue left
In mortal man,—nay, women had done better.
Oh, Jonathan, thy glorious deed at Geba,
Put out unto unworthy usury,
Is lost in Gilgal's issue!

JONATHAN.

Yearn not o'er me.
What we have done, O king and sire, is ours,
Part of ourselves :—yea more, it will not die
When we shall, nor can any steal it;
For honor hath that cleaving quality,
It sticks upon us and none may remove it,
Except ourselves by future deeds of baseness.

SAUL.

We never were so poor since we grew rich.

JONATHAN.

We will grow richer than we yet have been;
And, from this need, yet heap up such abundance,
That we shall wonder why we ever sorrowed
At this petty pilfering.

SAUL.

"Pilfering"! that's the word.
Yes, Jonathan, we have been meanly pilfered;
Rats have been stealing the grain from out our garner:
Each runaway was a rat; and for seven days
An ancient friend still oped our granary door,
Then snapped on me the recuperated trap
That should have caught the vermin.

JONATHAN.

Rate not, Samuel.

SAUL.

He rated me too low when he rebuked me,
And talked of ban on us, when he his garment

Ought to have rent, and his white head with ashes
Covered at sight of what his tardiness
Had caused,—the dissolution of my ranks,
And the fair tower of a well-won prestige
Mouldering and all dismantled.—Let us go.

JONATHAN.

Let us take with us the remnant of our guard :
They shew the fairer from their comrades' foulness.

SAUL.

I have lost all faith in others: they will be home
Before us; if not, I'll drive them but not lead them.

[*Exeunt.*

END OF THE SECOND ACT.

ACT III.

SCENE I.

The Country near Michmash.   Time, evening.
Enter GLORIEL *and another* ANGEL.

ANGEL.

My errand done, I must return above.
Farewell.

GLORIEL.

Farewell, sweet cherub.
[*Exit* ANGEL.
Heaven works again for Saul,
Nor will allow him utterly to fall.
Where is that able but rebellious spirit,
Zaph, ruler of the band that haunt the earth
To compass Satan's malice ?   At the pole
I lately saw him sitting.   Him and his band
I will compel to be my ministers
On the Philistines, whilst that I myself
Inspire with hardihood Prince Jonathan.
[*Enter another* ANGEL.
What news ?

ANGEL.

Zaph's hovering over Palestine:
I have dogged him from the morning until now.
I think he knows he's watched.

GLORIEL.

Go fetch him hither.
[*Exit* ANGEL.

Now let a blast from out the deep arise
And push behind him; for he will not come
Unless compelled.
   A Tempest suddenly arises, and ZAPH *is driven in followed by the* ANGEL.

ZAPH.

What dost thou want with me?

GLORIEL.

To-morrow let the day break gloomily,
And, at the hour when I shall instigate thee,
Enter the Philistine garrison at Michmash,
And so infatuate them that each man
Shall take his fellow for an enemy.

ZAPH.

Cannot thine own do this? I'll not obey thee.

GLORIEL.

At the same hour, let all thy company
Wander beneath the surface of the ground,
And simulate an earthquake; and let some
Emit low moanings like to those you utter
When, lonely meditating in hell's cavern,
You feel yourselves undone.

ZAPH.

Insult me not, old comrade. Gloriel,
Think that I once thine equal was in heaven,
And spare me, then, this drudgery. Cannot one
Of my band perform the trick with the garrison?

GLORIEL.

Thou hast mine orders, and obey them strictly.
Remember, there is naught betwixt us now
Of high respect and deep consideration;
And old equality has for ever vanished.
                            [*Exit* GLORIEL.

ZAPH.

Thou pitiless cherub! punctilious angel!—but
I must obey thee;

For thou hast power given thee to subject me.
Alas, that ever such exorbitant might
Should to one spirit o'er another be given!
May the gnawing fires of hell, spirit, yet exhaust thee;
And mayst thou feel, some day, the bitterness
Thou now inflictest on me. Curse thee, thou tyrant;
May Acheron yet torment thee. This will rankle;
And I will thwart him much for this.
Ah, if the God that made us would be neutral,
Or would abandon him as He hath done me,
Then he should be the slave, and I the tyrant.

[*Exit.*

SCENE II.

A solitary place near Gibeah. A ravine near, and on the opposite side of it the Philistine Garrison at Michmash. Time, the morrow of the preceding day. Enter two HEBREWS.

FIRST HEBREW.

Let's die at once; let's go provoke the Philistine
To end us, for now life is void of charm!
Deride me not; all nature is in horror;
The cheerful sun in shame avoids this land,
As joy avoids our hearts.

SECOND HEBREW.

It is a gloomy morn; a gloomier
I never saw;—but 'tis not true the king,
With all his court, has fled into the desert:
He Gibeah holds, and seems to keep at bay
(Though, with his means, it only is a seeming)
The enemy, who menace him from Michmash.
But come, some wine would do us both a kindness;
Let's to the "Eschol," where, I know, are soldiers
Of the Philistines drinking: we will cheat them
At a game of hazard, for the maid shall watch
And give us signals, while she stands behind them
And brews our negus.

FIRST HEBREW.
                    Let us go and pray.
            SECOND HEBREW.
No, better wine to drive our care away.
                    [*Enter a young* PEASANT *carrying a coulter.*
                    PEASANT.
Is it morning, sirs? for yet the sun's abed,
And has a vile, black nightcap on his head.
What an abominable teaster is this heavens!
This sky is as dismal as mortality.
Ah, me!   [*Filling the bowl of a pipe.*
        Man is a pipe that Life doth smoke,
            As saunters it the earth about;
        And when 'tis wearied of the joke,
            Death comes and knocks the ashes out.
Something with a moral in it so easily comes
In these sad times, sirs.
                    SECOND HEBREW.
                        Yet thou art not sad;
Thy face spells fun.   Good morrow, hind.
                    PEASANT.
                                Ay, ay.
    [*Exeunt the two* HEBREWS, *and enter a third from the ravine.*
Thou art a Gilgal swallow!
                    THIRD HEBREW.
                            Hound, my sword
Is in the Philistines' keeping, or I'd slay thee!
I'd rip thee up; fellow, I'd serve thee out;
I'd broach thy kilderkin; I'd stop thy crowing;
I'd find thine inmost bowels!
                                        [*Exit.*
                    PEASANT.
                    Ha, ha! the foe,
Having taken from us our warlike tools, yet leave us
The little, scarlet tongue to scratch and sting with.

Well, swords are dangerous things in angry hands;
And my coulter would have done but awkward fencing.
     [*Singing*.
I'll down with my coulter unto the foe's forge,
Lay my hand on his bellows, my eyes on his gorge;
And think, could I span it, oh ho! could I span it!—
Never mind, boys, never mind, boys, but some day we'll plan it.

I cannot crackle up, I cannot sing;
This gloomy morning quite extinguishes me.—
I'll get a light at Solomon's as I pass;
And if his hoydens try to tumble me,
I'll charge them with my coulter.
    [*Exit, descending the ravine, and*
Enter JONATHAN *and his* ARMOUR-BEARER, *the former pacing to and fro.*

ARMOUR-BEARER.

The day's as lowering as are Israel's fortunes;
And it, or they, or both combined, oppress me,
For I'm as gloomy as the sky is, or
As Jonathan.—Alas, poor prince, how changed!
Once he would jest with me, or chat on trifles
Of home or heart, disdaining not to tell me
His boyish loves; and shew me how to use
The spear and dart, how best to draw the bow,
How bear the shield, and how, with rapid fences,
To make the falchion hoarsely growl i'th' air:
But not so now; as a deserted mansion,
He dwells absorbed in cold and stately grief,
And half against me shut. Gilgal's vile field,
And the east wind of Samuel's threatening,
Seem to have withered in him sense of pleasure:—
No wonder! Unto all so kind he was,
So open; it makes me melancholy when
I think upon the sunshine of the past,
And I return—if not for shelter, yet
In very madness—to the drizzling thoughts
Engendered by the present. I would he'd speak;

E

His bearing so disturbed appears and threatening.
I like it not; now sudden standing still,
Fixed in some dark and earnest reverie,
Now off at quickened pace. He's muttering,
And casts his eyes towards heaven;—I will accost him.

    [*The* ARMOUR-BEARER *approaches* JONATHAN.

JONATHAN.

Come, let us go over to the Philistine's garrison;
It may be God will help us. Fear not, come;
For there is no restriction on the Almighty
To work by many or to work by few.

ARMOUR-BEARER.

Alas, he's growing demented!   [*Aside.*
What would your Highness do if you were there?

JONATHAN.

I cannot tell thee yet; but come and see.

ARMOUR-BEARER.

'Tis desperate; cast from you the idea.

JONATHAN.

No; 'tis an inspiration.

ARMOUR-BEARER.

                "Madness" call it,
Bred from your disappointment and galled heart.
Your highness broods too much: adversity
Hath fretted you as harness frets the steed
That is as yet unbroken, it inciting,
Even by its first, uncomprehended touch,
To violent and self-injurious efforts
To cast it off, which only make the Tamer
To strengthen it, and rudelier ply the bit
'Till the proud beast consents to do his paces.

JONATHAN.

No, never shall we consent to the Philistine!
Peace. Though the iron curb be in our mouths,—

No smith allowed by our politic foe
To forge new arms, nor to repair the old,
The very ploughshares, that make war with earth
And rip up its brown bowels, being bound
To be engendered in their licensed forges,—
We never shall be tamed to slavery
By the Philistines, whom we oft have driven
Across the borders, like a frantic steed
Rushing car-bound across the rugged plain,
And badged at mouth and nostrils with a beard
Of mingled blood and foam. Men are not cattle.

ARMOUR-BEARER.

Being greater, they are thence exposed to evils
That the low brute escapes; even as high hills
Do suffer blasts of which the plain feels nothing :
Pardon me, so much the more may you, being higher
In station than the rest of Israel,
And more endowed than most with the fair gifts,
But dangerous impulse of an ardent mind,
Greatly err than I. My life is naught, but yours
Is much, or I had not withstood you. Think,
The times are evil, and what influence
There may be hovering in this dismal air,
Or thoughts pernicious coming from the clouds,
Wherein, 'tis said, hide demons, nothing know we :—
Suffice, that your intent wears shape suspicious.
Haply this trusted inspiration comes
From some bad spirit, who would tempt your Highness
To instant death, or unto what were worse,—
The sad estate of prisoner to the foe,
Who, by slow process might to death's shores lead you,
Or hurry you from hence into the sea
And drown you as a sacrifice to Dagon ;
Or, should their vengeance merge in policy,
Spare you to manacle the hands of Israel,
Who might not dare to strike your captors, lest

She should but bruise herself in bruising those
That, holding you, could every future blow
Retaliate by nameless cruelties
On their great hostage, and of which intent
We should be warned.

JONATHAN.

Then I must go alone.

ARMOUR-BEARER.

You are not bent?

JONATHAN.

I am.

ARMOUR-BEARER.

Then take me, though
It be to the mouth of sure destruction: I
Can only perish, or live and with you suffer.

JONATHAN.

Fear not.

ARMOUR-BEARER.

Lead on; I'll follow you whither you will.

JONATHAN.

God will precede us.   Bring with thee our arms.

ARMOUR-BEARER.

I will, and use them to the last, if need be.

Having arrived at the bottom of the ravine.

ARMOUR-BEARER.

The garrison seems quiet.

JONATHAN.

Happy omen!
Now wear a moment a foul traitor's front:
Seem timid but be brave: affect misgiving,
But have within thee steady confidence,
For we must shew ourselves now.   Mark, if they cry,
"Wait till we come to you," we will stand still,
And not ascend to them; but if they say,

"Come up to us," we will go up to them,
For God will have consigned them to our hands.

They commence climbing towards Michmash; and its garrison, observing them, are hailed by JONATHAN.

JONATHAN.

What, ho!

A SENTINEL.

Who are you?

JONATHAN.

Hebrews.

THE PHILISTINES LAUGHING.

Ha, ha, ha!

SENTINEL.

Crept from your holes!

ONE OF THE GARRISON.

Come up to us and we will shew you something.

JONATHAN (*to his* ARMOUR-BEARER).

Follow me; they are ours.

JONATHAN and his ARMOUR-BEARER, *climbing on their hands and feet, disappear. Presently clashing of swords heard from the fortress, and great uproar, mingled with a rumbling noise, as of an earthquake. The scene changes to the Gibean side of the ravine. The tumult and noise as of an earthquake still heard.*

A HEBREW SENTINEL, *gazing across the ravine.*

What sound do I hear, as if the earth on sudden
Roared like the ocean, and the clang of arms
Coming from Michmash? and, most singular,
Behold the whole Philistine garrison
Come tumbling like a torrent on the field.
What meaneth this? Arms glance along like lightnings;
Helmets and shields, and heads and bodies bare,
Dance in confusion;—I'll inform the king.

[*Exit.*

SCENE III.

Mignon, in the furthest part of Gibeah.

SAUL, *seated under a pomegranate tree, and with his troops around him. The sound of the earthquake heard, and that of the fighting, faintly.*

SAUL.

Number our band and see who is absent. Quick;
I hear the sound of action and severe.

           [*Enter the* HEBREW SENTINEL, *running.*

SENTINEL.

The King, the King! where is the King!

SAUL.

           Lo, here.

SENTINEL.

Your Majesty, our foes are fighting, but
With whom I know not. Over all the field
The tumult spreads like fire among the stubble.
The earth, too, seems to shake; and I believe
I hear a noise that is not made by man,
So strange it is and dismal.

    SAUL, *to those who have been counting the soldiers.*

           Who is missing?

    Another SENTINEL, *running in.*

Up, up! our foes are stirring; arms on armour
Ring, and strange thunder mutters o'er the ground,
Which either God or man is causing tremble.

    AN OFFICER, *to* SAUL.

Jonathan is absent, and his armour-bearer.

    SAUL, *to* AHIAH *the Priest.*

Bring hither the Ark of God.

The Ark is brought, and AHIAH *the Priest having laid his hand upon it,* SAUL *and he converse together, during which the noise increases.*

SAUL, *to the Priest.*

Withdraw thine hand.

AHIAH.

The Lord hath not yet spoken.

SAUL.

He calls us by the earthquake to the fray.
To succour Jonathan let all away.

[*Exeunt omnes in haste.*

SCENE IV.

The country near Beth-aven.
Enter a group of HEBREWS *of that part. The noise of the pursuit heard.*

FIRST HEBREW.

Joy! the Philistines flee. Our countrymen,
Prisoners whom they had taken in their forays,
And who at Michmash did for them their drudgery,
Have turned upon them; by prince Jonathan
Surprised, who, nimble as the mountain roe,
With his huge armour-bearer, sweeps along,
And cuts off every knave that hails from Gath.
And, see, the king comes yonder, and brave Abner,
Mowing the foe down like two mighty scythes;
Naught leaving unto those who follow them,
Except to stumble o'er the swathes of dead.

[*Exeunt, and enter*

SAUL, AHIAH, SOLDIERS *and* PEOPLE, *the latter wearied and panting.*

SAUL.

Let none eat food till evening, that revenge
May glut itself, and the etherial maw
Of the starved soul be gorged ere bodily need
Be served.—Let this be known, and death the doom
Of him who disregards it.

[*Exeunt.*

SCENE V.

A wood, with honey on the ground.

Enter, panting, a crowd of people and soldiers, who seeing the honey are about to eat of it.

A SOLDIER.

Taste not, for so the King with oath adjured us,
Under the heavy penalty of death.
Onward, and heed not your hot, throbbing veins;
We'll eat when eve comes and no foe remains.

[*Exeunt, and enter* ABNER *and an* OFFICER.

ABNER.

Now I must rest awhile; I can no longer
Pursue nor kill. Why should I also die
Of very weariness, and o'ertake i'th' grave
The souls whom I have thither sent to-day!
Ah, there is honey yonder on the ground,
Cool to allay both thirst and hunger.

OFFICER.

Taste
It not: the King refreshment hath forbidden
Till evening falls and with it his last enemy:
I die myself of toil, but let us on.

ABNER.

'Tis hard, but from temptation let's begone.

Exeunt, and enter JONATHAN, *who dips a reed which he has in his hand into the honey, and while he is eating enter soldiers.*

FIRST SOLDIER.

Oh, cease, your Highness, to partake of death!
The King hath strictly charged us not to eat
Till evening, and has cursed whoe'er should do so.

SECOND SOLDIER.

He hath, that we might intermit not slaughter:
He hath indeed;—oh, had we seen you sooner!

JONATHAN.

'Tis done; and 'twas a foolish interdiction!
My father hath trouble made for many; and thwarted,
By this stern ordinance, his own intention
Of full destruction! See how I am refreshed
By tasting but a little of this honey:
How much, then, greater, could we have eaten freely,
Would the ruin of the enemy have been!
Say not that you have this misfortune seen.
[Exeunt.

SCENE VI.

A wooded part near Aijalon. Time, evening.
SAUL, JONATHAN, ABNER, AHIAH, OFFICERS, SOLDIERS *and* PEOPLE.

SAUL, *having cast himself reclining against a bank.*

Now for a little rest; for though my spirit
Is fresh, my body has no longer vigor.
Bring me a drink.
[A SOLDIER *presents to him a cup of wine.*
No, give me water; I, to day, have poured
Out wine sufficient in the blood of foes.
[Water is brought and he drinks.
Sweeter, methinks, that draught is unto me,
Than ever was the warm, spiced juice of grape.
How little delights us when we truly need!
Sit, friends, for we are equals all to day.
Now bring some food, and let those eat who may.

ABNER.

I cannot eat, and yet I'm hungry too.

FIRST OFFICER.

Nor I.

SECOND OFFICER.

Nor I.

SAUL.

Pray you, do not forego
Some needful nourishment, through my example
Abstaining. Freely eat, and hoard up strength
To re-pursue the enemy before
The young moon has gone down.

AHIAH.

Low in the west
Even now she is, and from her lighted censer
Gives but a weak though sacred beam: same time,
The fragrance born of yon adjacent wood,
Along the dewy air diffusing incense,
Both ministers seem at this great sacrifice
And wonderful oblation of our foes,
Who, by miraculous power, this day have been
Discomfited and wasted.

SAUL.

Jonathan,
Why art thou silent?

JONATHAN.

Gratitude and weariness
O'ercome me.

SAUL.

Take some food, and be revived
While light remains for labor. See, the clouds
Clear off, and leave the expanse o'th sky serene,
Although obscure.

FIRST OFFICER.

This is the most romantic
Of all time's hours!

SECOND OFFICER.

Witchcraft now seems to hang
Between the horns o'th moon, that cannot shine
Through the vast, darksome chamber of the night,
Which now appears, to my imagination,
Upgiven to magic and the spells profane

Of sorcerers, and the hags whose bodies bend
Ever forward, from their long-continued gazing
Into caldrons of incantation.   Art thou not,
O Saul, afraid of the magicians' charms
Directed 'gainst thee for their rooting out?

SAUL.

I fear them not, nor anything that comes
Within the range of their claimed ministry;
Whether ghosts of the departed, or bad angels
Who ('tis affirmed) are sold into their service
For the price of their own souls: yea, if the Devil
Now stood alone by me on this dusk field,
I'd snub him with ill manners.   Yet the moon
Wears unto me the same weird aspect as
She wears to thee: and when I was a boy,
I was (as even to this hour I am)
Fascinated by the horror of this quarter;
Loving it more than when, her face expanding,
The dim equivocation wears away,
Until at full she languishes i'th' sky,
And shines down like an angel.

FIRST OFFICER.

　　　　　　　　　　Spectre-like,
And with a few spectator stars, she goes
Down westward, as if leading the obsequies
Of those of her idolatrous worshippers,
Who, by their own swords or by ours, have perished
Since broke this day's strange morn.

SAUL.

　　　　　　　　Hearken; the blast
Sighs through yon cypress' tops the dismal dirge
Of the remainder; whom their own cusped goddess,
Pale Ashtaroth, yon moon, shall from heaven's verge
See scud, like spectres, over the dim ground;
For soon we will re-urge the invader's flight,
Nor leave one breathing by the morning light.

　　　　　　　　　　　　[*Enter a* LEVITE.

LEVITE.
Your majesty, the ravening multitude
Eat from the quivering carcasses of the cattle,
Which they have summarily slaughtered on the ground,
And but half drained of blood; offending heaven.
SAUL.
This must not be : roll hither a large stone,
And let each man, whate'er he has to kill
Bring hither, and dress it lawfully in our presence.
Disperse yourselves awhile among the people,
And send all hither who have aught to kill for food.
[Exit the LEVITE.

Now my first altar to the Lord I'll build,   *[Aside.*
And Him at once propitiate, that so
He may continue this sudden prosperity,
That, like a copious, unexpected shower
After long drought, makes green my heart, long sere,
And withering 'neath misgivings. Ahiah, choose
From out the cattle the fairest for an offering.
[Exit AHIAH.

Let some an altar build, for it is meet
We did acknowledge this deliverance,
Heaven-wrought; and ere we gratulate Jonathan,
Chief warrior in this wondrous feat of arms,
Upsend the smoke of offering to the skies.
SAUL (*aside*).
There, with a conscience cleared, and 'suaged the fears
That ruffled the fair down of my existence,
Ere long let me resume the grateful toil
Of war defensive, and whose aim is peace.
[Turning to those before him.
Friends, ere the moon, gone down, shall us no longer
Enable to distinguish friends from foes,
We will retake ourselves to the pursuit :
The rallied (if any have rallied) we'll o'ertake,
And leave no sullying dreg of the invaders
Alive upon our soil at peep of morn.
[Acclamation, 'midst which enters AHIAH.

AHIAH.
Let us consult Jehovah; all draw near.

SAUL.
Ask whether I shall pursue them; and if so,
Shall I be able to destroy their remnant.

Whilst AHIAH *seeks an answer from God, enter two of* ZAPH'S DEMONS, *meeting.*

FIRST DEMON.
Ah, my gossip, art thou here?

SECOND DEMON.
Ah, old crony, pray what cheer?

FIRST DEMON.
Thinkest thou the Lord will say
Whether Saul shall further slay?

SECOND DEMON.
Pshaw! I've no vaticination.—
To us what's Saul and his probation?
Yet we'll stay and see the end on't,—
But so so, thou mayest depend on't,
For already I can spy
Trouble in the priest's dark eye.

AHIAH.
God doth not answer thee.

SAUL.
                And wherefore?

AHIAH.
I know not, but He is silent.

SAUL.
                What is the wrong,
And who is the wrong-doer? for, as God lives,
Although it were my own son Jonathan,
He for it should die.

[SAUL *pauses and none answer him.*
Now every one of you to one side gather,
And I and Jonathan will take the other;
Then let the lot be cast, which God dispose.
The people having retired to one hand, and the King and Jonathan to the other.
Lord God of Israel, give a perfect lot.
AHIAH *draws the lot, and the* KING *and* JONATHAN *are taken, the people escaping.*
How is it that evil must thus dog my steps! [*Aside.*
Now cast the lot between my son and me. [*Aloud.*
[JONATHAN *is taken.*
Now God assist me to endure my portion! [*Aside.*
Jonathan, what hast thou done? [*Aloud.*

JONATHAN.

I did but take
A little honey with a rod I bore;
And for this simple deed, then, I must die.

SAUL.

Oh, that my curse should fall upon myself!
Saul, Saul, rash man, now let the sceptre drop
Out of thy hands, for thou hast slain its heir.
Jonathan, my dear son Jonathan, thou must die.

ONE OF THE CROWD.

Oh, hideous wrong! what wouldst thou do, O King?
Thy son too,—God forbid! Shall Jonathan die,
He who began this victory? As God lives
Thou shalt not hurt a hair of him, for he
Hath worked with heaven to-day.

A great uproar, 'midst which the people rescue JONATHAN, *and bear him away.*

SAUL.

They break my oath,
Not I. Oh, Jonathan, thou art saved; but I
Had near destroyed thee! Foolishly I swore,

Forbidding to eat;—but who can see the end
Of many a fine beginning? Abner, see
Our sentries posted: speak not to me now.

                              [*Exit* ABNER.

Surely there is a blight within the ear
Forbidding me a harvest. Jonathan
May reap when I am dead; but I shall never
Garner within my bosom sheaves of peace.
Heaven hath a quarrel with me; Heaven
Surely denies perfection to my deeds.
Ye fast-appearing and sky-peopling stars,
Ye see me, in victory, mournful. But I'll rest,
And, early risen, return with speed to-morrow
To give to other enemies cause of sorrow.

                                      [*Exit.*

SECOND DEMON.

He's gone; and we to night must drop,
With all our band, on Pisgah's top.

                                      [*Vanish.*

END OF THE THIRD ACT.

ACT IV.

SCENE I.

Gibeah. An apartment in Saul's palace.
Enter ZAPH.

ZAPH.

The insult that proud Gloriel on me put
In the affair at Michmash, rankles in me;
Therefore, to spite him, I will set a spirit
Upon the soul of Saul. But softly, for
Here comes his guardian angel to expel me.

Exit in haste, and ZOE *crosses the apartment after him; then enter*
TWO OFFICERS *of the royal household.*

FIRST OFFICER.

Now, surely, we shall have a lasting peace;
For since the king arose from his prostration,
After the base desertion borne at Gilgal,
He has dealt around him such a storm of battles,
That all the enemies of our race are down,
And buried beneath his heap of victories.

SECOND OFFICER.

Talk of the devil and he will appear;
Though that's a saying ungracious towards the king,
Who can be very gracious when he wills.
He is coming hither to walk and talk alone,
And never is in company more to his mind
Than his own thoughts in words half muttered. Come.

[*Exeunt* OFFICERS *and enter* SAUL.

SAUL.

All have succumbed before me;—Móab, Ammon, Edom;
The Kings of Zobah, and the Philistines;
Nor have the Amalekites unhumbled gone:
None now dare spoil us, and my throne seems settled,
That Samuel said was given to another.—
Surely it was the peevishness of dotage
That to such outbreak prompted the old man.
Hither he comes :—there's something in his look :
What is the burden that he will deliver ?

[*Enter* SAMUEL.

What wouldst thou, Samuel ?

SAMUEL.

Jehovah caused me to anoint thee King
Over his people Israel; therefore now
Hearken unto his voice. Jehovah saith,
Go and smite Amalek; for I remember
How he laid wait for Israel in the desert,
As he came up from Egypt. Utterly
Destroy man, woman, youth, and maiden; infant,
Camel, ox, ass, and sheep; spare naught whatever.

SAUL.

Exterminate them ?

SAMUEL.

Utterly destroy them.

SAUL.

Women and babes, and those by years made helpless ?
Dearly indeed now will the children pay
For what their sires did in a long-past day.

SAMUEL.

Moses hath told us that the parents' sin
Upon the children should be visited :
And what are days to the Eternal ?

[*Exit.*

F

SAUL.

Samuel, thou art too imperious, or I am
Too proud and unforgiving !—No adieu
He deigned me, nor, with hands imposed,
Left me his blessing ;—but I can forego it,
And could with ease have now foregone his presence.
'Tis strange, this visit; it is very strange.
Why comes he unto me with God's commission
If I'm of God dismissed ? This looks dishonest ;
This contradicts his declaration of
My forfeiture of the sceptre,—that which often
Appears a prophecy hanging o'er me dire
One day to be fulfilled. I'll think no more
Of that ! Why was I shaken with words, when deeds
Have not the power to move me ?—Samuel, Samuel,
Either the Lord spoke not by thee at Gilgal,
Or speaks not by thee now. I have heard tell
Of hoary men being perjured ; of false prophets ;
Of lying spirits sent to them from the Lord.
None are beyond the compass of temptation.—
Haply the prophet and others have conspired
For my dethronement ; or they seek my life,
That they may gain possession of my crown :
Hence with this mandate Samuel comes to me
(Whom, haply, he has found too unobsequious),
Thinking that Death shall meet me on the field
Of this grim expedition. No, 'tis wild,
And horrible to think of ! Yet wild things
And horrible have happened. Ah, if there,
Indeed, be somewhere an ambitious wight
Now coveting my throne, let him beware ;
For if my eye should light on him, and know him,
I will not say the horror of his doom ;
But it should be appalling. 'Tis the mood ;
This is the very pitch of Heaven's harsh rhythm.
Though Gilgal feigned, herein I feel Heaven speaks
To me by Samuel. Mercy, hence, and, Sword,
Come forth and do the bidding of the Lord. [*Exit.*

SCENE II.

Before a City of the Amalekites.
SAUL, ABNER, HEBREW SOLDIERS, *and* KENITES.

SAUL, *addressing the Kenites.*

Haste, and depart from among the Amalekites,
Lest I destroy you with them.

A KENITE.

Our fathers once to yours assistance rendered.

SAUL.

They did, hence my good-will; escape at once.
[*Exeunt* KENITES.
Saidst thou the city was surrounded, Abner?

ABNER.

I did.

SAUL.

We will surprise it, then. Do thou
Lead on those at the rearward of the place,
Whilst I assault its front.—When we shall meet
'Twill be midway in a domain of death;
And we'll shake hands o'er a bank of bloody corpses.
Drive pity from thy breast; no quarter give,
For to destruction are devoted all.

ABNER.

All?

SAUL.

All.

ABNER.

Women and children, infants and hoary heads?

SAUL.

Even just-born babes that have not drawn the breast
Must die; and those that have not seen the light,
Within expectant mothers killed by fright.
There must no seed be left to raise new harvest.

Pity hear not though strongly it plead in thee.
Drown them in their own blood; pound them together,
And trample out the living fire of Amalek.
There I have finished ordinance as dire
As ever mortal gave. 'Tis Heaven requires
This rigorous execution at my hand,
Or I could not have given such fell command.

ABNER.

Oh, let us cover us with the cowl of night
When we perform it. Yet would that but little
Avail us; for at whatsoever hour
We paint this picture, its pervading crimson
Shall set the heavens on fire. Oh, Saul, oh, Saul,
What go we do? I dreamed not that our mission
Urged us so far into the realm of vengeance.

SAUL.

Go, now begin;—go, ere I cry out, "Spare!"
Go, and believe it to be but *man*slaughter
When women's and children's blood is shed like water.
[*Exit* ABNER.

Now let me tighten every cruel sinew,
And gird the whole up in unfeeling hardness;
That my swollen heart, which bleeds within me tears,
May choke itself to stillness. I am as
A shivering bather that upon the shore,
Looking and shrinking from the cold, black waves,
Quick, starting from his reverie, with a rush
Abbreviates his horror. Now to the deed.
Hebrews, come on; glut your dislike of old,
And curst be he who spares for love or gold.
[*Exeunt* SAUL *and* SOLDIERS.

SCENE IV.

The midst of the town. Noise of the massacre; which, having subsided, enter SAUL *and* SOLDIERS *from one hand, and* ABNER *and* SOLDIERS *from the other, meeting.*

SAUL.

Art thou with blood not blinded?

ABNER.

                    Thou look'st grimmer
Than I ever before beheld thee; even when Nahash
Thou huntedst down from morning until noon,
And dyed his flight-path red.

SAUL.

                    No more; 'tis done.

ABNER.

Would it were not! I hated the Amalekites;
But such a deed—

SAUL.

                    It is not thine, nor mine.

ABNER.

Thou knowest that if this had not been of God,
I had disobeyed thee.

SAUL.

                    I had not commanded
Without Heaven's sanction. Samuel stands alone
Herein responsible. Let us cut short
Our colloquy. Leave some to bury the dead,
Lest pestilence fill the air.—Cease grieving, man:
The agony is passed; the slain are easier
Now than the slayers: it is we want pity.
No one now suffers from thy trenchant blade.
The lambs which thou hast killed and wrapped in gore,
Sleep painless, and will wake to pain no more.

ABNER.

Who will not call me butcher!

SAUL.

What's done is done:
Moreover, have not I in this red pool
Waded as deep as thou? Be comforted:
Remember, when our fathers Canaan took
All to the sword were put: this is not new.

ABNER.

There's some relief in that.

SAUL.

Much, all sufficient.
Consider, too, men move not much our pity:
Men are our counterparts, and these were all
Hereditary enemies of ours.

ABNER.

But women! the resemblance of our mothers,
And of our sisters, as methought they seemed,
When, with their upraised hands and frantic looks,
They fled before us; or, without defenders,
In fathers, husbands, brothers, all cut off,
Stayed kneeling and bowed down their meek, white necks
Before us to receive the horrid scymetar.

SAUL.

I prythee peace; Abner, I prythee peace.

ABNER.

I often in my rage thought on my daughter.—
And, oh, to see the little ones, that those
Damned brutes carved up so cheerfully, or dashed
Against the stones their brains out.

SAUL.

Prythee peace.

ABNER.

I cannot hold.

SAUL.

Ah, I could rave, too, Abner.
But that I dare not let my thoughts have birth,
Much less array those embryo thoughts in words,
I should deliver me of such conception
As would appall the reverent ear of men,
And make me seem, even what I fear I am,
The Omnipotent's accuser. But let's cease,
And preserve silence from this very day
Touching this dreadful business: let our hearts
(Like smoky rooms) blacken with their down-pent grief,
But never let us willingly recall it.

ABNER.

Be it so; and whatsoever tint may wear
My other deeds, past or to come, I'll say,
Or bloody red, or be I ingrained black,
Herein I am white as childhood's innocence.

SAUL.

May Heaven hold both guiltless. Let us go;
The men are wondering at our parley. Come,
We have but begun; we must the race uproot:
Betake we to the horrible pursuit.

[Exeunt omnes.

SCENE IV.

Country near to Shur. An Amalekitish town seen in a state of ruin.
Enter two HEBREW SOLDIERS.

FIRST SOLDIER.

Let us put up our blades; for not a blade
Seems standing on the Amalekites' wide mead,
So ruthless have we mown down life thereon,
And, with the sudden sickle of our coming,
Reaped red, prodigious harvest of old hate.

SECOND SOLDIER.

From Havilah to Shur we have destroyed them.
By the reward that waits on deeds well done,
Will not Jehovah smile upon us now!

FIRST SOLDIER.

Doubtless He will. 'Tis pleasant, too, to feed
Thus the keen appetite of a gnawing grudge,
Whilst we perform the mandate of Jehovah,
And work with His Commission. 'Tis as though
We banqueted on meats, that, while they gave
The present palate exquisite delight,
We knew should furnish us with surplus strength
To last for many days; or 'tis as though
We feasted with soft music floating round us.
When I was killing, such thoughts came to me, like
The sound of cleft-dropped waters to the ear
Of the hot mower, who thereat stops the oftener
To whet his glittering scythe, and, while he smiles,
With the harsh, sharpening hone beats their fall's time,
And, dancing to it in his heart's strait chamber,
Forgets that he is weary.

SECOND SOLDIER.
       Even so
During this wild destruction I have found it.
It seemed as though some pliant, deep, bass voice
Made—whether the note was from babes' voices shrill,
Or frantic women's, or oaths or howls of men—
Harmony to each occasion.

FIRST SOLDIER.
      None are spared.
      [*Enter two other* SOLDIERS.

THIRD SOLDIER.
Yes; Saul hath spared their King.

FOURTH SOLDIER.
       And we have spared
The choicest of their cattle and their sheep,
As sacrifice to Jehovah.

FIRST SOLDIER.

         Is their King
Spared for a sacrifice?

    SECOND SOLDIER.

         Why hath Saul spared
Their King?

    THIRD SOLDIER.

     He hath not told us;—perhaps to be
A mockery for the rabble in Gibeah.

    FOURTH SOLDIER.

Dost thou not know that like affects its like?
The king has spared the king.

    SECOND SOLDIER.

         But we have not
The subjects spared who are our like. Besides,
We were to finish them: I have obeyèd
To my utmost.

    THIRD SOLDIER.

        So have I.

    FOURTH SOLDIER.

        And I, little thanks
To me. It is not in man's nature, more
Than it is in the beast's full, panting heart,
To spare his quarry when he's roused by hunting it.
There goes our king. How conqueror-like he stalks!—
And yet methinks that he is sorrowful.

    THIRD SOLDIER.

I could be sad too, but I shall not.

    FOURTH SOLDIER.

         Let us
Follow the king.

         [Exeunt.

SCENE V.

Ramah; an apartment in the house of Samuel.   Time, twilight.
An ANGEL *descends.*

ANGEL.

Saul's early piety having wasted quite,
Jehovah rues that he hath made him king;
And, so to inform the prophet, from heaven's height
I come descended on the evening's wing.
Here 'tis he sleeps, and soon upon his couch
Shall see me through the starry air approach;
For I to-night must access to him find,
And stamp on his, Jehovah's altered mind.
[ANGEL *vanishes.*

SCENE VI.

Near Gilgal.   Time, morning.
The army of Saul seen marching home.
Enter SAUL.

SAUL.

The morn opes wildly,—'twill be rain to-day.
I never marched so heavily, although
The gladsome rank and file dance on before me.
[*Enter* QUEEN.
My Ahinoam! what is it brings thee hither?

QUEEN.

Ask of the swallow what 'tis brings him to us,
And he will tell thee 'tis the approach of summer:
So thine approach has drawn me to thee hither.

SAUL.

Am I thy summer, my Gibean Queen?
But thou art not the swallow, Ahinoam;—

For, now I think on't, 'tis not happily chosen
Thy simile of that wanderer,—since he leaves us
At peep of wintry weather. Remember,
The swallow is a byword grown in Israel,
Since when my army fled, like birds of passage,
At Gilgal's sudden chill.

####### QUEEN.

        Forget that now.

####### SAUL.

I read thine eye. The Amalekites have perished;
None saved, save he who merited the sword,
Haply, beyond the others who were doomed
To feel its keen destruction,—even their king.

####### QUEEN.

Saul, thou art made a minister of vengeance,
And must perform thine office; but may God
Forgive my weeping o'er thy finished mission.

####### SAUL.

My morning star, let me wipe off these dews
That dim thee in this unexpected rising.
Ahinoam, far dearer than that star
Is to the hour of dawn, art thou to me
Now, when home coming gloomy though successful.
Lift up thine eyes upon me, love, and drive
From out of me my darkness.

####### QUEEN.

       Husband dear,
Haste home with me to Gibeah, where new sights
May cause you to forget what you've late seen.

####### SAUL.

I never can forget what I've late seen:—
Oh, I could paint thee pictures with my tongue
(Scenes drawn from out of Amalek's great anguish)
From morn till midnight, till thine eyes grew redder
Than blood itself with weeping. Forget them! no:

Such scenes resemble not the figures that children
Sketch on the stones, and that the rain outwashes.
Ahinoam, I am a soldier, and have seen
War many times; but all here seemed like murder.
Such cries of youths, such shrieks, such looks of women;
Such chorus of promiscuous sounds, imploring
Mercy from men,—nay, let me not such call them,—
Who met those melting sounds with hideous laughter,
And out of countenance grinned the encircling air,
That stagnant stood with horror.

QUEEN.

        It was wrong
To scoff at the poor wretches in their ruin.

SAUL.

Their ruin made the revel of our men;
Who've made the massacre a carnival,
And fleshed their souls yet deeper than their swords.
Pshaw! the broad multitude know nought of judgment.
Revenge, with them, was at the bottom of it;
Whilst sensuality rose to the top like scum.
Revenge is hunger of the mind, and hunger
Makes all things cruel;—yet the wolf not sports with,
But rends his victim, and his sharp head plunges
At once into its bowels. Oh, 'twas foul
Behaviour!—but I fear that most of men,
If they were licensed by divine decree,
Would change to demons, and for aught be ready.

QUEEN.

Beware lest thou blaspheme Jehovah, Saul.
His holy will depraves not those who work it.

SAUL.

It does when they exceed it. The dead they've stoned,
And made the Holiest's order an excuse
To glut their basest passions.—But I'll punish:
They shall sneak in at the back door of Gibeah;
Pageant there shall be none! I could not bear
To see thee smiling—and with thee all Gibeah—
On half those men.

QUEEN.

                          I see that they are flushed,
Even yet, and look as lewd as savage.

SAUL.

                                            Ay,
As Amalek's daughters, even i'th' agony, found them.
Babe-killers are a third of them by nature;
Nor e'er for Age felt reverence: oh!—but I
Ne'er held that men were noble, for, in truth,
There is a latent treachery in us all;—
Ay, and mayhap in woman; though I think
That in your essence you are gentle, and
Admire no bravery in men save that
Which has been married to a tender spirit,
That, like an indwelling angel, causes them
To grieve even while they punish. Such not these.
Look at the gazing fellows who are nearest us:
Blood-shotten are their eyes with rage, and, where
The wine has not the cheek incarnadined,
The tawny jaundice mantles on the skin,
And speaks of yet-edged malice. I am sorry
That thou hast stolen from Gibeah to meet us;
For, in their vain and ignorant misconstruction,
Thy coming here may seem to mean glad welcome.

QUEEN.

'Twas love for you that did impel me hither.

SAUL.

I know it; but, sweet chuck, return at once:
Go back, dear wife, and wait me still in Gibeah.

QUEEN.

And must I be discharged so soon? and when
You are moody too,—for I can see you are troubled.

SAUL.

Not much, love, now: so let us separate, for,
On thee attending, I could not compel
This force to march 'tween discipline's strait borders.

QUEEN.

I see 'twas foolish to forestall your coming,
And disallow your soldiers' natural frenzy
To ebb yet lower down the bank of time
Before their greeting; but I'll say farewell:
To-morrow you will rest in Gibeah.

SAUL.

I hope so, darling; and by that time, surely,
These men will don their old and lying faces,
And from their mistresses and wives conceal
The dark truths of their nature. Now, farewell,
And better fare for th' love that brought thee hither.
[*Exit* QUEEN.
'Tis well she's gone! for, staying, she might see trouble.
Even now, I have within me a misgiving
That I have hurt myself in sparing Agag.
[*Enter* SAMUEL.
Mayest thou be blessed of the Lord, O Samuel!
Lo, his command given by thee is performed.

SAMUEL.

What meaneth, then, this bleating of the sheep
And lowing of the oxen that I hear?

SAUL.

The people have brought the choicest of the cattle
And sheep, to sacrifice unto the Lord;
All else destroyed they.

SAMUEL.
     Thou unhappy man,
Listen, and I will tell thee what the Lord
Said unto me last night.

SAUL.
    Say on.

SAMUEL.
     When thou
Wert humble and yet void of pride, God chose thee
To be his chief o'er Israel; then why

Hast thou not been obedient since? and when
He sent thee to extirpate the Amalekites,
Why hast thou not obeyed Him, but allowed
Thyself to make exceptions, and take spoil?

SAUL.

I have obeyed Him; I have executed
The Lord's behest. The Amalekitish King
I have brought captive; and have all his subjects,
Man, woman, youth, and babe, put to the sword.
Their cattle, dead or dying, strew the land;
Except a few which should have been destroyed,
The choicest, which the people brought on hither,
As sacrifice unto the Lord thy God.

SAMUEL.

Hath God in sacrifice and in burnt-offerings
As great delight as in obedience given
To his command? Know, that to obey is better
Than sacrifice; and that to hearken to Him,
Is more acceptable than the fat of rams
Unto Him offered: for rebellion
Is all as bad as is the sin of witchcraft;
And stubbornness is as injustice, or
Idolatry. Hence, since thou hast again
Rejected God's commandment, so He thee
Hath finally rejected from being king.

SAUL, *aside.*

How shall I answer this? Oh, Ahinoam,
Well that thou left'st me when thou didst! It is
For thine and Jonathan's sake I'll humble me.
Down, heart; down to the dust, if it must be so.

Aloud.

I have done wrong; I have not perfectly
Performed my errand; for I have deferred
Unto the people, granting their request
To save some cattle. Pardon me, and now
Go back with me, that I may worship God.

SAMUEL.

I will not go with thee; for thou again
Rejected hast God's voice, and He doth thee
Reject from longer being king o'er Israel.

SAUL.

Thou shalt not leave me thus: stay, I command thee!

SAMUEL *turns to go away*; SAUL *seizing him by the mantle, which rends in*
SAUL'S *grasp.*

SAMUEL.

Spirit perverse, and ready to do evil,
Thus hath God rent from thee this day the kingdom,
And given it finally unto another,
Better than thou. Remember, the strength of Israel
Lies not, nor will repent; nor is He man
To change his mind.

SAUL.

      I do confess my sin!

SAMUEL.

That comes too late to stay thee on the throne.

SAUL.

Too late! Is there no pardon in the world?—
Why, I myself dispense forgiveness, even
To culprits who have forfeited their lives.
Is not thy God as merciful as his creatures?

SAMUEL.

He mercy shows to thousands who do keep
His great commandments.

SAUL.

     They who keep them need
No mercy. Say, what have I done that calls
For this huge penalty now twice denounced?—
Omitted what, which cannot yet be done?
He has not said that which thou hast declared.
Thou art mine enemy, art jealous of me,

Wouldst wish to see me trip and tumble down.
Prophet, I now impeach thee. Why didst thou linger
Away frow Gilgal, and, when I supplied
Thy lack, come thither and ban me for my trouble ?
And wherefore com'st thou now in this proud style,
Requiting me for toil and life imperilled,
By second deposition ?—and forsooth,
Because some sundry sheep and calves and beeves
Yet snuff the air,—of which there is abundance,—
And a poor realmless king still lives to weep ;
Or curse, in secret, thee, myself, and God,—
The obvious triad who (for an offence,
Not his, but his dead ancestors') have conspired
To dash him and his idols. Answer these
Strong accusations; then come here, and with
Thine own soul pure arraign me.

SAMUEL.
God arraigns thee.

SAUL.
Nay !—and yet take the cattle, and take Agag
And kill him out of kindness. I know thou lovest
Not kings; so lovest not me, although I am
One half of thine own making :—hence it is
That I've endured thy schooling; for I cannot
Forget the early days of our acquaintance,
Ere thou hadst learned to chide me.

SAMUEL.
I still love thee,
Even in this thy last and deep disaster.

SAUL.
Is this sincerely spoken ?—if it be
Give me some proof : my anger towards thee dies.
Say that Jehovah is not wrath.

SAMUEL.
How can I ?
For He hath cast thee off.

SAUL.
                        But not for ever :—
Such cannot be for aught that I have done,
Or aught that I've omitted.—Or if He has,
Still honor me before my people's eyes,
By me accompanying to worship Him.

SAMUEL.
Lead on; but never more a favor ask me.

Exeunt, and enters soon a SUBALTERN, *who paces to and fro ; and presently a confused noise arises.*

SUBALTERN, *stopping suddenly.*
What means that hubbub ?
Here comes one who can scarce contain himself.
                        [*Enter a* SOLDIER.
What now ?   Thou look'st surprised.

SOLDIER.
                        No wonder, when
The gentle Samuel has executioner turned,
And finisher of our labor.   Agag is
No more.

SUBALTERN.
                        Has judgment, then, been so exact
That it has not allowed one doit of mercy,
Though 'twere to have been bestowed upon a king ?
This is not true :—and how of Samuel ?—pshaw !
I Agag saw but now and he was living.

SOLDIER.
He lives no longer,—not at least 'mongst men.
Agag is now a ghost, and would not know
The carcass that three minutes ago contained him.
So felled it is, so lopped, so strewn on th' ground,
The bird, his soul, now would not know the tree
That it for forty years has sat and sung in.
He'll pipe no more.

SUBALTERN.
Did Samuel order his death?

SOLDIER.
He summoned to him the idolater, who came
Bareheaded, and yet delicately, forth;
Approaching him, and, with forced smile, exclaiming,
" Surely the bitterness of death is passed!"
But Samuel cried aloud, with kindled eyes,
" As thy sword hath made woman childless, so
Thy mother shall be childless among women,"
Then hewed him into pieces.

SUBALTERN.
Is't possible?

SOLDIER.
Come with me, and I'll shew thee him divided
Into five Agags,—ay, and more. Let's reckon:
His hands are off, that sought to save his head,
Which is disparted; and his arms and shoulders
Are carbonadoed, minced; and gashed his loins,
And all the cunning ways and means of life—

SUBALTERN.
A curse upon thee! hold.—Why Saul and Samuel
Even now to worship went. I'll not believe thee.

SOLDIER.
What, not believe! I tell thee that from worship
Samuel arose and slew him; and away is gone
Saul to Gibeah, and Samuel back to Ramah,
And certainly in mutual displeasure.

SUBALTERN.
With this division 'tween the Throne and Altar,
Israel can never prosper.

SOLDIER.
Wilt go see Agag?
Thou'lt say he makes no handsomer a corpse
Than any of his subjects.

Exeunt, and re-enter near. SOLDIERS *looking at the remains of Agag. An altar still smoking in the distance.*

SUBALTERN.

Oh, horrible! This deed had better become
Saul's blood-stained hand.

SOLDIER.

Thou saw'st him whilst he lived;
Wouldst know him now that he is dead?

SUBALTERN.

His own
Wives would not know him, who should know him best.
Poor wretch, but this sight melts me!

SOLDIER.

Pity him not;
He would have done as much for thee and me,—
Ay, or for Saul or Samuel. Listen how
The ground, after the soaking draught of blood,
Smacks its brown lips. It seems to like royal wine
Beyond small-beer leaking from beggar's veins.

SUBALTERN.

All sceptreless he lies, and none to bury him.
Sceptre! he has no hands wherewith to wield it.

A SPECTATOR SOLDIER.

No: but he has two heads, or something like them;
So, were he living, he might wear two crowns.
His face is cloven like a pomegranate:
See how his eyes distend, and gape his jaws!

SUBALTERN.

Ay, stricken with terror at Samuel's sword, his spirit
Seems to have leaped out both at doors and windows.
Gather his scattered relics, and them cover
O'er with his bloody robe, and let it be
His purple pall.

While they are gathering his remains.

'Tis a dread dissolution!
Yet even as was his life. Let us begone;
I hear the recommencement of the march.

[*Exeunt, and enter two* DEMONS.

FIRST DEMON.

Now let us down to hell; we've seen the last.

SECOND DEMON.

Stay; for the road thereto is yet encumbered
With the descending spectres of the killed.
'Tis said they choke hell's gates, and stretch from thence
Out like a tongue upon the silent gulf;
Wherein our spirits—even as terrestial ships
That are detained by foul winds in an offing—
Linger perforce, and feel broad gusts of sighs,
That swing them on the dark and billowless waste,
O'er which come sounds more dismal than the boom,
At midnight, of the salt-flood's foaming surf,—
Even dead Amalek's moan and lamentation.

FIRST DEMON.

He's lost, but not as we. I've neither pity
Nor spite concerning him; for who can pity
Others in that which his own self endures
In greater measure? Amalek is strange
To his vicissitude; but he will grow
Inured to it, even as others have grown,
At length, inured to theirs. Rememberest thou
When, with those vast, inexorable rains,
Jehovah drowned the people of this world,
How long they lay upon the lumeless deep;
How long they drifted through hell's gates; how roared
Their grief?

SECOND DEMON.

I do;—but wherefore trifle we?
Say, whereunto shall we betake ourselves
To pass the hours, until we are compelled
Again to drop into our fiery prison?

FIRST DEMON.

Let's first go bathe us in the Atlantic Sea;—
Or stay, who's coming? It is my fair friend
Peyona, Malzah's lover.—Thou knowest Malzah:
Him, the facetious spirit, who, with mirth
Infectious, doth at times provoke half hell
To snap their fingers both at it and heaven.
I will accost her. Malzah was lately grown
Groundlessly jealous of her; for sure never
More constant creature than herself e'er fell
From light,—indeed, from thence she did not fall,
But wandered freely to our gloomy pit
After her lover, whom to seek was ruin.

[*Enter* PEYONA.

Peyona, my pale pilgrim, whence art thou?

PEYONA.

Tophet. Whence thou?

FIRST DEMON.

The Land of Amalek.

PEYONA.

'Tis said, that since the days of Jonathan,
Who conquered this, there has not been such slaughter.
You know, not I, the cause o'th' carnage; but
These mortals are continually frantic,
Or with desire, or changes of the moon,
Or lust of power, or lapses into rage
At their own wrongs, or those their fathers left them,
To school them into malice.

SECOND DEMON.

Even so
This hour, from Havilah to Shur is red
As Eygpt was, when we, with heaven's angels
(Beneath the forms of Moses and the Priests)
Contending in the gamesome lists of magic,
Changed all her streams and lucid pools to blood.

PEYONA.

Ha, ha! those were the days of frolic! Malzah laughed
For a whole century afterward. He would titter
While in his sleep, and, kissing and caressing,
Call me his frog, or louse, or pretty serpent.
And once he smote me such a blow, that I
Still bear the mark on't; for he dreamed he saw
Me, fascinated, speeding through the jaws
Of one of Aaron's sacerdotal hydras,
At which he aimed the blow, that fell on me.
Have you not seen him lately? for I seek him:
'Tis many a day since I beheld his face.

FIRST DEMON.

Yonder he comes, if I may know his gait.

PEYONA.

'Tis he indeed. How this would once have joyed me!
But now I almost fear to look upon him.
You'll stay and greet my mate?

FIRST DEMON.
        Excuse us, for
We are on eve of urgent business; so
We will not stay to greet him, least he should,
With mystic charm, seduce us to his vein,
And lead us, bound, to fields of dissipation.

Exeunt FIRST *and* SECOND DEMONS, *and enter* MALZAH, *stepping to the measure of his own words.*

MALZAH.

Home to Gibeah the king is gone,
With God's grace off, and man's dudgeon on.
O yes, he is gone; yes, home he is gone,
And I there to meet him will surely make one.
Ahinoam, his Queen, will wonder and pine;
His servants will pity, and some shall divine;
And I will all hear as midst them I steer,
And take from my hearing my strategy's line.

PEYONA.

I've watched thy folly.

MALZAH.

                  Ah, one embrace!—But stay :
What brings thee hither?   [*Enter* ZOE.
                  Here comes a Puritan.
        [*Exeunt* MALZAH *and* PEYONA, *hastily.*

ZOE.

Hell's ministers avoid my path,
As though I moved in latent wrath;
But I, on melancholy wing,
Muse on my own late ministering.
'Tis ended now; 'tis ended now;
And I unto the issue bow.
On Saul himself be all the blame.
Saul could not more attention claim :
A stronger influence from me
Would have destroyed his liberty.
His fault was found in his own heart :
Faith lacking, all his works fell short.
I for him sigh,—why should not I ?
I loved him when to me first given;
But I'll forget him now, and fly
Again unto my seat in heaven.
        [*Exit* ZOE, *and re-enter* MALZAH *and* PEYONA.

MALZAH.

I do believe thee;—nay, I know thou'rt true.
I am the very Ass of Acheron
To have brayed thus in thine ear. I promise thee
That I will snort out no more jealousy :—
Yet when I doubt thee, perhaps I love thee most.
Come, let us kiss ere parting.   [*Kisses her.*
                Peyona,
The scents of heaven yet hover round thy lips,
That are a garden of well-watered sweets;
Which I must leave now for the arid desert
Of vexing Saul.

PEYONA.

I know thy taste for mischief;
And all love's round, from this to summed desire,
Glads thee not more than does occasion offered
To gratify it. What thing is that?
[Pointing to the corpse of Agag.

MALZAH.

A pie;
But made, methinks, lass, when the cook was angry.
Look on it, for 'tis worthy thine inspection:
It is concocted of a certain king,
Agag by name. His bloody, stiffening robe,
Around it thrown, makes a fine encrustation.
Upon this grand updishing of his kingdom,
He is brought in at the last as the dessert,
And is served up in a most royal fashion.

PEYONA.

Oh, canst thou jest at such a hideous sight?
I'll go no nearer to it,—no, not I.

MALZAH.

We must now rip ourselves asunder. Come,
Bid me farewell again; and I'll expire,
Till quickened in the resurrection of thy countenance.
Farewell, my squeamish, ever-gentle goblin.
[Exit PEYONA.

I like not blood myself, and such dread carving
Makes one both sick and savage: but 'tis true
(For I beheld this tragedy performed)
These priests delight to school and humble kings.
Ay, ay, dead tyrant, this is degradation:
The flies already take thee for a dunghill.
Faugh! who'd stay here that doth rejoice in nostrils!
Now, over sweeter fields and running brooks,
I'll follow Saul, who has just lost his relish
For man-killing; grown surfeited and sick,—
As well he may, after his bloody courses.
I'll follow him and see how he'll take bitters. *[Exit.*

ACT V.

SCENE I.

Gibeah, an apartment in the palace.
Enter SAUL and an OFFICER of State.

SAUL.

To make and to unmake me at his pleasure!
Tell me not that he grieves;—he's glad at heart.
Let him beware; his office shall not shield him,
As the strong glove o'th' hedger shields the hand
That shears the tree it planted. Let him heed,
Lest, in attempting to blow out the flame
Which he hath kindled, it do fierce consume him.
Now get thee gone.
                              [*Exit* OFFICER.
                    Thus with denunciation
I'll meet denunciation, as might i'th' welkin
Thunder meet thunder. Bann'd as heaven's rejected!
If I rejected be, I too may have
Rejected; for I feel that I am changed.
Revulsion cold, and hot resentment, fill me.
I am as he, who, to his enemy
Having made fair offers, spurned with proud disdain,
Pays his disdainer with malicious scorn.
Is it the skies I scorn? Oh, no; for who
So hardy as to scorn the Omnipotent?—
Samuel I scorn, for he unjust is towards me!—
Yea, Heaven unjust is too.—Oh, peace, my tongue.—
And yet I am indubitably changed:
My heart now never beats up heavenward.

Once was I as a bird that took slight soars;
Now never mounts my soul above the ground.
I have no God-ward movings now: no God
Now, from his genial seat of light remote,
Sends down to me a ray. Yet I'll endure:
Though now 'tis night, 'twill break again to day.

[Exit.

SCENE II.

The neighborhood of Gibeah. Time, before daybreak.
Enter ZAPH *and* ZEPHO.

ZAPH.

Zepho, our spirits come not: what's the matter?
Surely they cannot have been intercepted!
I know that heaven's haughty ministers
Are more than ever upon the alert.
Be watchful; for I apprehend intrusion,
Either from Gloriel or from his troop.

ZEPHO.

Nor Gloriel, nor any of the minions
Who with him wear the livery of heaven,
And who have lately shewn such zeal to thwart us,
Shall steal upon your session whilst I'm sentinel.

ZAPH.

Why are my spirits late?   *[A cock crows at a distance.*
                                  Hark; chanticleer
Breaks with his voice the bubble of the night.
Even now the dawn is in the east fermenting.

[Enter ZAPH'S DEMONS *hastily.*

Is this the hour that you were summoned for?
Marshal yourselves about me; and now, Zepho,
Around about us wing continually,
And warn me if thou hear'st aught.

ZEPHO.

I will fly
So swiftly round you, that I'll be a fence,
Like the Divine, in every part at once.
[*Exit* ZEPHO, *and enter* MALZAH.

ZAPH.

Welcome, Malzah; welcome, sprite;
Welcomer than longer night
Just now would be! What hast for me?

MALZAH.

Tidings of the royal Saul,
King of Israel.

ZAPH.

Shall he fall?

MALZAH.

I deem he will, for much he dares.
Twice he has tripped half unawares;—
Twice, in spite of Zoe's cares;
She who late did him defend:
Her guardianship is at an end.
If thou wilt, I'll at him venture.

ZAPH.

Go, brave spirit, strive him enter.
[*Exit* MALZAH.

It grows too light:—lo! withering are
Both Jupiter and the morning star:
And, lo! Aurora peeping there
On the eastern eaves,—of her beware;
For that her pale, untinted ray
May light our enemies this way.
So, with low voice, and accents brief,
Tell me, conjointly and in chief,
What ye have suffered, or what done
To spread the power of Acheron.
Me answer all;
And let your quick words muffled fall.

ALL.

Master, master, some disaster
Hath befallen us, but much more
Hath success; and mortals sore
We have troubled, having doubled
Evil, latent in their core.

ZAPH.

This is well; 'twill gladden hell.
Pass away and work it more.
      [The DEMONS *vanish.*
Zepho, hither :
       [Enter ZEPHO.
The spirits are gone, and for the ether
I am ready.

ZEPHO.

On my shoulders take thy seat.
    *[*ZAPH *vaults upon* ZEPHO'S *shoulders.*
Sir, be steady !
Whither shall I bear thee fleet ?

ZAPH.

I have business, if I choose,
Beckons me to Tartarus;
But I will not :—to the moon
Let me now be carried soon.

ZEPHO.

When last there thou soon grew'st weary,
'Twas so full of valleys dreary ;
Nor thereon a rood of sea
Wherein thou mightest mirror thee.
Let's to Limbo.

ZAPH.

Then to Limbo : in a trice,
Lay me in th' Fool's Paradise.
         [Exeunt.

SCENE III.

Ramah. Time, night. A room in Samuel's dwelling.
SAMUEL sleeping. A mild radiance breaks over him.

ANGELS, *softly chanting.*

Silence, deaden; slumber deep,
Closer yet his senses seal;
For the Lord comes in his sleep
To him, his dread will reveal.
Samuel, reverently attend;
Cease to sigh with frequent gust;
Lo, Jehovah down doth bend
To converse with mortal dust.
Listen, seer,
To the Lord's voice low and clear.

VOICE OF THE LORD.

How long wilt thou lament for Saul,
Rejected from his regal height?
Fill now thy horn with oil, and go
To Jesse the Beth-lehemite;
For I have from amongst his sons
Provided to myself a king.
One after mine own heart is he;
And from out his line shall spring
A greater than himself to be.

ANGELS, *chanting.*

Waken, prophet, ere 'tis day;
Waken, prophet, and away.

SAMUEL, *awaking.*

No hope, no more probation now, for Saul!
I must depart; this vision was divine.—
Yet Saul will kill me if he know my errand.
They tell me that he rages, and in chief
'Gainst me.

VOICE OF THE LORD.
Fear not fierce Saul; to Beth-lehem go,
And with thee take a heifer fair:
To sacrifice it unto me
Say is the end that brings thee there.
Then, consecrated, to the feast
Bid Jesse and his sons to go;
And from amongst them him anoint
Whom I that hour shall to thee shew.

SAMUEL.
It is enough: now, Saul, I fear thee not!—
Though thou canst never be by me forgot.

[Exit.

ANGELS, *chanting.*
Angels, let us swift return
To our shining seats on high:
Lo, the rosy-fingered morn
Paints our passage up the sky.
Let us fly
Heavenward through the orient sky.

[The light fades out.

SCENE IV.

Gibeah. Interior of SAUL'S *Palace.*

MALZAH, *footing it to the measure of his own words.*
God's permitted me,
He's admitted me
Into king Saul's heart;
Wherein shall work strange wickedness,
Ere I from it depart.

Hory, gory, already Saul's story
Hath a tragical chime;
Hory, gory, how Saul's glory
'S perishing in its prime!

Ha, ha, ha! it shall be my aim
To drag him into crime.

I've him visited,
Improvisited
Him with his first rage;
And from his groans and threats I do
Some merriment presage.

Himble, nimble! never so nimble
Since fell I from on high;
And whilst I'm out, I'll take a route
And ramble up the sky.
Ha, ha! ha, ha! ere this, on earth,
I've seen a dancing bear;
But naught, in pure, exalted mirth,
That could with me compare.
I'm happy, very; I'm growing merry;
I'm in a mood most rare;—
Shall I the empyrean pierce to see
If heaven still hangeth there?
Yes, were it not the roarer of all jests,
To up and peep at the outside of heaven?
Beyond all questioning, it would be so:
Therefore I'll treat Saul with becoming leisure,
For business still should alternate with pleasure.

[*Exit gaily.*

SCENE V.

BETH-LEHEM. *A spacious apartment with preparations as for a feast.*
SAMUEL, ELDERS, JESSE, *and others who have been called.*

SAMUEL.

Now bid thy sons come hither that I may see them.

[JESSE *motions to one who goes out, and* ELIAB *enters.*
Surely the Lord's Anointed is before him!

VOICES OF ANGELS.

Hesitate, thou man of God;
Tarry, venerable seer;
For the Lord's Anointed yet
Is not, as thou deemest, near.
Rate not Eliab by thine eye,
Tall of stature, stern of mien;
Worth by outer show's unseen,—
God the heart sees; pass him by.

[ABINADAB *enters*.

Also this of lordly port;

[SHAMMAH *enters*.

Likewise this of equal sort;

[*Seven other sons of* JESSE *enter consecutively*.

And the seven that, in vain,
Enter in a gallant train.

SAMUEL.

Are all thy children here?

JESSE.

The youngest still remains and tends the sheep.

SAMUEL.

Send for him: we will not eat until he come.

[*A young man goes to fetch* DAVID.

VOICES OF ANGELS.

Over field and over brook
Runs the swift and wondering hind;
David, with excited look,
Hurries hither fleet as wind,—
Lo, he's here!

[*Enter* DAVID.

Note him, seer:
On that head shall sit the crown.
Rise, anoint him; for 'tis he,
Who, though now unprized, unknown,
Famous shall hereafter be.

SAMUEL (*after having risen and anointed* DAVID).
Now let us eat, for I must soon be gone.
      JESSE.
Thou wilt not tempt the night?
      SAMUEL.
       'Tis always day
To those for whom Jehovah lights the way.
I too long linger from the shades of Ramah.
   [*The repast being finished, all depart except* DAVID.
      DAVID.
What meaneth this? why am I singled out,
The youngest born, for this unusual honor?
Why am I consecrated? to what end?
I'm lost in wonder; and where'er I turn
My eyes I see the same. Alas, I fear
Eliab is not my friend, although my brother;
For he does eye me with vexed, haughty looks.
My sire says nothing; and the elders smile;
While Samuel brake not silence on its meaning.
Fear mingles with my joy. This is the Lord;
And I must wait till He shall make that clear,
Which is left dark by his departed seer.
            [*Exit.*
    VOICES OF ANGELS.
Joy! 'tis done; and royal grace
Now are David's and his race;
Saul, who from him good hath driven,
Up to evil influence given.

SCENE VI.

Interior of SAUL's *Palace at Gibeah.*
MALZAH *hurled in from above, and lying prostrate.*

      MALZAH.
Oh, hurt, unutterably hurt!—dashed, dashed
To pieces!

And yet I half forgive the Hurricane-Sender,
When I consider that He has but swept me
Whither I meant to come. He might have pitched me
To Tophet, 'midst the laughter of the fiends.
But I will be revenged, even yet, for this!
'Tis the most scandalous assault e'er known;
Most unprovoked. Merely because I
Flew up toward heaven, I'm cast down in this fashion.
'Twas a slight trespass. Oh, these throes!—oh, oh!
I've got a twist somewhere about my reins;
One that will hold me, perhaps, a thousand years.
Oh, to be lithe and sound again!—oh, oh!

[*Rising.*

Now the rigidity that haunts the age
Of mortals hampers my aërial sinews.
I'm stiff already, and I shall grow stiffer.
Oh, oh! but now I ache. A thunderbolt
Would not have so disabled me. What next?
God is not love, but malice. Never mind;
I can bear malice, and be cruel too.
I'll go seek Saul and vex him while I'm savage.

[*Exit, and after a while re-enter.*

I cannot do it!
Nay, nay; I'll brave Zaph's uttermost displeasure.
What hath Saul done to me that I should plague him?
It goes against my heart and conscience, thus
To rack his body and deprave his mind.
Oh, how he groans, and sighs, and swears, and reasons!
Nay, by the pith of goodness yet left in me,
It me unfiends to see and listen to him.
Give me a ground of quarrel with him; let
Me know that he habitually derides us,
Or that he charges us with the corruption
Of his own heart, as many do with theirs,
And I will trouble him to Zaph's desire.
Or pit me against a standing enemy,
An angel; bid me to insult the Dreadest,

And I will do it : but for this poor king,
I have no provocation to sustain me
I'th' process of his injuring. Ah, who comes?
Beautiful 'tis; yet I was once as fair!

[*Enter* ZELEHTHA.

ZELEHTHA.

Thou unassiduous and errant spirit,
Go·and plague Saul.

MALZAH.

Not at thy bidding. No!

ZELEHTHA.

To him, and leave him not until the hour
When thou hast done thy work.

MALZAH (*aside*).

I must obey; I know I must. Curse her!—
Peace; I believe she knows my inmost thoughts.

(*Aloud.*)

How long wilt thou enthrall me? I'll not obey thee;
I am Zaph's minister, not thine. I am
The serf of Lucifer; and I will pay,
For I do owe, no service to Jehovah.—
Oh, look not on me; I will go vex Saul.

[*Exit, followed by* ZELEHTHA.

SCENE VII.

The same.

SAUL (*now possessed by* MALZAH), *rushing in wildly*.

What ails me? what impels me on, until
The big drops fall from off my brow? Whence comes
This strange affliction?—Oh, thus to be driven
About!—I will stand still: now move me aught
That can. Ah, shake me, thing; shake me again

Like an old thorn i'th' blast! 'Tis leaving me;
Oh, that it were for ever! Oh, how long
Shall this fierce malady continue, these
Dread visitations? See, 'tis here again!
What's here again? Or who? Here's none save I;—
And yet there's some one here. 'Tis here, 'tis here,
Within my brain :—no, it is in my heart,—
Within my soul; where rise again black thoughts
And horrible conceptions, that from hell
Might have come up. All blasphemies that my ears
Ever heard; my horridest ideas in dreams;
And impious conceits, that even a fiend
Methinks could scarcely muster, swarm within
Me, rank and black as summer flies on ordure.
Oh, what a den this moment is my breast!
How cold I feel, how cruel and invidious.
Now let no child of mine approach me; neither
Do thou come near to me, Ahinoam,
Their mother and the wife I dearly love;
For now the universe appears one field
On which to spend my rancour. Oh, disperse,
Fit, nor return with thy o'erwhelming shadows!
Oh, that it would begone and leave me in
My sorrow! Surely 'tis enough to live
In lone despair. To reign is care enough,
Even in rude health; but to be harassed thus
By an unnamed affliction;—and why harassed?
Oh, why am I thus harassed! I have heard
Of wretches raging under sharp remorse;
Of cruel monarchs, in their latter days,
Falling a prey to an accusing conscience;
But why should I, whose faults smite but myself,
Be thus tormented?

[Enter the QUEEN.

QUEEN.

Oh, be soothed, my Saul;
My husband, oh, my king, be calmed.

SAUL.

Am I not calm?

QUEEN.

You were not lately: far off I heard you; yea,
Your servants must have heard you.

SAUL.

Let them hear me,
Since God will hear me not. I tell thee, wife,
I'll on Him call no more, nor sacrifice.

QUEEN.

Oh, speak not thus!

SAUL.

I will thus speak.

QUEEN (*weeping*).

Alas,
What shall I do!

SAUL.

Ay, what shall I do too!
I have no tears to shed as woman hath:
My grief must burn within me, or o'erflow
In tragic deeds, or those foul blasphemies
Which, from my soul's ooze, are uplifted by
My horrid agitation. Weep? No, no.
And yet I have wept too, but secretly.
Ay, ay, convulse me once again, strange forces.
Whate'er thou art that rends me, I defy thee!
Ah me! to be thus clutched! Ahinoam!
Help, help; pray for me, Ahinoam.

QUEEN.

Hear me,
Jehovah; hear me for my husband! Oh,
Rescue great Israel from his gusty pangs;
Cure his distemper, lighten his sad heart;
Assuage, O God, assuage his torment, or
Let me endure it and to him give ease.

SAUL.

Oh, wife, it is not these corporeal pains—
Though they are past description—that unman me;
But 'tis the horrid o'erthrow of my mind,
My will's harsh subjugation, that doth humble me.
I know the strength of man: I know a spasm
Can paralyse it; I know his cogitation
May fail at an impertinent idea:
But to have the soul swallowed up of its own self,
Like ocean by its own devouring sands,
Or the clear sun high in the firmament,
Thence downwards sucked and quenched in a volcano,—
Oh, no stouthearted courage can brave that.
I would that I could guide my thoughts! but no;
The king's most lawless subject is himself.
His thoughts have lately strangely scorned his rule.
They are as shifting winds that scorn the sun;
And fickler than the April hours they are:
Some fair enough, some sorrowful, and some
I know not what they're like, nor whence they come;
Inconsequential, so like imps of hell,
That I would not be their progenitor
For half my crown. No, no, I loathe
Such inspirations, in me but not of me;
Things that seem to me on the hot winds blown
Of some infernal desert; scorpions, dragons;
Inbreathings, no acknowledged brood of mine,
By thought on thought begotten.—Dry thy tears;
My paroxysm is ended for to-day.

QUEEN.

Would that you had some cure!

SAUL.

                Would that I had!
But let us hence; I am no longer mad.

                                        [*Exeunt.*

SCENE VIII.

An Apartment in the Palace.
The QUEEN *and a* PHYSICIAN.

PHYSICIAN.

His majesty's general health seems to me perfect;
For, save when he is suffering in the fit
(When I have marked his pulse most riotous),
His frame exhibits no symptom of disease.

QUEEN.

No? Looks his eye as clear and bright as ever,
As healthful his complexion? Is his voice
Strong, nor ever rumbles hollowly in his breast,
Like spirit speaking from a sepulchre?
Does he never seem to sigh without occasion?
I hear him groan throughout the livelong night;
And he informs me that he's vexed with dreams,
Wherein a form seems ever beckoning him
To rise and follow it to violent deeds;
Or, in his otherwise sound slumber, something
Beats at the doors and windows of his senses,
Urging for entrance. Tell me what these mean.

PHYSICIAN.

Whate'er their meaning, they are of one complexion
With his day's paroxysms. This much I know,
[*Enter* SAUL *unobserved.*
His Majesty certainly hath a mania,
An intermittent mania, but of such
Unusual kind, that I divine not yet
Of its true nature, and, hence, hesitate
To treat him for it.

SAUL.

Look deeper than the skin;
Then find me amongst thy compounds or thy simples,
An anodyne for undeserved distress.

Doctor, I have a stubborn melancholy;
Move it, and I will make thee king of physic.

PHYSICIAN.

Your Majesty bids me exercise an art
That I profess not: but as water droppings
Slowly remove whate'er they fall on, so
May the cadent moments of your Majesty's life
Gently remove your trouble.   Time is the skilfullest
Physician and tenderest nurse.

SAUL.

      But memory
Is time's defier.

PHYSICIAN.

      To know, is not to suffer
Always; for wrongs, like men, grow weak when old.—
But I'm too bold, your Majesty.

SAUL.

      I have heard say
That, toward the west, a people live believing
There is a river that can wash the past
From out the memory.

PHYSICIAN.

     I've travelled 'mongst them:
But they believe 'tis only after death
That those dark waters can avail the spirit;
Which, losing the remembrance of past evil,
Resigns therewith the memory of past good.

SAUL.

I ask not such oblivion!   But hast nothing
That can avail a mortal whilst he lives?
What are the dead to thee!

PHYSICIAN.

      Your majesty,
Herein I cannot help you:—I have no opiate
That can assuage the anguish of the spirit;

Nor subtle, fine astringent is there known
Can bind the wanderings of a lawless fancy;
No soft, insinuating balsam that
Can through the body reach the sickly soul.

SAUL.

Hast naught, then, in thy dispensatory?

PHYSICIAN.

I've sedatives, narcotics, tonics too—

SAUL.

Give me a tonic for the heart.

PHYSICIAN.

The King
Is strong of heart, or he had not delivered
Us from our enemies as he hath done.

SAUL.

O Prince of flatterers, but Beggar of doctors,
How poor thou art to him who truly needs!
The mind, the mind's the only worthy patient.
Were I one of thy craft, ere this I'd have
Anatomized a Spirit; I'd have treated
Soul-wounds of my own making; and, especially,
I would have sought out sundry wasted wretches,
And striven to cauterize to satisfaction
The gangrenes of their past.—Ye are imposters;
All said, ye are imposters; fleas.—Skindeep
Is deep with you: you only prick the flesh,
When you should probe the overwhelmèd heart,
And lance the horny wounds of old despair.
Away; Death is worth all the doctors.

PHYSICIAN (*aside*).

I'll speak the truth to him whate'er the result.
(*Aloud.*)
My liege, forgive me, for you have encouraged
Me, by your gracious freedom, to be bold:
You have an evil spirit from the Lord.

SAUL.

Ay, I am filled with evil whilst my fit
Continues, and do scores of murders then,
In fancy, and, in my excited hour,
Abominations work for which there is
No name in the vocabulary, whose worst
Expressions seem soft terms of innocence,
Compared with the big syllables required
To express me fully, when, in cruelty
And guile, the very soul of Moloch and
The machinations of the cunningest fiends
That walk the bottomless pit, and therein ply
Their fruitful fancies to deceive the world,
Move me 'midst black temptation.   Oh, I breathe
Then the live coals of hell, and all my heart
Glows ruddier than Tophet's angry noon,
So bloody is my soul and wrapped in sable.
Say, what's our cure?

QUEEN.

     Oh, fail not now his need !

PHYSICIAN.

Music can make the raging maniac gentle
As is the slumbering babe ; and hold the demon
In thrall until he smile like to an angel,
And creep from out his victim to the air,
To walk enrapt and harmless on the earth,
As erst he trod the blue abyss of heaven.

SAUL.

I envy him his dole: a minstrel seek
Me then.

PHYSICIAN.

    Your majesty, I have seen a son
Of Jesse the Beth-lemite; an excellent player;
Handsome and prudent, and religious also.
He keeps his father's sheep: his name is David.

SAUL.

Straight send a messenger to his father, bidding
Him send his son to the court.　　　　[*Exit* PHYSICIAN.
　　　　　　　　　　　　Dost hear, sweet,
How that the Devil is subdued by sound?
He cannot be all evil then; for music
Moves but that portion of us which is good.
Nay, dry thy tears. Come, come. Sweet medicine
Were music, and effective I doubt not;
For I remember, lately, when possessed,
Wandering beyond the limits of the garden,
Into the wood, upon a breezy day,
The sound of the swift brook assuaged my madness,
That, as I stood absorbed upon the bank,
Ebbed from me in unconscious, tender sighs.
　　　　　　　　　　　　　　　　[*Exeunt.*

SCENE IX.

The Garden of the Palace.
Enter two DOMESTICS.

FIRST DOMESTIC.

How is the king to day?

SECOND DOMESTIC.

　　　　　　　　　He's furious;
None dare approach him, and the very dogs
Shrink from him howling as they cross his path.

FIRST DOMESTIC.

Oh, horrible! a king to be so vexed!

SECOND DOMESTIC.

I met him even now, and he did fix
His eyes upon me in such savage sort,
I turned to avoid him; but he followed me
With vigorous strides, and on me poured hoarse curses,

Hissing 'twixt each like a serpent.   Horrified,
I looked behind me, and him saw returning
Upon his steps; yet his deep growls I heard,
And a sound as if of horrid chidings, that
He seemed to reply to in an abject sort;
And cast himself at last sheer on the ground,
And struggled 'mongst the shrubs like to a dragon,
Dust covered and as contending with a foe;
Then writhed in helplessness as if o'ercome,
And, panting, lay at last supine and moaning.

FIRST DOMESTIC.

What didst thou then?

SECOND DOMESTIC.

      I dared not reapproach him.
I stood and watched him till he seemed to sleep;
Then came I hither.

FIRST DOMESTIC.

      Dost thou think that he
Will awake, and, prowling in his mood malicious,
Come stumbling here upon us?

SECOND DOMESTIC.

      Heaven forefend!
For he would not respect us:—nay, 'tis said
That madmen are most bitter against those
Whom most they love in their clear hours of saneness.

FIRST DOMESTIC.

Hearken! what sound is that?

SECOND DOMESTIC.

      It is the harp
Of the stripling David, whom the king hath sent for
To soothe him in his hour.   See where he sits,
Like to a youthful angel on the mount
In Paradise.   The queen hath set him
Hard by the lattice of the royal chamber,
So that the king may hear him and be taken
In his own lure.

FIRST DOMESTIC.

       But will the evil spirit
Permit him to approach its enemy?

SECOND DOMESTIC.

I've heard all spirits—fallen ones as well as they
That are unfallen—have delight in music,
It being that which gave most zest to heaven.
Listen, is it not sweet?

FIRST DOMESTIC.

        'Tis more than sweet;
'Twould soothe a tiger, or the wretch that droops
Beneath despair, or him whose soul is chafing
Against itself at some sharp irritation;
Even as doth the squall-smitten and vexed sea's
White, boiling waves. 'Twould lift that back to hope,
This back to peace.

SECOND DOMESTIC.

     Lo, where the king comes back!
How formidable he seems!—but now thou'dst think
Him tame, hadst thou but seen him lately. Mark him.

FIRST DOMESTIC.

I do, even in fear; for yet his lips
Are muttering, and roll his cloudy eyes.
I hope he will not pass us; he's dangerous yet.

SECOND DOMESTIC.

He will: this way he comes with heavy steps;
Stooping, and with his tongue lolling out and bloody.
Alas, how brutalized, how laden with sorrows!
He feels his degradation, and he snorts,
Shaking his uncombed and luxuriant locks,
Like to an angry steed that meditates
To throw its rider.

FIRST DOMESTIC.

       I am terrified
To look upon him.

SECOND DOMESTIC.
       He is smeared and foul
With stains of earth, and foam clings to his lips;
Clenched are his fists, and, vertical his arms
Working consentive to his heavy tread,
He seems to pound both earth and air.
    FIRST DOMESTIC.
           And is
That Saul, our king, our royal master?
    SECOND DOMESTIC.
Austere he always looked, yet always noble;
But now, abstracted of his manly gait,
And champing at the bridle of the fiend,
He's dreader than the rank and brindled boar,
Whose sharp, white tusks are draped with liquid gore.
We are safe; but I would not now be within
Yon chamber where the young musician sits,
For a year's wages.
    FIRST DOMESTIC.
        Thitherward he turns.
He has caught the sound, and due appreaches it;
But whether in dudgeon or in softening temper,
I cannot tell. He hesitates on th' threshold.
    SECOND DOMESTIC.
He is like the ox that snuffs the slaughter-house
Before it enters.
    FIRST DOMESTIC.
       He has entered now;
And may heaven grant this music may assuage him.
    SECOND DOMESTIC.
It either will, or else the more enrage him.
Come let us hence.
              [*Exeunt.*

SCENE X.

A Chamber of the Palace. DAVID *playing on his harp.* SAUL *enters and listens, and at length* DAVID *ceases.*

SAUL.

Still more, still more: I feel the demon move
Amidst the gloomy branches of my breast;
Even as a bird that buries itself deeper
Within its nest at stirring of the storm.
         [DAVID *plays again.*
Were ever sounds so sweet!—where am I? Oh,
I have been down in hell, but this is heaven!
It grows yet sweeter,—'tis a wondrous air.
Methinks I lately died a horrid death,
And that they buried me accursed and cursing.
But this is not the grave; for, surely, music
Comes not t' reanimate man 'neath the clods.
Let me not think on't! yet a fiend fierce tore me.
Ah, I remember now, too much remember;
But I am better: still methinks I fainted;—
Or was the whole a fearful, nightmare dream?
Nay, am I yet not dreaming? No; I wake:
And, as from dream or as from being born,
Without the outcry of a mother's travail;
Or, as if waking from a reverie,
I to myself am ushered by strange music,
That, in its solemn gentleness, falls on me
Like a superior's blessing. Give me more
Of this sweet benefit.
       [*After having listened again.*
Who is this stranger? Yes, I know him now.
'Tis not a heavenly spirit, though so like one,
With hovering arms poised ruddy o'er the harp,
As o'er the landscape the aërial bow:
It is the minstrel youth from Bethlehem;
In form, indeed, surpassing beautiful.

Methinks he doth address himself to sing:
I'll listen, for I love him as he sits.
Rapt, like a statue conjured from the air.
Hist.
   DAVID *sings, accompanying himself on his harp.*
  Oh, Lord, have mercy on the king;
  The evil spirit from him take;
  His soul from its sore suffering
  Deliver, for thy goodness' sake.
     SAUL (*aside*).
He for me prays.
  Oh, heal thine own Anointed's hurt;
  Let health again to him be given;
  And breathe upon his troubled heart
  The balmy sense of fault forgiven.
     SAUL (*aside*).
I would not hide my faults; amen.
  Great God, thou art within this place;
  The universe is filled with thee:
  To all thou givest strength and grace;
  Oh, give the king thy grace to see.
     SAUL (*aside*).
What have I done deserved the loss of grace?
I cannot say " amen ";—and if I did,
My feeble amen would be blown away
Before it had reached heaven. I cannot say it:
There disbelief takes prisoner my tongue!
  As after winter cometh spring,
  May joy unto his soul return;—
  And me, in thy good pleasure, bring
  To tend my flock where I was born.
     SAUL (*aside*).
So able, yet so humble!
    (*Aloud*).
     David, no;

Thou shalt remain and be mine armour-bearer.
What, wouldst thou seek again the idle downs,
Midst senseless sheep, to spend the listless day,
Watching the doings of thy ewes and rams!
Thou shalt go with me to the martial field
And see great deeds thereon.
Myself will teach thee military lessons;
To tell the enemy's numbers; to discover
His vulnerable points; by stratagem
To draw him from his posts of vantage; how
Swift to advance; how to surprise the foe;
And how to leaven others with thy courage;
How win from Ammon and the strong Philistine
The double prize of vengeance and renown;
And how at last to drink aright, out of the
Goblet of a victorious return,
The blood-red wine of war.
Meantime, thy lyric pleasures need not end;
For the fair maidens of the court affect
Music and song. Go now and tell the queen
Of the advantage thou hast been to me.

[*Exit* DAVID.

How potent is the voice of music! it
Is stronger than a king's command. How oft
In vain have I adjured this demon hence!
Oh, music, thou art a magician! Strange,
Most strange, we did not sooner think of thee,
And charm us with thy gentle sorcery.

AHINOAM (*entering and rushing to his arms*).

My regal Saul; my dear, recovered lord!

SAUL (*embracing her*).

Kiss me, dear wife, though I am smeared and foul.

AHINOAM.

Oh no, thou art not foul to me; no more
Than is the tiger, with his brindling stripes
Foul to his mate, or leopard with his spots,

Or than the kingly lion to his love,
When, with dishevelled and still-lifted mane,
He stalks back from the chase into his den:
Yet come unto your closet now with me
And cleanse yourself from these degrading stains.

SAUL.

More fair than in thy fairest flush of youth,
Now in thy ripened womanhood, that bears
To me such duteous harvest! Love, we'll keep
This shepherd youth at court; so, if need be,
He may again his wondrous skill display,
And chase the demon as he has to day.

AHINOAM.

A debt we owe him it were hard to pay.

[*Exeunt.*

SCENE XI.

Within the Palace.
Enter a Military OFFICER *and a* COURTIER.

COURTIER.

It is most wonderful.

OFFICER.

'Tis so indeed:
This youth hath made the king a king again;
Whose evil term hath day by day grown shorter,
Till 'tis no more. Thanks to that noble shepherd,
Who, with the engines of his harp and voice,
Has, since his coming hither, planned and laid
Such heavy seige to this king-entering demon,
That now our master stands erect and sound;
His royal mind's strong citadel being freed
And purged from evil influence.

COURTIER.

Oh, great joy
I feel at this deliverance!

OFFICER.

          Abner wept,
Nor could restrain his tears for very bliss,
To see his royal cousin look so bravely,
And bear his helm as wont was 'fore the troops,
Who, with their myriad tongue-blast, rent the sky
And shook the marble base of Gibeah.

COURTIER.

I saw the Queen, too, watch him from her window,
With looks composed of gladness, pride, and love;—
Yet wherein some misgiving seemed to lurk
And check her exultation.

OFFICER.

       She's discreet,
As he is brave; more timorous, and less sanguine
Than he (even as she should be, being woman).

COURTIER.

Jonathan was at the review.

OFFICER.

         Yes; at the side
Of his great Sire he moved, as if he meant
Preclude all other tendance.

COURTIER.

          Possibly
He was suspicious of an access, even
I'th' very midst and presence of the soldiery.
'Twas somewhat rash so soon to venture forth;
Yet very like the king. What age is the moon?

OFFICER.

I know not; con the calendar.

COURTIER.

         Not now:
I go to attend the Princes and Princesses,
And greet them on the end of their distresses.   [*Exit.*

OFFICER.

Ha, ha! how sudden shoots this bolt of peace!
I wish, my blooming, jaunty sprig of clover,
Your joy may last, and their distress be over.

        [*Exit, and enter* MALZAH.

MALZAH.

Music, music hath its sway;
Music's order I obey:
I have unwound myself at sound
From off Saul's heart, where coiled I lay.
'Tis true, awhile I've lost the game;
Let fate and me divide the blame.
And now away, away;—but whither,
Whither, meantime, shall I go?
Ere long I must returned be hither.
There's Jordan, Danube, and the Po,
And Western rivers huge, I know:
There's Ganges, and the Euphrates,
Nilus, and the stretching seas:
There's many a lake and many a glen
To rest me, as in heaven, again;
With Alps, and the Himalayan range:—
And there's the Desert for a change.
Whither shall I go?
     I'll sit i'th' sky,
And laugh at mortals and at care;
(Not soaring, as before, too high,
And bring upon myself a snare;)
But out my motley fancies spin
Like cobwebs on the yellow air;
Laugh bright with joy, or dusky grin
In changeful mood of seance there.
The yellow air! the yellow air!
He's great who's happy anywhere.
To be the vassals and the slaves of music,
Is weakness that afflicts all heaven-born spirits.
But touch whom with the murmur of a lute,
Or swell and fill whom from the harmonious lyre,
And man may lead them wheresoe'er he wills;
And stare to see the nude demoniac
Sit clothed and void of frenzy. I'll begone,
And take a posy with me from Saul's garden.

 [*Exit; and soon re-enters bearing a huge nosegay, and thereat snuffing.*

Shall I fling it in the earth's face, from whence I took it!
Albeit I've seen, perhaps, flowers as mean in heaven.
Well, I will think that these are heaven's. Alack,
This is a poor excuse for asphodel;—
And yet it has the true divine aroma.
Here's ladslove, and the flower which even death
Cannot unscent, the all-transcending rose.
Here's gilly-flower, and violets dark as the eyes
Of Hebrew maidens. There's convolvulus,
That sickens ere noon and dies ere evening; and
Here's monkey's-cap.—Egad! 'twould cap a monkey
To say what I have gathered; for I spread my arms
And closed them like two scythes. I have crushed many;
I've sadly mangled my lilies. However, here
Is the august camelia, and here's marigold,
And, as I think, i'th' bottom two vast sunflowers.
There are some bluebells, and a pair of foxgloves
(But not of the kind that Samson's foxes wore).
That's mint; and here is something like a thistle
Wherewith to prick my nose should I grow sleepy.
Oh, I've not half enumerated them!
Here's that and that, and many trifling things,
Which, had I time, and were i'th' vein for scandal,
I could compare to other trifling things,
But shall not. Ah, here's head-hanging-down narcissus,
A true and perfect emblem of myself.
I'll count it my own likeness; and so leave it
For delectation of my radiant mistress,
Who, lieu of keeping watch and ward o'er me,
May keep it over my pale effigy.
                                    [*Drops the narcissus.*

Oh, hang her, hang her!
I'll hang this matchless rose upon my lips,
And whilst I'm flying will inhale its breath.
                                                [*Exit.*

END OF THE FIRST PART OF SAUL.

SAUL.

SECOND PART.

PERSONS REPRESENTED.

SAUL, *King of Israel.*
JONATHAN, *Saul's Eldest Son.*
ABNER, *Saul's Cousin.*
DAVID, *A Young Shepherd, and afterward King of Israel.*
JESSE, *David's Father.*
ELIAB, *David's Brother.*
GOLIAH, *The Philistine Giant.*
JOKIEL, *An Aged Member of the Royal Household.*
JARED, *A Youthful Member of the same.*
AHINOAM, *Queen of Israel.*
ZELEHTHA, *An Angel.*
ZAPH, }
ZEPHO, } *Demons.*
MALZAH, *The Evil Spirit of the Lord.*
COURTIERS, OFFICERS, SOLDIERS, MAIDENS, &c.

SECOND PART.

ACT I.

SCENE I.

Gibeah. Interior of the Palace.
Enter JOKIEL *and* JARED, *the latter having been some time absent.*

JARED.

Now that we are at leisure, thou canst tell me,
Somewhat at greater length, how fares our house:
How the clouds float in'ts sky; which one looks threatening.
What minister in the sea of state affairs,
Or in his own particular bay of office,
Hath struck a rock or run his craft ashore;
Who is wrecked for ever, who stranded in disgrace,
Who riding now the waves with oar and sail,
And who just foundered. Come; the king is better.
What next? How fares the stripling David?

JOKIEL.
                                   Oh,
Gone home: he pined for home, and the clear brooks
By Beth-lehem.

JARED.
             Thou sayest not so! he took the king
Vastly.

JOKIEL.
    Ay, so he did; and cowed the Spirit
That did so sore torment him, that, at length,

'Twould flee before the opening of the strain,
That was prolonged to charm the royal ears ;
While all the household did suspend its cares,
And post itself on stairs and passages
To banquet on the sounds.—But he is gone.

JARED.

Alas, that he should go ! Such a brave youth !—
So handsome too !

JOKIEL.

He hindered labor.

JARED.

How ?

JOKIEL.

Even from the cellars to the garrets, all
The palace's industrious economy
Worked under a dull clog on every wheel ;
And every operant shuttle of the loom
Would catch and stop mid-way as he went by it.
He was the song of the fat, smutted slut,
As she knelt scouring (and, with labor, sweating
Into) her own greasy kettles ; and the maid
O'th' chamber murmured his euphonious name,
As she stroked down the milk-white coverlet ;
While minxes from the town and country near,
Came, rank and zealous, to serve for naught the Queen.
Nor were the ladies of the court much better ;
They scarce concealed their loves ; and antique maids,
Gazing abstracted, browsed upon his cheeks,
And drank long at the clear brook of his eyes,
'Neath some excuse of empty colloquy.
The youthful damsels I have caught—ha, ha !—
Peering from lattice corners at him, and
Each other pulling thence, that each might view
The Adolescent, and, with wanton image,
Tenant the empty chamber of her mind ;
Or the desire-scorched desert of her soul

Invade with Ishmaelites of unlawful thoughts,
To rove at leisure o'er her virgin rock,
And love unwatered fancy.

JARED.

Ah, poor youth!
Unfortunate in his excess of fortune:—
An idol kissed away by its adorers.
Well might he flee to Beth-lehem!

JOKIEL.

Well indeed;
And well indeed men were not fairer formed,
Or, by the ark, the world's work had stood still,—
Yea, the whole garden of our State run wild;
Our household flower-beds gone untrimmed, whilst women
Had on us hung like bees on honeyed flowers.
Oh, they are fond, they are fond,—but not of thee
This David hath been to us key and mirror
To unlock the nature of woman, and to shew it
Uplighted to our eyes.

JARED.

Thou art a cockscomb!

JOKIEL.

Hast thou a weapon that can cut a comb?
Art thou aware the Philistines are approaching?

JARED.

No.

JOKIEL.

Then I tell thee; and I tell thee also,
That on to-morrow Saul goes forth to meet them.
I tell thee truth; there's bloodshed now in train,
And, though thou fight not, thou mayest scratch the slain.
Let us go; thou lookest enlightened.

[Exeunt, and enter SAUL.

SAUL.

Philistia's forth again, and our pale swords
Must blush once more i'th' livery of war.

With instant speed we'll meet the foe half way.
He shall not say that he hath wasted us.
My army from me melt not now away
As at accursed Gilgal. Many a field
Of slaughter hath inured them to death's terror:
They fear not violent end; and discipline,
Combined with stern selection of each man,
Hath made my standing legions thrice the value
Of raw, unbroken levies. So let come
Again these martial traders of the shore,
To be driven back as they have been before.
[*Enter* ABNER.

ABNER.

All's ready for the march.

SAUL.

Then we'll begone.
Hast parted from thy wife?

ABNER.

I have not.

SAUL.

Nor
Thy children?

ABNER.

No.

SAUL.

Then do not: like me, go
To this arena of uncertain strife
Without leave-taking or of child or wife;
For of all things that may unnerve a man,
Is thinking we may never meet again.
[*Exeunt.*

SCENE II.

A sylvan country.
Zaph *seated, and* Zepho *standing near him*

ZEPHO (*aside*).
My master seems but ill at ease to-day.

      ZAPH (*musing*).
Zepho,—
      ZEPHO.
What says my master to his servant?

      ZAPH.
        Zepho,
The Jewish king now walks at large and sound,
Yet of our emissary Malzah hear we nothing:
Go now, sweet spirit, and, if need be, seek
This world all over for him:—find him out,
Be he within the bounds of earth and hell.
He is a most erratic spirit, so
May give thee trouble (as I give thee time)
To find him, for he may be now diminished,
And at the bottom of some silken flower,
Wherein, I know, he loves, when evening comes,
To creep, and lie all night, encanopied
Beneath the manifold and scented petals;
Fancying, he says, he bids the world adieu,
And is again a slumberer in heaven:
Or, in some other vein, perchance thou'lt find him
Within the halls or dens of some famed city.
Give thou a general search, in open day,
I'th' town and country's ample field; and next
Seek him in dusky cave, and in dim grot;
And in the shadow of the precipice,
Prone or supine extended motionless;
Or, in the twilight of o'erhanging leaves,
Swung at the nodding arm of some vast beech.

By moonlight seek him on the mountain, and
At noon in the translucent waters salt or fresh ;
Or near the dank-marged fountain, or clear well,
Watching the tad-pole thrive on suck of venom ;
Or where the brook runs o'er the stones, and smooths
Their green locks with its current's crystal comb.
Seek him in rising vapors, and in clouds
Crimson or dun ; and often on the edge
Of the gray morning and of tawny eve :
Search in the rocky alcove and woody bower ;
And in the crow's-nest look, and every
Pilgrim-crowd-drawing Idol, wherein he
Is wont to sit in darkness and be worshipped.
If thou shouldst find him not in these, search for him
By the lone melancholy tarns of bitterns ;
And in the embosomed dells, whereunto maidens
Resort to bathe within the tepid pool.
Look specially there, and, if thou seest peeping
Satyr or faun, give chase and call out " Malzah !"
For he shall know thy voice and his own name.

ZEPHO.

Good ; if I catch't not, no more call me swift.

ZAPH.

Go now, my spirit.

[*Exit* ZEPHO.

I yet will feed the hungry grudge that gnaws me !
I will set Malzah upon Samuel,
Whom, if my spies report to me aright,
Now Gloriel guards 'gainst Saul with half a legion.
Never can I forget that angel's scorn,
And taunt at my despair-wrung moans in hell.
Naught save revenge can make my sick soul well.

[*Exit.*

SCENE III.

The Hebrew camp amongst the Hills by the Valley of Elah. Time, after midnight.

Enter SAUL *and* ABNER.

SAUL.

Let discipline be strictly kept. Remember,
Fertile are these Philistines in war's wiles;
And much experience hath made them apt
At seizing on advantage. Still our tactics
May balance the goodness of positions, which
At present lies with them. Thou seest that they
Respect us; for they dare not leave their heights,
But wait, instead, until we shall leave ours,
And, in the open and exposing vale,
Deploy defenceless; but which shall not be
Till I forget all warlike policy.

ABNER.

So be it; for we can wait, since all behind
Are ours, and glad to minister to us:
But, for his food and warlike store, the foe
Must either steal or for them homeward go.

SAUL.

And yet it irks me that I here must stand
And watch your small encounters; nor the less
Does it arouse my still impatient blood,
Knowing that beyond they rob us, and that this
Audacious Giant comes, and, day by day,
Defies us with his challenge, whereat I
Perceive our men's souls sinking; and at times
I fear some ambushed ill is in delay,
As formerly at Gilgal. We still doubt
Fortune, and, wert not madness, would assail
Th' Philistine ere the dawning; for we wait

Not now the enquiring of the Lord. Say, Abner,
Say, art thou not afraid to follow one
Who leads you in his own unaided might?

     ABNER.

Sometimes. And yet full many a field we've won
Under thy banners since no sacrifice
Them consecrated, or divine assurance
Gave to our people courage not their own;—
People, not soldiers; for thou art the first
Who made in Israel soldiers, and hast bidden
Them follow war and learn it as a trade.

     SAUL.

It is a trade, a terrible trade too!
Whilst, with the ambition of the human soul,
And greediness of the insatiate spirits
Of many,—to say nought of honor, and
Of stern religion, neither of which can
Allow unto their claims a compromise,—
I see not how the world can well forego it,
At those recurring, violent occasions,
When the distempered bodies politic
Of neighboring states shall, to the surface, throw
Their evil humours. What is thine opinion?

     ABNER.

'Tis scarce for luxury men fight; neither
Is it for conquest always, nor to throw
Away home tyranny, nor break foreign yoke.

     SAUL.

One half the pleasure there is in this world
Seems, unto me, evolved and spun through pain,
E'en as some sweet medicaments and syrups
Provided are through filthy processes.

     ABNER.

'Tis true this very pang of war brings with it
Delight.

SAUL.

Much did I feel of that once, Abner;
But now, the buoying wings of novelty,
Shorn down or plucked, together with my spirits
Much maimed by priestly treachery and scorn,
(Yet by that very scorn I'm strengthened,) now,
When comes heroic war, my blunted mind
Feels little more than the pressure of its care;—
Yet welcome care; ay, welcome priestly scorn;
Ay, welcome treachery, which I scorn to fear,—
'Tis what I have scorned, and will scorn, to fear:
For what I am, I am because I've scorned,
Not God himself, but the haughtiest hierarchy
That ever sought to be paramount i'th' world:—
Moreo'er, these ills now keep me from one greater.

ABNER.

And what is that?

SAUL.

Oh, the old malady,—
Devil possession. War abroad me keeps
In peace at home. Thou understandest me?
Oh, Abner, Abner, 'tis no easy thing
To be demoniac, yet to act the king.

ABNER.

Cousin, I thought that you were quite delivered
From that sad harrassment!

SAUL.

I have been charmed
Awhile by music; and the trumpets' din,
The clang of arms, and all this warlike care,
Divert me: so the fiend now lays not hold
Upon my soul: but, when this war is o'er,
He will return and me torment the more.

ABNER.

Alas!

SAUL.

Pity me not; but wonder why
I am in that plight that doth provoke thy pity.

ABNER.

Jehovah's ways are dark.

SAUL.

If they be just, I care not.
I can endure till death relieve me,—ay,
And not complain; but doubt enfeebles me,
And my strong heart, that gladdeth to endure,
Falters 'neath its misgivings, and, vexed, beats
Into the speed of fever, when it thinks
That the Almighty greater is than good.

ABNER.

Beware how thou dost charge Him who hath made thee!

SAUL.

I did not crave my making; did not solicit
To be a ruler. What I am, I am
Perforce: yet would I loyally perform
The work imposed upon me by my Maker
And Samuel; would faithfully discharge
The functions that, thou knowest, I never sought.—
Lo!
Did I not hide myself amongst the baggage
At Gilgal's great convention, and had need
To be sought out, and, in a manner, dragged
Before His crowded bar, and, like a proud
Criminal, to stand confessed, and be admired
For this unusual stature? What have I done
Since then? what left undone? I've sacrificed;—
And had I not apology? I spared the king
Of Amalek; and Samuel afterwards slew him.

ABNER.

Samuel never looked less like himself than then.

SAUL.

He did become an executioner. Oh,
I could have run between him and the blade
That did make ready the poor, fainting king
For th' shambles!

ABNER.

And yet 'twas retribution.

SAUL.

Pshaw!

ABNER.

He had made women childless, Samuel said;
So should his mother be childless among women.

SAUL.

Have we not all, who draw the sword, so done?
Shall not Philistia's mothers curse again,
Ere long, our arms that shall bereave them? Shall
Not Israel's matrons do the like, and howl
By hill and valley their young darlings slain?
Thrice helm thy head; for soon will at it beat
Such storm of curses, both from sires and mothers,
As thou hast never seen the counterpart of,
Not even when darts came at thee thick as hail.
'Twas retribution?—oh, no more of that;
Or the great ghost of Amalek will rise,
And stand before us with grim-eyed rebuke.—
But wherefore this? Now to the left, and I
Will take the right, to see that our sentries walk,
And take no sleep, ensconced in cosy crannies;
And snoring bass to dream-tuned symphonies,
And strains engendered by the mountain winds.
Good night.

ABNER.

Good night. A storm seems nigh at hand,
Will scarcely let our weariest guards doze; even
Those of them who have learned to keep their watch
A-walking but not waking.

[*Exeunt.*

END OF THE FIRST ACT.

ACT II.

SCENE I.

The Country near Beth-lehem. DAVID *tending his flock.*

DAVID. [*Sings.*

Father, father, let me go
To the battle-field!
Why should I not strike the foe,
Why should I not weapons wield?
Why may I not bear the shield,
Draw the fatal bow?

[*Enter* JESSE.

JESSE.

Son, cease to long for danger.

DAVID.

Listen, Father;
(And be not angry with me;) are not our days
All numbered for us? It would seem to me,
The field of battle is as safe a place
As is this quiet and unhazardous mead,
Where naught more hurtful comes than the sheep's tooth,
Or hoof of ox, or heedless tread of men,
Fatal to flowers.

JESSE.

These are mysterious themes.—
But whether this unhazardous, quiet mead
Be even as the noisy, crowded scene
O'er which war-chariots drive, or not, be sure,
War is not man's true trade. To till the soil,
Excel in arts, not arms, and unto all

To do the deeds of love and charity
In fear of God, are our whole duty: these
Do and thou shalt be happy: every other
Pleasure but ends in pain. Know, he whose hand
Is red with human blood, must not approach
Jehovah nearly,—a plain evidence
Of war's essential evil. Wouldst thou wish
In youth to play the slayer ? Lo, the day
That dawns blood-red matures in wind, and fades
'Midst drizzling rains spread o'er the gloomy west,
Or goes 'fore lightning bellowing down the darkness,
A warning for all morrows:—hence, do thou
Extinguish this red spark that may consume thee,
And far from violence live content. As day
Now fails serene, so doth the Peaceful's life.
Moreover, have I not three sons already
(Surely sufficient for one parent's part!)
Assisting Saul to drive back the invader ?
Then wherefore should I offer thee, as yet
Uncalled for by his terrible conscription ?
But be content; for thou shalt start to-morrow
Full early for the camp, and take thy brothers
Something, and bring me tidings of their fare.

DAVID.

I thank you for thus granting half my wish.

[Exit JESSE.

As a coiled cane, when suddenly unloosed,
Rebounding, quivers, throbs my heart with joy.
Oh, night, be brief that keeps from me the morn !
I long, filled with presentiment, to be gone.
To go is well; to stay there would seem better.
I'll even now my flock lead toward its fold.—
How light the heart whose weight is from it rolled !

[Exit.

SCENE II.

The Hebrew camp overlooking the valley of Elah.

SAUL (*entering*).

No surer sign have we of deep respect,
Than when our enemies, all mannerly,
Preserve their distance; for 'tis certain that
Familiarity not only breeds,
But manifests contempt. They still their tops
Of vantage keep, nor half-way in the vale
Invite us to shake hands. How different once!
Now are we at a balance in the scales,
And this great issue shall determine soon
Which of us kicks the beam. Their giant still
Comes to insult us; but he's a harlot merely,
Sent out before them to decoy us down
Into the bottoms, whither, if we venture,
They, doubtlessly, intend, full fledged, to swoop
And terribly embrace us.

[*A noise heard.*

There he bellows,
With voice like to a gong's, his proud defiance.
Why do my officers oppose me, when
I seek to meet this bully? for it seems
As though his challenge were meant but for me,
Who, though not his, am of gigantic mould.
Perchance I honor this event too much;
Yet would dear to me as a victory
This braggart giant's demolition be.
There is no mettle left in Israel
Or 't were not thus. I grow impatient:—come,
Soon giant slain or battle's general slaughter;
Come, victory won, or come loss of my daughter.

[*Exit, and enter Hebrew* SOLDIERS.

FIRST SOLDIER.

Goliah is forth again! come on and look.
By heaven, he groweth bigger every day,
His voice more thunder like.   Come, and look down
Into the valley, and see him, in his mail,
Move like a fulgent cloud.

SECOND SOLDIER.

        Does one with a shield
Precede him?

FIRST SOLDIER.

        Yes, and looks no bigger than
A child, compared with him.   Hearken again:
This is the second time to day.   Attend.

SECOND SOLDIER.

Not I; I'm weary of his insult, that
For forty days hath now continued thus.

THIRD SOLDIER.

Oh, might some Samson pull him to the ground!

SECOND SOLDIER.

What, wouldst thou have the land shake with his fall!
For it would be as though an armèd tower
Were toppled to the dust.

FOURTH SOLDIER.

        Oh, shame to us!
Is there, then, no one who can with him cope?—
None in our army dare accept the duel?

THIRD SOLDIER.

None dare except the king, and all the army
Excepteth him from entering the lists.
'Tis said that he with Abner quarelled because
The latter did withstand him, even to force;
Holding him when he would have straight gone down
Into the valley to the huge Philistine.

FIFTH SOLDIER.

It was a madness in the king to think
Contend with one, excelling him even more,
In size and strength, than he therein doth others.

THIRD SOLDIER.

And yet he would have done it; and now says,
Whoe'er shall kill the giant he'll enrich,
And give his daughter unto him in marriage,
And make his kindred free.

SECOND SOLDIER.

        His majesty
May spare his singular bounty, since the giant's
Mien will prevent all comers, for he looks
Terrific at this distance. His threatenings boom
Up hither like to fearful prophecies,
And do dishearten all our host, which now
Thinks the most ordinary Philistine thing of terror.

        [*Enter a* SIXTH SOLDIER.

The monster is retiring.

SECOND SOLDIER.

        Then we'll go
And eat our dinner. Let him mind, or yet
We will eat him, the uncircumcisèd sinner.

Enter a Hebrew SOLDIER *named* JOB *and* DAVID *talking together.*

THIRD SOLDIER.

Stay!
Again his challenge is loud upon the wind.

SECOND SOLDIER.

Then let the wind it answer; what care we?
Can caring crop a cubit from his stature?

DAVID.

Of whom thus speak they?

JOB.

Of a giant, whom,
When thou'rt returned unto Beth-lehem's maids,
Thou mayst declare to them that thou hast seen,
And say what grim foes soldiers do encounter.
Goliah is his name, and forth he comes,
Each day, to stalk like horror in the vale.
He is so tall he'd reach thee from a tree,
And stronger he than a rhinoceros;
Nor looks the hyena or the wolf more cruel.
He surely must have been begot in blood,—
Some ever-angry tigress suckled him;
For when he looks about him, unaroused,
So fierce and fiery is his gaze, his eyes
Are like unto a turret's windows, which,
While flaming faggots crackle on the hearth,
Receive a portion of the ruddy light
That dances on the walls.—None dare approach him.
Listen, and tell me what thou thinkst thou hearest.
For what thou'lt hear will not appear like man's:—
Indeed, 'tis said the devil was his father.

DAVID.

I hear a sound like that of distant thunder.

JOB.

A thunderer he is; and his huge mail,
Whene'er he moveth, is a heaven of lightnings.
Listen again and tell me what's the tune.

DAVID.

'Tis lower, and comes up like weak moan of beeves.

JOB.

'Tis said he eats a beeve each day to dinner.

DAVID.

But now 'tis swelling like the sound of torrents,
Even as I have often stood and heard them,
When, swollen with rain, they've down the gullies galloped
To plunge themselves in Jordan.

JOB.

                                  How is't now?

DAVID.

Dying away, like the receding wheels
Of chariots o'er the valley. Let me see
This giant: come, and shew me him near hand.

JOB.

Not nearer than this top:—I dare not venture
Upon the crags, lest, chancing topple from them,
He should devour me, as a wild beast would
A tame one in its den.

DAVID.

                        Art thou so faint?

JOB.

All faint before him; for, where'er he comes,
Our men from thence retire.—I wonder thou,
Even at Beth-lehem, hadst not heard of him;
For he this forty days hath challenged Israel,
To send him down her champion. List again;
He is defying us.

DAVID (*after having listened*).

                    What says the king
To this?

JOB.

                    He says that whosoe'er shall kill
This proud, insulting monster, he'll enrich;
Give him his daughter, too, in marriage, and
Make all his family free.—But who'd descend
For riches, wife, or freedom, to the dead?

[*Enter* DAVID's *brother* ELIAB.

DAVID.

Oh Israel, where is thy valor! Then has none
Yet offered to remove from us this shame?
For what is this uncircumcised one,
That he for forty days hath been allowed
Defy the army of the Living God!

ELIAB (*roughly*).

Why art thou come down hither? and with whom
Hast thou left in the wilderness yonder those few sheep?
I know thy vanity and carelessness;
Thou art come hither but to see the fight.

DAVID.

Do I offend thee with my presence? or have I
Spoken indignantly without a cause?
To fight with this Philistine I am willing;
And let the king straight know it.

FIFTH SOLDIER.

        My brave youth,
Thy words are folly's. Why, our stoutest soldiers
Shrink from him: he would trample thee to death;
Yea, crush thee as a beetle 'neath his feet.

DAVID.

Yet take me to the king.
           [*Laughter.*

THIRD SOLDIER.

       I'll take thee, boy;
Though I fear he'll think thou comest to insult him.
       [*Exit along with* DAVID.

FIRST SOLDIER.

This is the very stripling that at court,
With harpen strains, allayed the king's distemper.

SECOND SOLDIER.

Nay, he has caught it; he is mad:—come on!
Come on, come on! all ye who love a joke.
       [*Exeunt all the* SOLDIERS.

ELIAB.

Now shall we be the scoff and sport of Beth-lehem!
Why has my old, fond father let him come?
I'll go and see him now dismissed ashamed.
           [*Exit.*

SCENE III.

Interior of the royal tent.

SAUL *seated, with* OFFICERS *about him. Enter* ABNER *leading* DAVID.

ABNER.

Your majesty, behold your servant David;
The same who, with his harp's mild ministration,
Did exorcise your spirit's gloomy rage,
And purge to cheerful health your dull-eyed grief.
You know him not; look on him, for 'tis he.

SAUL.

I know him now: he's changed. Come near me, David.

[DAVID *advances and the* KING *takes him by the hand.*

My soother, my young friend, my shepherd boy,
Who drew me from the witchery of the moon,
How hast thou fared since I beheld thee last?
Thy father, is he well? thy mother too?
Did she not weep when thou departedst from her,
And flung away the crook to grasp the sword?
Now is the time to be a soldier: art
Thou come for that, or, with thy suasive harp,
To turn our warfare's dissonance to chords?
Harsh is the music of these days of force,
And rough as is their business. The loud bugle,
And the hard-rolling drum, and clashing cymbals,
Now reign the Lords o'th' air. These crises, David,
Bring with them their own music, as do storms
Their thunders,—no inspiring hymn, no psalm,
The handmaid to devotion; no winged fugue,
No song, no merry catch, no madrigal;
No tender strophe, nor solemn canon;—but
The sharp alarm, the call to boot and saddle,
The big hurrah o'th' onset, and the irregular
Chorus on th' fire-spitting steel; all of them sounds

Rousing to the already-bated spirit,
But to nice ears offensive. Thou dost see
At present we have no time for vagaries,
Nor leisure for soul sickness:—but inform us
What brings thee from thy favorite Beth-lehem.
If thou wouldst be a soldier, thou art welcome:
Yea, whatsoever be thy wish or errand,
Peace and my heart's best favor be upon thee.

DAVID.

The kindness of your majesty o'ercomes me,
Piled upon memories of your former goodness
My gratitude is greater than my words,
Then let a deed more eloquent speak for me.
Vouchsafe unto me yet one favor more ;
That, like a gamester, staking it, I may
Win, of one whom you hate, so great a sum,
That I may you in some small part repay,
In coin of service, and yet owe you more,
Of love and gratitude, than now I do.
Grant I may cope with this vain giant, who,
With insolent challenge, puts your host to shame.

SAUL.

My ardent, fond, uncalculating boy,
Thou knowest not what thou askest. His breath alone
Would sweep thee from his path: he would disdain thee,
As doth the lion carrion disdain ;
He would not fence with thee, but on thee seize,
And crumple up thy tender frame like paper ;
Or lift thee with the engine of his arms,
And on the ground, close to his mail-clad feet,
Dash out thy brains.—No, no ; thy father never
Shall say that we to slaughter sent his son.

DAVID.

Yet hear me speak.

SAUL.

      Thou speakest not wisely, **David**.
He with his spear, which is like a weaver's beam,
Would stop the dancing shuttle of thy life.
Nay, stand not thus imploring with thine eye:
To send thee doomed forth to contend with him,
The fatal mockery would ever on my conscience
Sit waste and haggard, and dash my happiest moments;
Yea, ghastly, gibber to me in my sleep,
That I had murdered thee. My strongest captains
Dare not encounter him; then dream not thou
To kill him, or to bring him to me bound;
Thou but a youth and uninured to arms,
Whilst he is more than man, and has been trained
Up from his youth to do heroic deeds.

DAVID.

Your gracious majesty, forgive me, but,
Thus kneeling, I must urge my suit. Oh, hear me!
You know me not yet fully, deeming me
Only prevailing with the harp and crook;
Yet once, when I my father's sheep was keeping,
There came a lion from the wilderness,
And unawares took from my flock a lamb,
Which, soon as I perceived, I chased the robber,
And the lamb rescued from his jaws; and when
He turned on me, I seized him by the beard
And killed him: I also slew a bear;
And this Philistine soon shall be like them.
Fear not for me, your majesty; I know
The Lord, who saved me from those savage beasts,
Will likewise from this giant.

SAUL.

       But, my child,
The lion and the bear were but as kids
Compared with this Philistine!

DAVID.

It was God
Who made the strength of each as nothing to me;
Who made the lion's armed, distended jaws,
And shaggy throat, but fatal to himself;
For 'twas thereby I caught him, and him pressed
In such an irresistible embrace,
That soon he rolled his dull, protruding eyes,
And fixed them upwards on my face in death.

SAUL.

Go, go; and may God too go with thee; but
I trow that I shall see thy face no more!
He, who assisted thee to do these deeds,
May thee assist to do one greater. Go;
I shall await the issue here in horror.
Abner, wilt see him clothed with mine own armour.

[*Exit* ABNER *and* DAVID.

My heart misgives me. 'Tis not yet too late;— [*aside.*
But what if Heaven have sent him? He shall go.
Now each retire to solitude and pray [*aloud.*
For that heroic boy. He who no faith
Has got to wing and plume his dart of prayer,
May groan a low petition, that some angel,
Walking the earth, may shoot it unto heaven.
At once let's separate and wait the event,
Each in the company of his own suspense.

[*Exeunt the* OFFICERS.

I'm full of thoughts that will not now be uttered.

[*Disappears in the shadow of the tent.*

SCENE IV.

A part of the camp near the royal tent. A Sentinel *pacing.*
Enter Hebrew Soldiers.

FIRST SOLDIER.

Is he retired yet?

SENTINEL.

Who?

FIRST SOLDIER.

The Giant.

SENTINEL.

No.
He is seated on the ground; and as a tawny
Lion, just waked and weltering in night's dew,
Shines in the morning's beam, so he in noon's.
Why does he not return?

FIRST SOLDIER.

Because he smells
The prey.

SENTINEL.

What prey?

FIRST SOLDIER.

A youth of Beth-lehem,
Who goes to him to be killed.

SENTINEL.

What dost thou mean?

FIRST SOLDIER.

I mean even as I say,—a Beth-lehem boy,
A crazy lad, who goes to him to be killed.
The king put on him his own armour; but
It was too large and heavy for him, so,
Naked and armed with but a sling he goes,
And stones from yonder brook.

SENTINEL.

Was ever such
A duel?

SECOND SOLDIER.

See, our serried soldiers stand
Breathless and fixed like statues, or as woods
Sleeping in the brief calm before the storm.
We cannot see our Champion; but he's winding
Down the hill side, for thither the Giant turns
His angry eyes. Lo, how he watches him!
And now he rises up;—and now again
He is seated. Hark! he is calling on the youth.

THIRD SOLDIER.

The king is much to blame in this,—
To let a stripling go where powerful men
Declined to venture. Listen how the monster
Growls, less in rage than in his disappointment,
At such a trifling quarry. He is cursing
The youth now by his gods, and now, in scorn,
Calls for an arrow of some babe of Gath.
But the youth answers not.

GOLIAH (*down in the valley*).

Now, by great Dagon,
Where have they found thee, dumb approaching fool?
Presume no further;—dost thou hear me, boy?
Back to thy king, thou idiot. Am I
A dog, that thus thou comest to me with staves?
Thou cattle-driver, back, and get thee gored
To death by thine own herd;—no nearer me.
Dost thou despise my warning? Hear me, young
And listless strayer; get from these dread bounds,
O'er which, to every Hebrew, I have hung
Death's bloody banner. Still approaching? Then
I'll let thee walk beneath destruction's archway,
Into the vaulted and sepulchral den
Where lie all thy forerunners. Come, boy, come;

L

Come unto me, and, with my naked hands,
I joint from joint will rend thee, and thy flesh
Give to the birds and beasts to be their food.

SENTINEL.

May heaven forfend!

SECOND SOLDIER.

      Hist, for the shepherd's answering.

DAVID (*heard*).

Oh, boastful giant, impious son of Gath,
Trust not too much in thy prodigious strength;
Nor in thine armour, that, till now, has been
Invulnerable unto mortal dint:
Nor scorn me for my youth and seeming weakness.
Complete in arms and covered o'er with mail,
Thou comest to me; but I come unto thee
In the name of Him who is the Lord of Hosts,
The God of Israel's armies, whom thou hast
Defied. He will deliver thee this day
Into my hand; and I will take from thee
Thy head, and give your army's carcasses
To the wild beasts and birds, that all may know
That there is certainly a God in Israel,
And that this is His battle.

FIRST SOLDIER.

          Bravo, boy!

SENTINEL.

See; now the monster rises in his rage.

SECOND SOLDIER.

He needs not stride so; for the youth retreats not.

SENTINEL.

Now let us all send prayer apace to heaven,
Mightily pray, for the champion of our country.

THIRD SOLDIER.

The shepherd runs to meet the angry monster.
Ay, whirl thy sling, poor wretch,—ay, leap along,
A-toward Death's fist like to a bounding ball!

[DAVID *slings a stone, and* GOLIAH *falls.*

SECOND SOLDIER.

Great heavens! now shall the sparrow pierce the eagle!
Surely the days of miracles are returned;
For who had counted that this youth could sling
A pebble through that cincture of thick brass?

SENTINEL.

We thank thee, Lord; we thank thee, God of Israel!

FIRST SOLDIER.

That youth is or the devil or an angel;
Either an angel or a youngling devil!
Oh, he's an angel, or should be so enrolled.
That shepherd's worth his weight in purest gold!

[*A great shout heard.*

SENTINEL.

Hark, how the army shouts! and see, the shepherd
Is standing on the carcass of the giant,
That lies like one of their own stranded hulls,
While the rude blows of his own scymetar
Assail him; as the yet stout, lashing storm
Beats on the wreck that shall no more go seaward.

SECOND SOLDIER.

His head is off; and that same tongue of his,
That long hath uttered threats too great for mortals,
Shall brag no more, for ever. Silently he died;
Or the great groan with which his savage spirit
Left the huge body, was o'erwhelmed and drowned
I'th' clangour of his falling.

FOURTH SOLDIER.

                                              Little thanks:
He surely made quite noise enough when living;
For not a man hath heard his proper tongue
For half the day during this month or more;
Either by reason of the Giant's brawling,
Or brawls concerning him amongst ourselves.
I would as lief live near the boiling ocean,
Or in the neighbourhood of a cataract,
Ay, or in hearing of a brace of mothers
From morn till evening quarelling o'er their brats,
As be compelled again to let my ears
Be made the thoroughfares unto his bluster.
I always hate a man whose voice is loud;
I always hate a man whose mien's imperious.
And as for armour, doth it not make war
A heaviness, a mortal sweat and toil?
What razor-like, fine-ground and polished swords
Hath it not turned, with horrid hack, to saws!
What aching arms hath it not given us all,
Whilst we in vain have striven to hit the joint!
And many a hapless devil, being down,
Hath perished like a turtle on its back,
Because he could not, more than it, arise.
I hate a man that stalks in panoply,
And would much rather meet a ghost by night,
Than see, a mile off, one of those by day.
I always did suspect, when I beheld
Such men approaching cap-a-pie, that they
Were cowards or else bullies; and this giant
Hath in this guess confirmed me.   Break his bones
Three several times have I been nigh to choking,
From being startled, when in earnest dining,
With sound like to a coming avalanche,
When it has only been his Ugliness,
Vomiting insolence upon our host,
As he descended down yon mountain's side.

SAUL.

The heedless villian ! our forces have grown lean,
From being stayed by him amidst their meals ;
Him whose main use was only to devour,
And eat us up like a huge caterpillar,
And spread a locust-famine o'er the land,
On which like a huge locust he's now lying.
Why did he not lie there a month ago ?
I do assert that we have been abused ;
I say this giant was a mere marsh-fire,
A bugaboo, a come-up-salt-flood meteor,
A down-fallen comet, a hither-shotten star,
A mere mock-sun, a thing as false as moonshine ;
In short, a mere audacious will-o-wisp,
A mere innocuous, polished jack-o-lantern.

SENTINEL.

Peace, and prepare thee for the coming fray.
The imperious trumpet and the rattling drum,
With clashing cymbals, to arms bid us come:
And, oh, now listen, for a murmuring wail
From Ephis-dammim sweeps across the vale.
Here are Saul and Abner hastening ; let's away.
Yon sun will set upon a bloody day.

Exeunt, and enter the KING *and* ABNER *rapidly, the former speaking.*

SAUL.

Now that their hearts are up, lead down thy men
Into the vale, which soon shall roll in blood ;
Unless the foe, astonished and alarmed,
Shall keep their heights, which, if they do, we'll storm,
In spite of storm of rolling stones and darts,
And drive them homewards, should they turn their backs ;
If not, provoked and hurried to yon brink,
This sweeping yawn shall be to them their grave.

ABNER.

I never saw our army's heart so swell.
I do believe (such ecstacy has risen)
That they this hour would strive to carry hell,
And, sacrilegious, storm the heights of heaven.
[Exit.

SAUL.

Too much reflection would arrest the world.
Why should we not attack them? I will go down
With Jonathan into the perilous yawn.
[Another great shout heard.
The changeful souls!
Because one man appeared whom no one man
Dared cope with, why, forsooth, more than a month
They stood immoveable as stupid stocks:—
Now, when that one man's dead, and, by a youth,
Before their eyes, shewn to be vulnerable,
There is no holding them; but they must rush
Pell-mell into the dangerous valley, and thence
Mount, all disordered, up the opposite steep,
Nor wait for their commanders. I have known
Ere this, a simple chimera stop men
Even as a wall of brass, when, to their ardour
Unchecked by fear, realities were less than
Fences of yielding air.
[Exit; the noise of the army increases, and then dies away.

SCENE V.

Within sight of Ekron. Time, evening of the same day.

SAUL (*entering and sheathing his sword*).

There take thine insult back, thou proud Philistia;
Through Ekron's gates take it, besmeared and bloody.
Art thou not satisfied? Art restless yet?
Come to the field again of Ephis-dammim,

For thou mayest easily find it by the clue
Of thine own dead and wounded. Lo, they stretch
Hence to the tented field, and all the road
Is rendered vocal by their sore distress.

[Enter ABNER.

Brave Abner, my true cousin !

ABNER.

Is my liege
Unhurt? Is whole my great Commander? Oh,
Too rash this day hath been my kinsman Saul.
Thou far too reckless of thy life hast been,
And, with unwarrantable hardihood,
From the meridian 'till eve hast sought
The hottest fight, and over Israel's borders
Hurried the obsequious war, that did so lately
Sit heavy at her heart.

SAUL.

O'er Elah's vale
Too long the bold Sea-Eagle brooding sat.

ABNER.

But suddenly it rose, pierced with one arrow,
That was the prelude to a myriad others
Which fatally o'ertook it. Cousin, cousin,
Victory still rests upon our house; or, rather,
Is thither wafted from the sky by some
Vicarious angel, who, in Samuel's stead,
Conducts her down and gives her to thy hand,
Still to assure thee of the doubted throne.
Fear not henceforward, my anointed sovereign.

SAUL.

Fear not for me; my faithful captain, fear not;
But let the signal blast be loudly blown
That calls our wearied men from the pursuit.

[Exit ABNER.

I'll still extinguish fears, as men young fires
Extinguish, even by stifling them; for fears,
Like fires, are things which are, yet ought not be,
To honest men.

[Enter an OFFICER.

OFFICER.

The chase grows slack, my liege;
Yet never knew Philistia such a hunting.

[Exit.

SAUL.

To hunt and to be hunted make existence;
For we are all or chasers or the chased;
And some weak, luckless wretches ever seem
Flying before the hounds of circumstance,
A-down the windy gullies of this life;
Till, toppling over death's uncertain verge,
We see of them no more. Surely this day
Has been a wild epitome of life!
For life is merely a protracted chase;
Yea, life itself is only a long day,
And death arrives like sundown. Lo, the sun
Lies down i'th' waters, and the murky moon
Out of the east sails sullen. 'Tis the hour
Of fear and melancholy, when the soul
Hangs poised, with folded wings, 'tween day and night.
Now grow I sad as evening, yea, as night;
And boding cometh, like eve's mournful bird,
Across my soul's lea, doleful to my heart.
Therein, alas! now new misgivings rise
At Abner's well-meant but superfluous words,
That, lieu of stilling fears with sense of safety,
Stir doubts of danger; as a friendly hand,
In the repose and hollow of the night,
Officiously stretched forth to scare one fly
From a sick sleeper, might upraise a swarm
To buzz and to awake him. Down, black bodes,
False flies! or, if ye will not settle, come

And singe your little, silken wings at lamp
Of this great victory.

Exit. The recall begins to sound, and soldiers pass over the stage with appearance of great fatigue.

FIRST SOLDIER.

Never welcomer than now was that recall,
So tired am I with slaying and pursuing.

SECOND SOLDIER.

Thrice have I fallen myself in felling the foe;
And twice I've lain me down awhile to rest,
Amongst the dying and the dead Philistines.

THIRD SOLDIER.

Would that we might bivouac upon the ground;
And not hie homewards, as 'tis whispered round.

[Exeunt, and re-enter SAUL along with an OFFICER.

SAUL.

Bid some to minister unto ours who lie
In doubtful plight 'twixt life and death; and see
That all our wounded be sent after us;
For, after some refreshment, we shall thread
Our way, by starlight, home amongst the dead.

[Exit OFFICER.

'Twill be a weary road, and slippery;
For the waterspout that came up from the sea
Hath poured amain its rent and shattered volume,
And soaked the route with blood.

[Enter an AIDE-DE-CAMP.

AIDE-DE-CAMP.

Your Majesty, the chase has stayed itself.
The foe exists no more, except in Ekron;
Where he has sought a shelter and a refuge,
Wasted and wearied by this dread pursuit.

SAUL.

There let him lie and ease his panting sides.

[Exit AIDE-DE-CAMP.

Out, idle terrors!—nay, by hell and heaven,
There's something in it! Ah, what is there now
Stood in the vestibule of my conception,
Or from me there a rood, I know not which?
It is the form of the heroic David,
Crowned, and with Israel's sceptre in its hand.
Out, Phantom! It is gone; but where it stood
Glares with vexed flames, as if they would convince me
That what I've seen was real. Ye quick fires,
If ye would shed a light upon my mind,
Display some secret to my understanding;
If, by your friendly and unnatural splendour,
Expose some latent danger to my rule,
Inform me with your dumb but luminous tongues;
(That wave and wag as if in mockery,
And now, even whilst I question you, low flicker;)
Say, if ye have aught to tell me for my good.
All's darkness now, like hell, from whence this came.
Ye binding hoops that gird the cask o'th' soul,
How have ye burst and out of me let reason!
I was not once thus liable to panic,
Nor troubled with wide-waking, daylight visions.
Then why in this hour befooled?
It is the brooding on the one sad thought—
The echoing of the Samuel-uttered doom,
Which even now, when I was hopeful, wafted
Me unto my old lunes upon a sudden—
Thus drags me back unto my former self;
Even as a thing which, long pressed out of form,
Does, after 'tis restored to its true shape,
If that which holds it be removed, start back
All foul and crumpled to its old mis-figure.
Away, and let me this forget:—'tis evil,
And comes from, or may lead me to, the devil.

[*Exit.*

SCENE VI.

Ephis-dammim. Interior of a large tent.

SAUL *and* JONATHAN, *seated.*

JONATHAN.

Your majesty, see who comes, and with what burden,
Hung like a pendant to his valiant hand.

[*Enter* ABNER *and* DAVID, *the latter carrying the head of Goliah.*

ABNER.

Now, cousin, now behold a frontispiece,
Such as will nature not soon make again.
Now scrutinize your enemy in safety.
How like a slumbering lion's head that seems!
I could believe Goliah's spirit dreamed
Again within that dome of cogitation.
Who would not choose to dream in such a chamber,
Although within the precincts of death's palace!
'Tis like to some grand ruin overgrown
And half concealed by herbage. View him well,
Upwards from the foundation of his chin.
Observe that shaggy beard, those locks that cover
The hand of David as with coils of chains.
Was't not a sin to kill so fine a beast?

JONATHAN.

Who shall hereafter trust in his own strength!

SAUL (*aside*).

Yes, or henceforwards in his proper eyesight?
Yet like him as he's like himself, that vision.

(*Aloud.*)

Lay down thy trophy on the dais, David.
Implacability is not for mortals.
Pity now moves within me, and I feel
A solemn reverence at the sight of that
Fine relic. How august it seems in death!

David, that trophy, I confess, is thine;
But be it, with its fallen carcass, buried.
His armour will record his bulk, and shew
The volume of thy hardihood, as long
As brass endures. He was an armèd galley,
He was a laden argosy; and thou
But little knowest the treasure thou hast cast
From out the hold of his enormous frame.
His spirit was prodigious as his form;
And generous, for he warned thee from him: hence,
Cast no indignity upon the brave,
But lay that visage in a decent grave.

DAVID.

Even as your majesty will. He shall be covered
Up by the earth; but all his blasphemous boasts
Shall be remembered to his evil fame.

SAUL.

Leave that to those who shall come after us:
But, for ourselves, to life let punishment
Be limited; 'gainst none be urged the suit
Of vengeance after death. Remember that
We all are evil-doers; and should justice,
Intent to accuse us of our numerous faults,
Vindictive follow us to the courts of death,
All entering them would certainly be cast.

DAVID.

Your majesty is wisest; but was not
This giant an idolater, and a foe
That did invade and strive to enslave the land?
Doubtless he was:—still, now my ire is passed,
Him and his memory I can from me cast.

SAUL.

You both shall be remembered, long as might
And bravery retain their high reputes.
But let not malice in thy young breast linger.

Full many things are best forgot; and all
The dross of life, men's vices and their failings,
Should from our memories be let slip away,
As drops the damaged fruit from off the bough
Ere comes the autumn. It were wise, nay just,
To strike with men a balance; to forgive,
If not forget, their evil for their good's sake.
Thus cherishing the latter,
We shall grow rich in life's pure gold, and lose
Only its base alloy, its dross and refuse.—
But wherefore stay we on the field, while Gibeah
Awaits impatient our triumphal entry?
For by this time our messenger is there.
Abner, precede me;   [*A sound of a trumpet heard.*
(Hark, the clarion peals!)
And let these young braves follow at our heels.
      [*Exeunt* SAUL *and* ABNER.

    JONATHAN.
Thou seem'st not glad, my friend and future brother.
Art thou, in fancy, bidding to thy home
Farewell? Or art thou musing upon one
Of Beth-lehem's maidens, who, till thy return,
Restless endures the rack of tender thoughts?
David, thou must no more consort with swains;
Thou must no more return to Beth-lehem.
Farewell, now finally, to tending sheep,
The shepherd's crook, and to the pastoral pipe:
The martial sword and spear, the post of trust,
And this well-won alliance, now await thee.
Why didst thou leave the court?—But this exploit
(Even as an unexpected billow should
Return a drifted bather to the shore)
Hath rendered thee again unto our house.
Come nearer, David; speak unto thy friend.

    DAVID.
Pardon me, prince, but I am dubious:
I know not whether I've displeased the king
In bringing on this trophy.

JONATHAN.

       Fear not, David;
Fear not my father's words, dear mate in arms,
But with me follow him to Gibeah,
Whither thou goest in Jehovah's conduct;
Jehovah, whose directing providence,
From Beth-lehem's quiet but inglorious nook,
Has led thee to the camp at the due moment;
The camp which is the entrance to the court,
The court which still is rife with praise of thee.
Oh, thou art worthy of its utmost praise!
Oh, thou this hour appearest to me fair!
Thou, with thy flinty pebble of the brook,
Hast from the giant's mail struck out a flash,
That plays on thee like to the lightning on
A marble idol, making it resplendent.
We shall, I fear, an idol make of thee.
I fear we shall be tempted thee to worship,
Who hast already found a golden shrine
And ruby temple in our heart's affections.
Oh, David, genius makes the world its vassal.
Oh, do not wonder that I thus extol thee.
I would not be extravagant, nor would I
Willingly flatter thee,—not I,—but thou,
By this most glorious duel, hast become
The shining centre of our kingdom's shield,
And drawn bright favor on thee from the might
And majesty of Saul. Speak, David, speak.
No longer stand in shady pensiveness,
When o'er thee hangs the royal ray serene;
Yea, the full glory of a heaven of honor.
Speak to me, David; answer me, I pray thee.

DAVID.

What shall I say unto your gracious highness,
Except that gratitude doth penetrate me,
And cause me to forget his majesty's check;
Even as the tepid breathing of the spring
Drives out the inlodged winter from the earth.

JONATHAN.

Oh, do not thus respond to me lukewarmly!—
What shalt thou say? Listen, and I will tell thee.
Say that we are henceforth in friendship joined;
That in the lists of amity, henceforwards,
With offices of kindness we will vie.
Say, wilt thou cope with me in friendship, brother?
Wilt thou not now accept of my love-challenge?

DAVID.

Too generous Prince, I do believe thou lov'st me;
And I love thee, but with a reverence
Engendered by thy station, and abase
Mine eyes before thee; even as the flame
Which, though of the same element, doth yet
Abate and fade as on it shines the sun:
For, Jonathan, although thou deemest me
To be so worthy, still it matters not;
For well I know (and rue) that perfect friendship
(However we may strive to join ourselves)
Will not vouchsafe its lacing, golden cords
To bind disparities. Forgive me if
I speak too plainly. I am not thine equal:
I'm but a shepherd though I've slain the giant.

JONATHAN.

David, not so; thou art a warrior
Upon whose arms the Lord hath deigned to smile.
It is not station in a gilded court
Which thou hast lacked; nor that which I do lack,
A long and legend-covered pedigree;
But noble deeds, and noble natural powers,
That give the stamp and value unto man.
Try us by these; then say whether we are not,
In all the traits wherein consists true likeness,
More wrought to be as castings from one mould,
Than, oft, the fashioning in one womb doth give
Of temper and exterior resemblance.

DAVID.

Jonathan, thou dost compel me to thy wish.
I did esteem thee ere I saw thee, and
Desired to emulate thy daring deeds.

JONATHAN.

Then vow to me, (for with a vow I'd bind thee,
Even as fondest lovers bind each other,)
Vow to me friendship, and I'll vow again;
Let's friendship vow, and let Heaven say " Amen."
Hear now, ye angels, if such hover o'er us,
And shed sincerity upon us both;
That this intended covenant may be,
Like as your sacred selves are, strong and blessed.
David, I offer thee perpetual friendship,
And, therewith, such large measure of my love
As I have never given before to man.

DAVID.

Which I accept; and offer in return,
What you have always had, fidelity;
And add thereunto, by your free gift laid,
A love not given before to man or maid.

JONATHAN.

Enough. Now let us hence, and leave grim war;
And haste to Gibeah, where rejoicings are.

[*Exeunt.*

SCENE VII.

A sylvan country between Ephis-dammim and Gibeah.
A sound of females singing merrily. Enter SAUL *and the* OFFICERS *of his staff.*

SAUL (*entering*).

Our land this year receives a second spring,
So rife it is with gay and bird-like carol,
Proceeding yet from out our victory's grove;
That, as we journey, doth produce new echoes,
In widening series, breaking still anew.

What is it that these maids are uttering,
Who seem to me much more methodical,
In the wild elegance of their mazy mirth,
Than all before we've noted?

FIRST OFFICER.

Here they come.

Enter a group of young females singing and dancing, and with musical instruments.

(*Song.*)
Far as Ephis-dammim came
The Philistines, dreadful name;
But to meet them went the king,
And young David with his sling.

(*Chorus, with dancing.*)
Saul he has his thousands slain,
David has his thousands ten.

SAUL.

Ah!

(*Song.*)
In the vale 'tween mountains lying,
Came Goliah forth defying;
Fear came with him on our host,
But brave David stayed his boast.

(*Chorus.*)
Saul he has his thousands slain,
But David has his thousands ten.

SAUL.

This is the very creeping towards the height
At which he shewed near Ekron. Do my ears
Deceive me here, as there my eyes befooled me?
Keep calm, my blood.

(*Song.*)
Pebbles five from out the brook,
David to th' encounter took;
Fitted one unto his sling,
Sent it on its airy wing.

(*Chorus.*)
Saul he has his thousands slain,
David has his thousands ten.

SAUL.
Oh, now I rue I did not meet the Giant,
Or disallow the deed unto the youth.
I'll stop this chant.—Nay, let them finish their folly.

(*Song.*)
Lo! the Giant, pierced, fell dead;
Lo! the proud Philistines fled,
Chased by Saul, devoid of ruth,
And the handsome shepherd youth.

(*Chorus.*)
Saul he has his thousands slain,
But David has his thousands ten.

SECOND OFFICER.
See how the king's look lowers.

(*Song.*)
Nor till reached far Ekron's gate,
Doth pursuit its fury sate;
Then Philistia's daughters wail,
While with joy we load the gale.

(*Chorus.*)
Saul he has his thousands slain,
But bold David thousands ten.

FIRST OFFICER.
Speak to the king:
Perchance the fiend is entering him again,
For hell is in his eyes.

SECOND OFFICER.
It is too late.

SAUL (*aloud*).
Fools, tell what undiscriminating churl
Composed for you that burden!

SECOND OFFICER.

         Surely 'twas
A demon that then blew the trumpet of
The royal mouth, for it was hell's own peal!

FIRST OFFICER.

The maids have vanished; and the king, perturbed,
Stalks to and fro. Behold, he's struggling with
(Whether it be his own or from the Lord)
A spirit of wrath.

SAUL.

     Now let me curb mine anger,
Lest it should gallop with me off the field.

FIRST OFFICER.

I never saw his majesty so incensed.

SAUL.

Nay, this would spur the dullest steed to start,
And throw his rider too, scorning the bridle.
Hold hard, hold hard, though we should break the reins.
Honor a subject and insult the king!—
'Tis well the caper-cutting troop have fled,
And to a better purpose put their heels.
What next? blows follow threats. This was defiance;
This was the very pass and guard of young
Rebellion; these girls his saucy trulls.
Ah, I have been too lenient and secure;
But now the rigor of my reign begins.

FIRST OFFICER.

Mark him.

SECOND OFFICER.

     I do, I do: he's calmer now,
But wickeder. He looks more cruel than a tiger
When it hath couched it for the fatal spring.

SAUL.

Ay, ay, I'll note them; I will be abroad;
I will have spies in every town and hamlet:

For it is meet that it should be so, when
They keep a poet in these unpolished parts.—
This is the work of elder heads than theirs.
Why find I not the covert knave who wrote
Their pæan, and saw him asunder before their eyes?
But I'll be prompt henceforwards, and conviction
Shall hurry execution to his office :—
Yea, and suspicion shall be competent
To stand unchallenged and give evidence.
Go put our troops in motion, gentlemen:
These are but foolish hoydens after all.

FIRST OFFICER.

Let us not leave him though he so commands us.
He's hot within, though at the surface cooled.

SAUL.

'Twas David through the whole, and ever highest:
A studied theme.

FIRST OFFICER.

Look how he frowns again:
This bodes some ill.

SAUL.

To me they have ascribed
Thousands, but unto David tens of thousands;
And what more could he have except the kingdom?

SECOND OFFICER.

He walks and mutters, scarce knowing what he does.

SAUL.

I've been deceived; these also were but spectres.—
You go not, gentlemen: the song is ended.—
Woe unto Levi if he this inspired!

FIRST OFFICER.

Stay.

SECOND OFFICER.

No; we shall but draw on us his wrath.

SAUL.

Am I not in an after-dinner dream ?
No;
I doubt mine eyes, but I'll believe mine ears :
It cannot be that I am twice befooled.
Look, how my officers yet stand amazed!
I'll to the air give Ekron's vision ; but
Shall this dissolve away, like that, in doubt,—
This that enthralls its wondering witnesses ?
Go on before me, gentlemen, I pray you.

FIRST OFFICER.

Myself will dare him, to prevent worse issue.
(To SAUL.)
The king is moved by this hyperbole.

SAUL.

Hyperbole ! It was beyond all bounds.
What in this world shall now be counted pure,
When lies and treason pass through such sweet lips ?

FIRST OFFICER.

There is no conduit but is sometimes fouled.

SAUL.

Then angels' mouths may yield obscenity ;
And why should men strive to be nice and clean ?
Now straight to Gibeah urge. Along, along;
And bid the drums outroll their loudest thunder ;
And let the shrill pipes and the martial bugles
Swell to the uttermost. Be clashed the cymbals,
Let all the trumpets rend the sky together,
And bid our forces raise a general shout,
That this vile gust of harmony may be lost
In a loud storm and raging sea of discord.

*Exeunt, and presently a peal of trumpets, drums, cymbals, &c., mingled
with cheers of the distant soldiery.*

END OF THE SECOND ACT.

ACT III.

SCENE I.

The Alps. Time, night, with stars.
Enter MALZAH, *walking slowly.*

MALZAH.

So, so ; I feel the signal.
It seems to reach me through the air,
Urging me to Saul repair.
I wish 'twould cease ; it doth not please
Me now to terminate my leisure.
I was alone ; and here to groan
At present is my greatest pleasure.
I'll come anon ; I say begone ;—
What is the wayward king to me ?
I say begone ; I'll come anon.
Oh, thou art strong ; I'll follow thee.
[*Exit.*

ZELEHTHA, *entering in a little while.*

Lo, where yon demon, with increasing speed,
Makes his dim way across the night-hung flood,
Due to the Hebrew King, with onward heed,
Like to a hound that snuffs the scent of blood.
I'll follow him.
[*Exit.*

SCENE II.

Gibeah. A spacious apartment in the Palace. Time, the morrow.

SAUL (*entering*).

Now let hell work (or heaven) its will on Saul !
I am beset by a new demon ; for

That chorus haunts me, and from every other
Study my mind reverts to that foul lode-thought.
I know that I am not in health of body;
Hence may arise the sickness of my mind.
For I am seized with ague of the soul,
Now hot, now cold, now rage, now fear, in turns;
And sometimes I believe I feel my old,
My demon-ruled and fatal fit returning.
Oh, God, give me not up again to that!
David, young roe,
Out of the dangerous thicket of my thoughts!
I know the fit's around me gathering.
I cannot be deceived; I feel the true,
Alas, too true, awakening of the storm.
Oh, let my thoughts' course now turn far from David;
Lest, when the helm of reason no more guides me,
I run him down upon his life's young sands,
And voyage 'neath clouds of penitence ever after.
Come, ye benignant ministers of heaven,
Come, ye mid-region-dwelling genii,
Angels, or whatsoever be your name,
Whose hands, still charged with various dispensations,
Administer heavenly medicine to the world,
Come to my heart, and, with some blessed unction,
Assuage and mollify its growing ire;
Purge me of these unnatural suggestions;
Oh, disinfect me of these sad misgivings.
[*Exit, and re-enter.*
It cannot be; 'tis blackness all, and thickens,
And in it I must grope, howe'er I stumble.
Alas, I know not if I may not have
A too-substantial ground for dread of David.
Granting his image on the plain near Ekron
Were merely in imagination's mirror;
Yet its re-rendering by the insolent minstrels,
That seeming many-voiced corroboration,
Wherein true flesh and blood, at ears and eyes,

Forcing conviction onwards by two paths,
Did cry out loudly to the same dumb burden,—
What can be said to that, except to ask,
Is not this he to whom my throne was given?
Oh, horror! Oh, now blows temptation on me
Until I strain beneath the infernal gale.
Pour on me, hurricane; I can withstand thee.
Nay, nay; now hold. I will not—yet I will;
He shall not live to peril me. I go;—
Nay hold, rash fool; down with that bloody flag.
Oh, look not there, my soul, at that false polestar
Would coldly guide thee into a dark gulf,
From whence thou never couldst return to these
Waters of innocence,—of innocence
Though troubled. Alas, alas, thus insecure!
I deemed that I again was snugly housed;
When from the wilderness there comes a blast,
That casts my cabin of assurance down,
And leaves me in the tempest. Methought that spring
Was only just returning to my soul;
And here I pant in sultry summer air,
Wherein I feel the fiend wild floating round me,
Like a huge blowfly, and upon my spirit
Seeking to sow new horrors. Phantom, pity me:
Begone from me, without thee filled with sorrow.
Do thou not bring thy rough, black waves to sink me.

[*Exit, and re-enter wildly.*

He comes again; the fiend again attempts me.
Who is this thing that whips me into gall?
I know him now,—at last methinks I know him:
'Tis Spleen, 'tis Spleen; it is the Goblin Spleen;
Who still can find occasion, as can find
The spider corner where to hang its web.
David is now my occasion; David is
To me a boil, now greedily drawing to it
The humors of my long-distempered heart.
Oh, Spleen, thou art a devil of thyself,

And canst bring up Gehenna from the deep,
And therewith set on fire thy victim's soul.
Oh, Spleen, Spleen, Spleen, unnatural embryo,
That gnawest the womb that doth engender thee!
Wolf, out of me! Ah, have I named thee right?
Oh, 'tis a wolf, it is a devil, in me;
A devil that I cannot, dare not, name;
A wolf that seems composed of hell's black flame.
Burn, flame, what care I! Wolf or fiend, devour me.
Grow, fœtus, grow; rack violated Saul
With pangs more dire than woman's in her travail!
Spirit, grow riot; raise all Tophet in me;
Confusion, blindness, and barbarity.
Oh, oh!—Why should I moan if Heaven sends it?—
'Tis hell, 'tis hell; I hear her rumbling wheels,
That, when this outrage is accomplished, come
To bear me to the region of the damned.
I'll go and clamour unto Heaven to save me.
[*Exit, and re-enter.*
I am not heard: heaven's doors are closed, and will
Not open to my knocking. Oh, for war;
New cruise;—but, oh, for no young sharks of Davids
To swallow down my glory. But the hook
Shall stick in him.
Begone, begone, ye pleadings; I will not hear ye.
Why should I hear you when myself's unheard?
Why should I spare him when myself's unspared?
I've been by far too casuistical;
And casuistry would not let us kill flies,
Nor any other vermin. But I'll kill.
All Israel knows that I am under ban;
I am encompassed round with enemies,
And I will fight my way through though I murder.
Start not, my heart, at that outblurted word,
As might a steed recoiling from a serpent;
Beat not thus like a hammer in my breast.
Murder is only death, and what as death

So common? I will do it;—I must do it.—
It will not be so painful as I thought;
Anticipation ever is a cheat.
Ah, with what furlongs murderward I'm striding!
Hence, and with motion whirl my soul from David!
                                                [Exit, and re-enter.
Why, many a maid ere this has been defiled,
And many a brave youth has untimely perished.
The whole world dies. Yes, that's the way to think.
So probably thought Moses,
In killing the Egyptian; so thought Jael,
When nailing Sisera to the floor; so too Ehud
Whispered as tickling Eglon's ribs; and Samuel,
(Ah glad I am that I have thought of him,)
And Samuel when he too played the slayer. Yes,
But all these victims would have done as much
For those who did those deeds on them; but David—
Oh, 'twere ingratitude and tenfold murder.
Oh, oh, 'twere foul, 'twere foul!
Let me not stray into that vault again.
I'll go and strive to pray down these suggestions,
And ask Heaven's pardon that I entertained them.
      [Exit, and enter the QUEEN *and* DAVID, *the latter bearing his harp.*

                      QUEEN.

Oh, happy is it, David, happy that
Thou, his physician, art come with his disease.
I heard his voice; he cannot be remote.
Hie after him and be once more his healer.
                                                      [Exit DAVID.

Oh, sorrow riding pillion to joy,
Turning the latter to a mockery!
How long with Saul will this foul spirit bide?
When will Jehovah's wrath be satisfied?
Lo, here Saul comes, his visage fraught with ill.
I must begone; his very looks would kill.
                                          [Exit, and re-enter SAUL.

SAUL.

Why have I fallen again upon my knees,
And cast mine eyes in agony towards heaven?
No prayer of mine arose, no prayer I breathed.
I cannot pray; for that which should aspire
Rests 'neath despair, or turns aside at ire.
Why should I try to pray? I have not prayed
These years. Would cursing not avail me more?
For I have known men that have cursed out humours,
Like trampling out dispersed and dangerous sparks.
[*Enter* DAVID.
I'll trample out him, and be at peace;
I'll pin him to the wall.

DAVID *beginning to play,* SAUL *throws the javelin at him, which sticks in the wall, and* DAVID *escapes.*

Transport him to the grave, ye angels, now;
Bear him away, ye ministers who bore
The corpse of Moses; and as ye it buried,
That none know where it is unto this day,
So murdered David's ever hide away.
Ungrateful Saul! Poor murdered youth!
I'll look upon him though it sear my sight.
[*Seeing that David has escaped.*
Deception rules the hour, and hell or spleen
Hath made my skull a hall to riot in.
Now will he straightway go and tell the Queen.
Why, let him go and tell Gehenna's king;
Nor he nor other shall live to hold me in dread.
To the winds, remorse. They'll say the spirit did it,
And they'll say truly. Come forth, javelin, come;
To day, it seems, death is not David's doom.
[*Exit, and enter* MALZAH.

MALZAH.

Out of his hand the javelin flew,
And entered into the wall:—
Ha, ha, ha! there's a strange ado
When at such small game flies Saul.

He struck at David, and said t'was I :
He says I made the javelin fly :
He grasped it hard, and yet it flew :
Ha, ha! ha, ha! what an ado!
How mortals worry when they slip !
If they like us their souls would dip
And dye all o'er in one grand sinning,
We less should hear of their conscience-dinning.
Temptation, indeed! they need it not :
Whew, whew, let man go rot.

   [*Exit, but re-enter immediately laughing heartily.*
Oh, oh! oh, oh! here's a pretty jest.
I'll labor now, having had my rest :
His strange abuse has given me zest.
Ha, ha! ha, ha! I'll him re-fetter :
The next time he tries perhaps he'll do better.
Lo, here he comes; and, if right I spy,
He has still got David in his eye.
          [*Enter* SAUL.

SAUL.

What if I should dismiss him merely?
In that case he'd but spread abroad his glory
Amongst the people; as Samson's foxes spread
Their fire among the corn of the Philistines.

MALZAH.

Murder him, and there's an end.

SAUL.

Ah, was not that a voice? No; 'twas my own
Soul's echo.
            [*Exit.*

MALZAH.

 I will follow him.
        [*Exit, and re-enter soon.*
     Again
I've breathed him; he is nearly mad. What with
This new-born jealousy, and the cold envy,

Which, like the north wind on the winter fire,
Blows into rage the embers of the spleen
That nature kindled in him ere his birth;
And what with mine own goading influence,
He, as of old, but now with settled aim,
Broods in the palace, or in its grounds goes stalking
With his clutched javelin. I'll visit him
Again anon: meantime I will stay here,
Awaiting whatsoever shall befall,
Singing a little to tide my tedium.

[*Song.*

Ye melancholy dogs below,
Up hell's perpetual furnace blow
With general sighs; I pity ye,
But what is your distress to me:
In many sorts I count you better
Than I, who have escaped your fetter.

Here comes my royal maniac in my chains.
I'm here, yet riding in his brains.

[*Enter* SAUL.

SAUL.

I will extinguish him.

MALZAH.

What, me? Nay, nay.

SAUL.

I will extinguish him with this, and nothing,
Except some smoke and odour, shall remain;
Merely remembrance, and that a month's soft wind
Will bear away. The ungrateful multitude
Remember for a month, and then forget.

[*Exit.*

MALZAH.

Very true.

Now Malzah may lie quiet, for the king
Needs no more seasoning to this temptation;
For he is simmering in such a pitchy caldron,

That he can scarce escape without defilement.
I shall not hurry him, nor broil myself.
His fire is hot, his loaf is leavening;
His broth I'll brew before 'tis evening.
I'll sing again, for now Zelehtha's gone,—
I hope to heaven, and to stay there; though
That is an aspiration for her good,
And I do wish her more than all the evil
That ever yet befell or saint or devil.
Ah me!

[*Song.*

There was a devil and his name was I;
From Profundus he did cry:
He changed his note as he changed his coat,
And his coat was of a varying dye.
It had many a hue: in hell 'twas blue,
'Twas green i'th' sea, and white i'th' sky.
Oh, do not ask me, ask me why
'Twas green i'th' sea, and white i'th' sky;
Why from Profundus he did cry:
Suffice that he wailed with a chirruping note,
And quaintly cut was his motley coat.—

I have forgot the rest. Would I could sleep;
Would I could sleep away an age or so,
And let Saul work out his own weal or woe:
All that I ask is to be let alone.

[*Song.*

Oh, to be let alone! to be let alone!
To laugh, if I list; if I list, to groan;
Despairing, yet knowing God's anger o'erblown.
Oh, why should God trouble me?
Why should He double my
Sorrow, pursuing me when He has thrown
Me out of his favor? Oh, why should He labor
Down lower ever thrusting me into Hell's zone?
Oh, let me alone! oh, let me alone!
Oh, leave me, Creator, Tormenter, alone.

Peace ; here comes Saul, more wretched than myself.
[SAUL *enters and slowly crosses the stage.*
Behold how swollen yet haggard is his face!
He doth remind me, as he hither stalks,
Of Lucifer, in his pent anger, pacing
Over the black and burning floor of hell.
He's charged ; so have worked in him the last drops
That I let fall upon his soul. Woe now
To whomsoever shall meet him. Now is my time:
I'll enter him, that he may work his doom,
And, peradventure, I get my release.
His mind's defences are blown down by passion ;
And I can enter him unchallenged, as
A traveller does an inn, and, when I'm there,
(He is himself now so much like a demon,)
He will not notice me. I will lie perdue
'Tween his own shadow's bounds; he will not see
Me, from the very darkness of his soul.
I'll couch within his gloom, like to a spark
Amongst combustibles. Again he's pregnant
Of an intent pernicious; and a throe
Again I'll give him, in a double sense,
To hasten his delivery.
[*As he is going* ZEPHO *enters.*

ZEPHO.

Hist, hist !

MALZAH.

Now, by all things, ill-timed! Would that thy heel
Just now were sticking in a trap of steel!
Wherefore at present comest thou stealing hither?

ZEPHO.

Tell in what kennel thou hast lately housed ;
For, save in that one, I in all earth's corners
Have lately sought thee. I am come from Zaph.

MALZAH.

Well, what wants Zaph?

ZEPHO.

To know thy speed.

MALZAH.
                    Thrice thine.
ZEPHO.
Zaph wants to know of thy prosperity.

MALZAH.
I never knew a devil that did prosper.

ZEPHO.
Now answer soberly: Zaph asks thy fare.

MALZAH.
I never knew a devil that fared better:
I feed on a king's sighs, do drink queen's tears,
Am clothed with half a nation's maledictions.
Am not I a lucky fellow?

ZEPHO.
                    Never saucier.
How goes the royal Saul?

MALZAH.
                    Oh, furiously:
He from a giddy tower lately jumped,
And nearly broke his neck;—he says I threw him.

ZEPHO.
Leave him, and turn on Samuel.

MALZAH.
                    I cannot do so.
I am in thraldom to a heavenly spirit:—
See where she comes!

ZEPHO.
            It is exceeding bright.

MALZAH.
So we were once; but now how dim!

ZEPHO.
                    There's hope
In that. Hast thou not seen
The snow upon some ever-shining summit
Precipitated to the dim ravine?

So may her order yet, for fault or freak,
From Heaven fall dimming into our dark hell.
I'll stir up Zaph to send unto thy rescue.
            [Exit.

MALZAH.

May Zaph be damned (as he assuredly is)
For sending thee, his henchman, here to quiz!
        [Enter ZELEHTHA.
I bade that prying fellow to begone;—
I'm diligent to be the sooner done.
            [Exit.

ZELEHTHA.

I'll follow him, or he'll o'eract his part.
    [Exit, and enter the QUEEN *and* DAVID.

DAVID.

Fear not for me, although his majesty
Is even as a chafed and senseless beast;
And standing in his presence no less risk
Than being with a lion in its den:
Should he again his lance against me wield,
Again the Lord will be to me a shield.

QUEEN.

Then take thy station here and ply thy harp.
Oh, David, do thine uttermost again
To exorcise from him this evil spirit.
Alas, I thought thy former minstrelsy,
And the employment of these latter wars,
Had healed his soul; so that a tranquil life,
Except those blasts that we expect to blow
Around a royal head, henceforth were his.
Begin, that he may hear thee ere he see thee.
Strike that old air composed before the flood,
And which has often calmed his boiling blood.

DAVID.

I will.
'Tis said it draws foul spirits, since 'twas played

Oft for them by their human paramours;
Whom, when they hear it, they believe returned
Up from the uncertain regions of the dead,
And so go forth to meet them.

QUEEN.
                    Here he comes;
Still armed, and now his lips all foam.
I'll fly, for he doth hate me in these fits.
                                   [*Exit.*

A javelin is hurled into the apartment and sticks in the wall; DAVID *escapes as before.*

SAUL (*entering*).
After him, fiend, that sit'st within me. Forth,
Infernal hound, and fetch him. Oh, thou false one!
                              [*Enter the* QUEEN.
Hast thou met David? Hath he told thee aught?
Bid him come hither;—or he had better hence,
For what I'll do I'll do.

QUEEN.
                    Peace, peace.

SAUL.
Ay, knowest thou why that trembling shaft is there?

The QUEEN *draws the javelin from the wall, and throws it out of the room.*

QUEEN.
Now, my dear husband, come and take some rest.

SAUL.
Yes, when I've done what I have vowed to do.
I am beneath the tyranny of a vow,
Which I will honor whilst I am eclipsed,
That I hereafter may have power to plead
I did it in the darkness.—'Tis the fiend:—
He darkens, yet illuminates, my mind,
Like the black heavens when lightnings ride the wind.

QUEEN.
Your sun will shine anon.

SAUL.

Tormentor, no!
I want it not to shine; let the wind blow.
Let me wreck all my foes, or else be lost
Myself upon this black and fatal coast.
Mad pilot, wouldst thou see me drowned i'th' vortex?—
Oh, it is I am mad; mad, mad is Saul.

QUEEN.

Then, if you know that you are mad, at once
Confine yourself within your chamber's bounds.
Come, for your slumber will betake you soon.
You will be happy when the spirit's gone

SAUL.

Gone!
When he is gone for ever. When will that be?
When will he go hence to return no more?

QUEEN.

Oh, fall not thus away: come, come.—What, would you
Cast yourself on the ground? Fie! burdened care,
Bent-bodied, better is than prone despair.
Nay, nay, revive; why, even now I spy
The faltering fiend departing at your eye.
Be Saul, be Saul again.

SAUL.

Ah, would I were again a quiet hind!

QUEEN.

And leave your sovereignty? You sleep, you dream.
Awaken, Saul, and be your proper self:
Return, return from this wild wandering.
Come home; your Troubler's gone: come home.—
Oh, fill that horrid blank upon your face;
Tear off therefrom that veil of lunacy;
Oh, cast that eye-bewildered stupor: Saul,
Shake off this creeping, death-like lethargy.
What, will you never be to sense recalled?

Help me, ye angels; help, Jehovah.—Saul,
What are your thoughts? Know you not where you are?
You are outside yourself, are disembodied;—
Oh, put your soul into that emptied frame!
Get from the weather; get within yourself.
Why stand you thus beneath unsheltering eaves,
Amidst a deluge of dread, pelting thoughts?
Come in, come in, poor king, into thyself;—
Saul, Saul;—oh, do not look so lost; oh, let me
Now lead you back to recollection: lo, 'tis I;
Lo, you are here though much perplexed: behold
You stand upon the threshold of yourself,
Yet know it not; look on it, 'tis yet fair;
Enter, and you shall find its furnishing
Is, even yet, such as becomes a king.

SAUL.

Nay, I am but a puppet, not a king.
Kings are supreme and uncontrolled, but I
Am under horrid slavery to a being
That I despise and loathe.

QUEEN.

       Forget it now.
Come, come at once to bed.

SAUL.

        Oh, Ahinoam,
Although I must acknowledge some past faults,
Can God permit this outrage yet be just?

QUEEN.

Renew not your old reasonings, but come
And take the sleep that follows on your fit.

SAUL.

Fit, fit!
'Tis strange this should seem fit:—why, had I killed him,
It had been written down murder; yes, and Samuel,
And haply this malicious goblin too,
Staying my passage to a city of refuge,
Had haled me back into Jehovah's wrath,

And Tophet of my conscience. Ahinoam,
There's something wrong in this recurring fit:
I will investigate it, I will dare
To question more than e'er I've done as yet;
Yes, I will question on till I am answered.

QUEEN.

Cease raving, Saul, and come; your mind needs rest,
And not the contemplation of an inquest,
Which, to the coolest, most impartial stranger,
Had need upconjure a black pause of caution,
Like to a ghost, to awe him from the inquiry.

SAUL.

No such ghost shall awe me; for I have known,
Yea, oft have in me, an upconjured ghost,
More terrible than any human terror,
And am not yet affrighted. What, shall I
Not ask from whence this comes? Shall I accept
Evil, nor seek to know its origin?
Shall I be dumb because great Samuel's spoken?
No!
I will demand, I will seek satisfaction;
I will have some, though bitter, pacification:—
Yea, I already to my soul have such
Obtained by fearless thinking. It is magic;
'Tis Samuel leagued with the remnant of the sorcerers.
Stand not aghast at my accusing him:
I would accuse the high, majestic heavens,
I would accuse the blue, etherial air,
If, when from my ablutions forth, I found
My person sudden smirched; say, wouldst not thou?

QUEEN.

I would not dare to accuse the sacred seer,
Of falsehood and deception.

SAUL.
     Then thou wouldst
Accuse thy husband. Well, so let it be;

No foolish reverence shall choke my suspicion.
Prophets are not beyond the freaks of poor,
Affronted mortals, any more than kings.
Why dost thou look upon me thus alarmed?
Thou wouldst expostulate? No, no, 'tis vain;
I will not hear even thee: I'll march right onwards,
Nor list to any charming; I'll escape;
And I will punish for what has been done;
I'll come upon my secret enemies,
And scatter them and their vile incantations.

QUEEN.

Oh, is the gamut of your heart played over?

SAUL.

Not yet, not yet. I have a clang of discords
Yet for thine ear. By hell, it makes me fierce
To hear the cant of silly dames and priests.
Those talk of right, and charge great heaven with wrong;
These dribble on my head their verbal spite,
And say 'tis th' thunder of heaven's waterspouts:
Those honor me, yet count me reprobate;
These send a fitful access unto me,
And name it the evil spirit from the Lord.
Out! out! shall I be silenced and beguiled
By a chicanery that drives me wild?
Wife, I am sane at present though uncivil;
But these reflections half bring back my devil.
I hear, methinks, him humming round my head:
Old hornet, cease. Wife, lead to bed, to bed:—
Would I could sleep,—would, would that I were dead.

[*Exeunt.*

SCENE III.

SAUL's *bedchamber.* SAUL *asleep upon a bed. Time, night. A lamp burning. Enter* MALZAH.

MALZAH.

He is now sleeping, but his fervent brow
Is all meandered o'er by swollen veins.

Across his temple one appears nigh bursting.
He breathes, too, heavily, and a feeble moan
I hear within him; shewing that his soul,
(Like to a child that's wept itself to sleep,)
Even in slumber, doth retain its trouble.
I am loth again to rack him; but I will,
For I am desperate to escape from slavery.
I will breathe hotly on his countenance,
And when he awakes and doth cry out for water,—
Which I will make his servants slow in bringing,—
I'll enter him 'midst his vociferations,
And goad him back to madness.
[*Approaches the* KING.

SAUL.

Oh, leave me, foul fiend!

MALZAH.

He dreams.

SAUL.

Thou art not from God.

MALZAH.

Alas, I am.

SAUL.

I have long thee withstood.

MALZAH.

Boast not too much.

SAUL.

Depart from me, horrible presence!

MALZAH (*advancing nearer*).

'Tis the wind that hath blown me against thee; 'tis fate
That I and thou thus for a season should mate.
[*Having breathed upon* SAUL'S *face.*
I love thee not, and yet too much I love thee,
To do my work effectually, I fear.
[*Breathes on him again.*
There, there.

SAUL.

Oh, to be pent in hell! I suffocate.
Veer, winds that from the red equator scorch me,

And let the north blow on me till I shiver.
Ah, for an avalanche of snow! Fall, flakes,
And blind me; cover me up, drifts; freeze, freeze.
Seize on me, blast, and hurl me into winter.

MALZAH.

Again I'll breathe on him.
[Breathes upon him.

SAUL.

Full threescore fiends and ten, each with a javelin,
Half-molten, and thrust through me from behind,
Chased me all up the burning lane from hell.
Some water, water, ho! Ah, here again!
Each with his brand swept through me, and dispersed
Now all of them back hissing.
[Waking.
Water! water!
What ho, bring hither water! Is there none
To watch me? Jonathan, Michal, Merab; where's
Ahinoam? Gone! Oh, ye are all
Forgetful of me, and my children take
Their ease and pastime whilst their father's dying.
Some water, water!—Oh, to breathe upon
Carmel or Ararat! Clouds, burst upon
My bosom, as upon their heads ye burst:
Pour on my head, ye waterspouts: cataracts,
Dash down my throat and turn me to an ocean.—
Ah, will there be no rain again, no dew?
To the dank vineyard! let me go and wallow,
Suck out, and trample out the freshness. Chained!
[Writhes furiously to break the chain.

MALZAH.

I'll enter him now, but not to do him evil,
But, out of ruth, to help him snap his chain.

[MALZAH *vanishes; and* SAUL, *having broken his chain,
rushes out.*

SAUL. 193

MALZAH (*again visible*).

I am not lazy, but I loathe to do
The work of Heaven.—Ah, here comes my lady!
I'll hide myself in Saul.   [*Exit in haste.*

ZELEHTHA (*entering*).

How quickly the defaulter flees away!
I'll follow him.   [*Exit.*

SCENE IV.

A vineyard. The moon shining.
Enter SAUL, *struggling with* MALSAH.

SAUL.

Creature, begone, nor harrow me with horror!
Thine eyes are stars; oh, cover them, oh, wrap
Them up within thy cloudy brows: stand off,
Contend not with me, but say who thou art.
Methinks I know thee,—yes, thou art my demon;
Thou art the demon that tormentest me.
I charge thee say, mysterious visitant,
At whose behest thou comest, and for what
Offences deep of mine: nay, nay, stand off:
Confess, malicious goblin, or else leave me;
Leave me, oh goblin, till my hour is come:
I'll meet thee after death; appoint the place;
On Gilead, or beside the flowing Jordan;
Or, if parts gloomier suit thee, I'll repair
Down into Hinnom, or up to the top
Of Horeb in th' wilderness, or to the cloud-
Concealèd height of Sinai ascend,
Or dwell with thee 'midst darkness in the grave.

[*Enter* ZELEHTHA, *invisible to* SAUL.

MALZAH.

I cannot enter him now; he does so set
And close his soul against me. Thou art not angry?

Give me commandment, and I now will rend
His body into fragments, and let out
His soul, for thee to do with what thou wilt.
       [Crawling abjectly towards her feet.
I will obey thee in whate'er thou biddest me,
So thou wilt look less stern. Shall I to hell,
And take him with me living, as to heaven
Went Enoch; or shall I put poison in
His food, or hang him on a bough; or may I
Entice him to his highest turret's top,
And cast him thencefrom; or, in human guise,
Insult him (for he is both brave and choleric,
And quails not at the wrath of any man)
Until he draw his sword, when I will pierce him,
Right through his heart, in quick and angry duel?
I pray you let me finish him, sweet mistress.
Shall I provoke him to excess in wine,
Until he die of fever and delirium?
Bid me to rise and work; for aught I'll do
To pleasure heaven and be dismissed by you.
I pray thee let me hurl him 'gainst the moon,
And leave him there to pine, and freeze, and shiver
Till he expire; or be it his hell for ever.

      ZELEHTHA.
Come.
      MALZAH.
I do implore thee let me kill him first!—
It cannot be that he shall live much longer;
Behold how gaunt he is. He would have killed
David, and, by God's law, the murderer
Devoted is to death; so let me be
God's instrument of justice; oh, do thou be
Just unto David, and to me show mercy.
     [Arising and following ZELEHTHA.
Inexorable angel, it were bliss to curse thee! *[Aside.*
    [Exeunt MALZAH *and* ZELEHTHA.

SAUL.

'Tis strange, most strange : how strange was its demeanour!
Would I had had the power to make it speak,
Albeit of mischief it leered forth a volume.
Or had I seen it sooner, that I might
Have known from whence it issued; whether it
Came from the fabled pit, straight through the earth,
Emerging even at my very feet, or
Glode level o'er the lea like a marsh-meteor,
Or down the air shot like a falling star
'Twas as fantastic as a thing of moonbeams,
And looked most wicked ; 'tis a son of murk,
Both by its mien and by its baneful work.
How it did come I know not ; but, at last,
It did appear to address itself to some one,
And crawled till it lay prone and agitated ;
Then rose and glided hence, like to a vapor
Attracted towards a cranny by a draught.
I shudder yet ;—but how have I grown steeled,
To have kept my senses in hell's very clutch!
Be still, ye trembling limbs ; post, fearful hour,
Into oblivion's arms ; perish, evil day,
And be no portion of eternity.
Thou dawnedst in fear, and hast expired in horror.
Oh, let me say no more upon this theme,
For I could utter impious things ; could pour derision
On prophets, I who've twice myself had vision.
Let me within ; yet not attempt to sleep,
Lest yonder creature 'twixt my curtains peep.

[Exit.

SCENE V.

An apartment in the Palace.

SAUL.

If, in my fiend-fraught frenzy, I had killed him,
It had been well ; 't had not my conscience burdened,
Yet lightened much my heart. 'Tis heavy yet,

For my presentiment is not unfounded.
My sudden aversion to him is an instinct,
Trustworthier than is fair inference
From his past services.   Why do I feel
This else irrational dislike of him;
That shameful and unmanly dread, yea, even
Horror, when he is present, except from that
Intuitive and warning sense of peril,
Which, even whilst we are disporting with it,
Prompts us to kill or cage the toothless cub,
Ere it become the fanged and terrible lion?
I once was but a herdsman, as he lately
Was but a shepherd.   The several distances
Between our first conditions and the throne,
Are equal; and Samuel hath withdrawn from me
Disloyally, whilst half the people's hearts
Go with him wheresoever he doth lead them.
May he not lead them to this martial shepherd?
Nay, they are there already!   Those accursed,
Choral, and tripping nymphs proclaimed it.   Now
All charmed away is the spirit of disagreement;
Which, in excess, is ever a nation's weakness,
But, in due measure, is the monarch's strength.
His popularity is universal.
Such a strange concord of opinion
Was never heard before in Israel,
That one long note of praise rolls through the land,
None making dissonance; and such spirits as those
Who at my own election scornfully asked,
"Can this man save us?" laboring 'neath the spell,
Either hang silent or join the general hum.
I have heard say (and I do half believe it)
That apprehension brings what 'tis apprehending.
How know I but that the capricious creature,
Who visits me and gives me up to passion,
Intended by this foul attack on David,
To goad him into treason?   That vile chant

May have brought into his soul the faggots of
Ambition; and this fiend of burning hell,
Couched in the flying javelin, have swept after
And put into his hand a torch of hope
Wherewith to kindle them. It was a sad
Unlucky deed, that of the other day!
Now, doubtless, he is conscious that I fear him;
And as a word, dropped in a hurried moment,
Will suddenly reveal a weighty secret,
So he will now my jealousy surmise.
Know we not, by the enemy's double guards,
The weak points of his camp? So David now
Shall have perceived where I am vulnerable.
Ah, it is hard to overcome dark dread!
I know that God is with him, and suspect
He hath deserted me, or I'd ne'er feared.
I'll end this dread of David, though I may
Have conjured up a chimera to torment me.
Hither he comes: I'm loth, yet I will do it.
         [*Enter* DAVID.
In a good time thou art come; we were of thee
Communing with ourselves. Thou shalt have Merab,
Our eldest daughter, given thee to wife;
Only do thou be valiant, and fight
Jehovah's battles for us. Art content?

DAVID.

Press me not, gracious king: what am I, and
What is my life or family, that I
Should be thy son-in-law?

SAUL.

      But we did promise 't
To him who should despatch the Giant Philistine.
But the Philistines are yet giants; and
Do thou assist me by thy valour, till we
Dwarf them to common men; for, by Jehovah,
We swear that we will humble the aggressors;
Nor shall there be between us peace, till we

Have bound them to the shores of their own main.
Thou dost not answer us:—why, then, be dumb;
And, growing in arms, our wish towards thee shall come.
We have determined, and the force and worth
Of our resolves thou knowest.—Let us forth.
(Aside.)
The worst is passed; and I will order so,
He shall his death to the Philistines owe.

[*Exeunt.*

ACT IV.

SCENE I.

A Room in the Palace. Enter JOKIEL *and* JARED.

JOKIEL.

Methinks this is about the time that Merab
Should have been given to David unto wife.

JARED.

That time is passed, and David little cares.
I tell thee David wishes not to wear
His earned honor:—whether of humility
It come, or if from policy, I know not.

JOKIEL.

Art thou not young? Dost thou not look abroad
With eyes that have but recently begun
To rub their smoothness 'gainst the roughening world,—
Even as the buttons of thy tunic rubbed
Against the desk whereat thou sat'st in school,—
And are they now so dull? Oh! blind, like all
This last generation! Why, man, the old cat
Can mouse a secret, yet, out of its hole,
And play with it, and kill and eat it too,
Before you youths can smell it. My son Jared,
Lend me the oyster-shell of thy right ear,
And in't I'll whisper thee a secret pearl.

David desires not Merab; but if Michal
Were offered him, 'twould warm his seeming coldness,
And, to the very sea-marge of his neck,
Like to the tide up to the ocean's brim,
At evening, 'neath the low and crimson sun,
Would cause blush out to view his simmering blood.

JARED.

I have myself remarked the specialty
Of his respect towards Michal. What he doth
For Merab and for all the royal house,
He doth sevenfold for Michal, and delights in
The supererogation.

JOKIEL.

Yea, he doth:
But 'tis no theme for runners of the palace,
Who straight will run it o'er all Gibeah.
It is not meet that I along with thee
Should crony thus, and take thy swinish ear.
It is not meet, that, touching David, I
Therein, like wavelets purling o'er a shell,
Should hint, assert, and, with prophetic tongue,
Declare what will be, or, at least, what might be,
If only those inflexible household gods,
Fathers, were kind.—Son, I speak feelingly;
Myself have been i'th' Giant-killer's case,
And could have wished the nymph of my desires
Would have betasked me like a very slave,
Yea, sent me into Egypt to make bricks,
Provided that I might have thence returned,
And baked them in the sunshine of her eyes.
I could have wished most terrible strange things;
Yea, most preposterous metamorphoses:
She unto me a lioness, and I, to her,
Her sole provider,—ay, her very jackall;
She, unto me, some rich, luxurious land,
And I, to her, as its entire flotilla,
That, driven by oar or hugged along with th' wind,
Unto its shores brought tribute. Lo, the king.

JARED.

He sent me from him to perform an errand.

[Exit, and enter SAUL.

SAUL.

Why lingered Jared with thee?—he was sent
On business for Michal, who lacks patience.

JOKIEL.

He is young, your majesty, and youth will have
Its gibes at tacit age. Your majesty,
Ere now, hath doubtless seen an urchin raise
A stone to throw at some poor harmless thing:
A dove it may have been, or, likelier,
Cat (and I own unto your majesty
That I, in youth, the latter have tormented),
That crossed his path, or whose himself he crossed,
Wandering to school, or on forgotten errand.
Even as wanton boys will missiles fling
At dove, or dog, or an espièd cat,
So passing youth will fling jests at meek age.
Your majesty, I know, will pardon me
This bold recital and high colloquy,
Wherein my tongue copes with your royal ear,
('Twas folly, truly, in me to return 't in kind,)
But the green fledgling who just went from hence
('Twas folly, certainly, to talk at all
In such nice matter) but we talked of Michal,
And how that David secretly admires her,
In secret pines, but dares not dream to have her.

SAUL.

Thou art officious, and thyself concernest
With things that are beyond thee. Go; the queen
Was asking for thee. Probably she wants
From thee some tale, whose telling may bring back
The slumber that has late too much forsaken her.
Attend her, but talk not to her of David.

[Exit JOKIEL.

I'll offer Michal to him for a snare;
And love shall lead him hoodwinked to his death:
For, as her dowry, I will ask a hundred
Foreskins of the Philistines. He shall fall
Yet by their hands, not mine. Welcome to Saul.
                                        [*Enter a* MINISTER *of state.*

SAUL.

Because we know thee powerful in persuasion,
We shall employ thee in a delicate case,
'Twixt Michal and our favorite captain, David.
Preamble it as thou wilt; say so and so;—
Say all the house of Saul admire and love him;
Say that the Queen's his friend, (as he well knows,)
And Michal too affects him; that ourselves
(Whatever may have seemed to the reverse)
Regard him with all favor: tell him this,
And counsel him to be our son-in-law.
Now to him straight, for he is ruminating
There yonder in the garden.
                                      [*Exit* MINISTER.

Let me not dwell upon this ugly business;
I love him though I act as if I hated.
'Tis not my nature, yet 'tis from my nature,
To which self-preservation is a law:—
Nor more its law than 'tis the law of heaven,
To Moses' added, making up eleven.
Sad is the fate that does to this compel me!
Sad, sad that he must be pushed on to slaughter;—
As sad to sacrifice my favorite daughter.
                                                [*Exit.*

SCENE II.

In the Garden. Enter the MINISTER *and* DAVID *conversing earnestly.*

MINISTER.

Nay, hear me further, and then answer me.
Is 't not the highest duty of the subject
To obey his king?

DAVID.

                                Doubtless it is my lord,
Granted the king command not aught forbidden.

MINISTER.
Even to the risking of that subject's life?

DAVID.
Such risk being for the king's or country's good.

MINISTER.
How much more, then, when such obedience is
Both for that subject's honor and the country's pleasure?
Now listen: Saul affects thee, though thou wert
By him passed by in Merab, whom, he knew,
Thou lovedst not, so declined to recompense thee
In coin of her, which, if he had done, would
But have defrauded thee, to whom her value
Came not at its full standard. Saul affects thee—
Whatever to the contrary has seemed—
And all the royal house admire and love thee;
Her Majesty, and (what is of much weight)
Not Jonathan alone, but all Saul's sons.
Do thou accept, then, should his majesty
Offer thee (as I believe is his intention)
The buxom, and yet proud and dainty, Michal,
Who, 'tis surmised, in secret pines for thee.

DAVID.
And thinkest thou it light for one like me,
Poor, and inheriting but some few sheep,
To mate in wedlock with the royal house,
That for its purse doth hold a kingdom's coffers?

MINISTER.
There's weight in that; but it may be removed,
If all the parties to the noble contract
Should will it: for what could withstand such triple
Engine of lovers' hearts and parent's soul,
With nation helping it away to roll?
No more at present; I will now begone,
But talk upon this subject more anon.   [*Exit.*

DAVID.

I do love Michal, and could go tend sheep
Again at Beth-lehem, might she go with me.
Oh, selfish David, wouldst thou then debase her?
Wouldst thou then cheat the king her royal father?
Who knoweth not the worth of his quick jewel,
To which his palace is the setting ring.
She burnishes the ingot of his court;
Yea, wheresoever in the court she moves,
Dispenses riches from her dazzling beauty,
'Till all flames like a mine.—I fear to indulge
What is even more than was my wildest wish;
For to be paid with her would overpay me.
This is the king's. Surely he would not trifle
With me in Michal as in Merab! Nay,
If he do ask me, I will even say, yea.

[*Exit.*

SCENE III.

The Royal closet. SAUL *and the* MINISTER.

SAUL.

Tell him that we require no other dowry
Than that which he can give,—a hundred foreskins
Of the Philistines; that we may have vengeance
Upon our enemies, which is to us
More precious than much wealth in gold can be.

MINISTER.

I know he will accept your proposition,
Prompted thereto by his own inclination;
For it is known to me that he has long
Loved Michal, and he fears not the Philistines.
I'll to him straightway; and return to tell you
That he is gone, intending to surprise them.

[*Exit* MINISTER.

SAUL.

May he himself be now surprised! At last
May the foul genius of disaster meet him,
That he return no more! I love thee, David,
But love Saul better. If he come back alive,
And bring with him the full tale of the foreskins,
Then shall I know that God or Devil's leagued
With him to fight against me.
[*Exit*

SCENE IV.

The Courtyard of the Palace.
Enter Two Domestics.

FIRST DOMESTIC.

Dost thou not know that joyful wedding glee
Again is at the threshold of the court?

SECOND DOMESTIC.

I do, and know that it within the palace
Shall enter if so happen; but the bridegroom
Elect rides such a sharp-edged hazard towards
Her, who is bought with a hundred males' dishonor,
That I much doubt within myself if he
A bridegroom e'er, in very deed, shall be.

FIRST DOMESTIC.

Fear not for David; for he hath around him
A panoply that no one sees, but which
Makes him invulnerable to the foe.
How often have we seen the king borne hither,
All pale and bleeding from the battle-field,
Suffering although victorious; whilst David always
From his recurring, bloody skirmishes,
Returns uninjured.
[*A sound of military music, and loud acclamations.*
Listen! 'tis his drum:
The air's heart beats; let's go, for he doth come.
[*Exeunt, and enter* SAUL.

SAUL.

He is returned, whom I wished not to return:
Living too and unhurt; fresh as becomes
A jocund bridegroom; and he with him bears
The bloody dowry, doubled, from our foes:
So that the pit I willed him to fall into,
And lose himself therein with death and darkness,
Hath proved an eminence, on which he stands
Like to a beacon lighted up afresh.
Men his augmented beam will see full soon,
And bless him seeing it; but I, like the moon,
Before the presence of the rising sun,
Shall wane and fade before this last deed done.
He shall have Michal, although much it cost
To see my child thus to me ever lost;
For sure I am that there can never be,
From me toward him, but covert enmity.

[Exit.

END OF THE SECOND PART OF SAUL.

SAUL.

THIRD PART.

PERSONS REPRESENTED.

SAUL, *King of Israel.*
JONATHAN, *his Eldest Son.*
ABNER, *Saul's Cousin, and a General in his Army.*
DAVID, *originally a Shepherd, now Saul's Son-in-Law, a General in his Army, and eventually King of Israel.*
JESSE, *David's Father.*
SAMUEL, *High Priest of Israel.*
AHIMELECH, *a Priest.*
ABIATHER, *his Son.*
DOEG, *an Edomite, Chief of Saul's Herdsmen.*
AHIMELECH, *the Hittite.*
ABISHAI, *David's Cousin.*
ACHISH, *King of Gath.*
MICHAL, *Saul's Daughter, and Wife of David.*
The WITCH of Endor.
ZELEHTHA, *an Angel.*
ZAPH,
ZEPHO, } *Demons.*
PHYONA,
MALZAH, *the Evil Spirit from the Lord.*
COURTIERS, MESSENGERS, ZIPHITES, SOLDIERS, SAUL'S ARMOUR-BEARER, &c.

THIRD PART.

ACT I.

SCENE I.

Gibeah. The Courtyard of the Palace.
Enter TWO COURTIERS.

FIRST COURTIER.

Three suns hath Israel now to warm and light her,—
Saul, Jonathan, and David; and her blood,
So liberally shed, shall be as rain
Upon her lands, henceforth thrice fruitful in
The doubled toil of husbandry secure.

SECOND COURTIER.

Auspicious is this marriage; and the more so
Because it promises that there shall be
No difference of privilege in the tribes.
Judah and Benjamin thus joined already,
Says that the other scions of our race
Shall, in due season, be engrafted on
The royal tree, that, with roots tempest-stricken,
Now gives us shelter 'neath its stately arms.   [*Exeunt.*

SCENE II.

An Apartment in the Palace.

SAUL.

" Defeat, defeat," the court pronounce in whispers;
" Defeat," they low pronounce with eyes depressed,

As if the dreaded truth were hung above them,
And unto it they raised not their regard,
Fearing to make assurance. Willingly I'd lose
A battle, so that he might lose renown.
But let me not receive this seeming angel,
Lest it should prove to be— [*A noise heard.*
What noise is that?

MICHAL, *rushing in.*

Oh, here he comes to tell you how the day,
Which we believed went lowering down on Israel,
Set in a flood of glory on our arms!
[*Enter* DAVID.
Oh, David, David, thou art welcomer
From this new victory, (which comes threefold
On us, late sat in fog of feared defeat,)
Than sunbeams in a dull November day.
Speak to him, father.

SAUL.

Thou art the minion, David,
Of the best fortune, whencesoe'er its source.
Yet had we heard reverse had come at last:
But, slow to credit it, we kept our mind
Calm and ebalanced 'twixt the dim extremes
Of chance defeat and likelier success;
Well knowing, if it were the former, that
We, with swift strides approaching the Philistines,
Would soon return it with high interest,
Paid down unto those warlike merchantmen.

DAVID.

No need of that: Jehovah never fails
To succour me; for in mine own strength never
Do I contend, but, mailed in faith and prayer,
Meet those grim warriors from the ocean marge,
Expecting ever thus to overcome them.

SAUL.

Thou'rt lucky in thy frame. To-morrow we
Will ask of thee particular recital

How the fight swayed, and how, as usual,
'Twas won : sufficient, now, to know 'twas won,
And that thou livest thyself to bear the news,
And, all unhurt, again art Michal's. Now
Hie home with her : 'tis wrong to take thee from her
So often in your newly-married days;
Which should be spent in soft and amorous fields,—
Sweet days that, spent, can never more return.
Go, go; this is not meet. I, for awhile,
Myself will keep these Philistines in awe,
And, for my health's sake, make a few campaigns.
Michal, go with him. See thou cherish him,
As doth become a young and duteous wife.

MICHAL.

David, let's go. At home we'll talk together;
And thou shalt tell me nine times over, love,
How went the course of this misstated field,
That has returned thee to me still unscathed.

SAUL.

Yes, tell her to the full : for women are
Most gluttonous in feeding on the tales
Their husbands tell them of their proper honor;
But little thinking, in the same sweet hour,
How many a wife deplores her spouse disgraced.
Go; such is war :—but ye can moralize
When ye are old and crusty grown like me.
       [Exeunt DAVID *and* MICHAL.
If I can hinder by delays, he shall
Not render a thank-offering for his victory,
Nor for his safe return. If I can cause
A breach 'twixt him and heaven, 'twill serve as well
As if he were, like me, beseiged by hell.
How now ?
         [Enter JONATHAN.

JONATHAN.

David, I thought, was here.

SAUL.
He was.

What wouldst thou with him?

JONATHAN (*aside*).

Question strange! [*Aloud.*] Why, nothing:—
Or if he were now here, I, perhaps, might greet him.

SAUL.

He has returned victorious, as usual:
The rumour of his overthrow was false.
Hadst thou been true unto thyself and me,
Thou hadst dipped into this new ray of sunshine,
And left awhile the sports of concubines,
To play at least another game with men.

JONATHAN.

Have I refused?

SAUL.

Refused! thou should'st forestall him.
But thou forgettest that thou art the heir
Unto a sceptre, that must be maintained
By those who wield it, or at length must drop
Out of their hands, to be ta'en up by him
Who is esteemed, both by himself and others,
(And proves it by his realm-protecting deeds,)
More able and more worthy to retain it.

JONATHAN.

I hardly this expected.

SAUL.
Ponder it.
Ponder upon it, my forgetful son;
Ponder't for thine afflicted father's sake;
Who must again to the wars: by day and night,
In heat and cold, in sunshine and in rain,
Walk the tent-covered field; and in his age,
When he should sheltered sit and counsel only,
Have both the planning and the execution
(Along with Abner) of all enterprises,

Or them resign to David,—to his heir,
More fit than thou to fill the regal chair.
Did I say "enterprise"? Alas, alas,
My sons possess it not, although I once
Believed them ablest of the sons of Israel
To adorn and keep the house which I have built:
But it must crumble, peradventure fall,
And bury in its ruins you and Saul;
Who hath his sweat and blood for nothing spilt,
For others founded and for others built.
But David goes no more unto the war.

JONATHAN.

I do beseech your majesty, if you love
Yourself, my mother, and my sister Michal,
Dismiss this dread of David from your mind.

SAUL.

I would dismiss him to the land of mind.
Knowest thou where that is? I tell thee, boy,
If he live thou diest. Dost thou wish to die,
Who knowest how sweet a life of glory is?
Now hearken what I say; and let it call thee
Back to thyself, like trumpet to the field.
Thou, whilst he lives, shalt no more glory taste;
For whilst he dazzles thou canst not be seen.
He is between us and the people: and
As a small matter held near to the eye
Hides the whole world besides, so David now
Hides all the merit of the house of Saul.
He shall be straight removed; I say he shall.
I tell thee kill him.—I had done it myself
But—

JONATHAN.

But why?

SAUL.

Because I will not do it, yet
It shall be done; and very quickly too:
So do it thou and ease thy father's soul.

Think not upon it, but do it.—Art thou craven?
'Twere but one less on earth, one more in heaven.
[*Exit.*

JONATHAN.

Oh, horrid counsel! Most ungrateful sire!—
But he is mad,—or the foul spirit hath
So venomed him by its repeated stinging,
That, when 'tis absent, still it in him works.
How black my father must esteem my heart!
A brother bid assassinate a brother.
No, though the victim were not my dear friend.
Shall I become a bravo, though my fee
Should be a father's bosom set at rest?
Rest! how could he then rest, with mind so guilty?
Ten thousand fiends would from that hour torment him;
And David's spirit, like a white-robed angel,
Would make them ply their task upon his conscience,
Till, in some moment of despair and anguish,
Down from these battlements he'd dash his body
To the earth, and soul to hell's perdition. Oh,
How can the soul of man become transformed!
How turn, self-changed, with black, ungrateful thoughts!
His son-in-law, his own child's husband,
My sister's spouse! him whom she loves so dearly,
And at whose frequent absences she chafes;
Whom when at home, nigh to unseemliness,
Binds with her arms and clothes with her endearments!
I will disclose this horrid scheme to David. [*Exit.*

SCENE III.

An apartment in the Palace.
SAUL *and certain* RETAINERS *of the Court.*

SAUL.

If you know one whom you believe I love not,
If he were near me lately, even in this palace,
Although he might be somewhat to me akin;

If there be such a one, deal with him as
You list. You know no enemy should live;
And whom I point out to your understandings
Should be no longer left to trouble me.
If you know such a one, crush him as you
Would crush a spider that you had observed
A-creeping towards me as I ignorant slept;
A spider that, although you were aware
It could not harm me, notwithstanding would
Deserve the death for rash and filthy vermin.

A RETAINER.

Your majesty, each would lay down his life
To purchase safety and repose for yours;
And him whom we deem detrimental to you
We would destroy.

SAUL.

     We understand each other.
Now go.
         [Exeunt RETAINERS.
  Ay, go, ye hypocrites; begone.
I could perceive they mocked me:—they 'll to David.
Well, let them go: and when they here return,
Should I discover in them aught amiss,
I'll send their ghosts to shew the way to his.
            [Exit.

SCENE IV.

An apartment in the House of David.
Enter JONATHAN, DAVID, *and* MICHAL.

JONATHAN.

Dear sister, for a while retire; for I
Have with me business to which no ear
Save David's must be privy.

MICHAL.

      Business
Should be transacted in its proper place:

The mart's for traffic, and the council chamber
Or royal closet for the State's great secrets.

JONATHAN.

Wise sister, leave us, for I must not tarry.

MICHAL.

I am most glad of that. Be light your theme
As brief, for I count you here a trespasser.

[*Exit* MICHAL.

JONATHAN.

David, I've heavy news for thee.

DAVID.

What, is the evil spirit on the king?

JONATHAN.

Nay, worse.

DAVID.

He is not dead?

JONATHAN.

No, but he seeks thy life; and now not in
His blind, demented fury, as I fear,
But in a cool, absurd antipathy.—
Nay look not so incredulous; 'tis true.
So hide thyself forthwith until the morning;
When I will join my father, as he takes
His early airing, and will speak of thee,
And tell thee afterwards what I have gathered.

DAVID.

Oh, my divining eyes! I saw he'd evil
Within him toward me ere I left the palace.

JONATHAN.

Leave here, too, quickly; hide thyself at once:
For his resolves are like unto sharp arrows
Already on the bowstring, and, whilst others aim,
His thoughts in deeds are shot.

DAVID.

                    I know his promptness:
I know too, that, of late, he loathes or fears me;

Me, who am ever prompt to risk my life
That his may not be perilled.

JONATHAN.
                    Speak not thus: but
Go, since thou knowest his act pursues his word,
As thunder lightning;—yea, far surer, for
Oft the report doth fail the flash, but never
His execution does his threatening.
Take not thy leave of Michal; I'll excuse
Thee to her. Go conceal thyself till morning;
Whilst I return and watch my sire, to save thee.

DAVID.
Far keener this than the Philistines' swords!
                                        [Exit.

JONATHAN.
He's in an evil and a bitter mood:—
But deep the sting goes of ingratitude.
                                        [Exit.

SCENE V.

The grounds of the Palace. Time, morning.
SAUL *and* JONATHAN *walking together.*

SAUL.
Wherefore art thou so silent?

JONATHAN.
                          Heavy thoughts
Hang on my spirit, as those murky clouds
Hang on the horizon; and as the sun's rays
Cannot now reach the vapor-covered ground,
Cannot my sorrow reach, in words, your ears.

SAUL.
What meanest thou?

JONATHAN.
                I have a sister Michal.

SAUL.

Thou hast, and what of that?

JONATHAN.

And she a husband.

SAUL.

I know it.

JONATHAN.

Whom you do wish assassinated.

SAUL.

Cover the conception with a fairer word;
And bring not unto me, in bloody grave-clothes,
The corse of David.

JONATHAN.

Deed as foul as that
Which, yesterday, was unto me suggested
Cannot be styled fair. Things are the same,
However daintily the tongue approach them.
Bitter is bitter, though the lips be not
Allowed to wry themselves thereat. Oh, father,
Let us not do that which we dare not mention,
And, for our future days, beget a monster
Of which the embryo merely and foreshadow
Already horrifies us. My dear father,
Towards David change your mind; and let down drop
To hell the vile suggestion, whence it came.

SAUL.

Thou knowest not what thou sayest; peace.

JONATHAN.

There is no peace when the black storm is muttering.
You would o'erwhelm our house by this foul deed;
Would so affront the cloud and wind of heaven,
That its already lowering indignation
Should burst and deluge you, your wife, and children
And in its whirlwind overturn your throne.

SAUL.

Thinkest thou so?

JONATHAN
                         Oh, think on his good deeds
Towards you and towards us all; think how his life
He jeopardised with the giant,—alone he slew him,
And none thereat did more rejoice than you.
He hath done you no ill since, but fought your foes,
While you have slept unperilled; and when here,
Back from the violent field and harsh alarms,
How fondly flows the music of his harp
To heal or sooth your ailment! You have no child
Of your own blood who is more dutiful;
And if your people love him, you no less
They love; but ever since he wed my sister,
His glory goes to augment the common stock
Of the young, royal house and dynasty,
Whereof yourself foundation are and root.
Why should you wish him slain then? Slay me and Michal;
But bring not on yourself and on our line
Their curse who shed a benefactor's blood.

SAUL.
Prythee no more; I have relented:
Though tenderness towards him, perhaps, is harshness
Towards thee and all our house. His life is safe.

JONATHAN.
And safer is our house, since this offence
Shall not rot its foundation.

SAUL.
                       Go thy way;
It was for this thou joinedst me.   [*Exit* JONATHAN.
                       We are weakest
When we are caught contending with our children!
Not tongue of wisest minister, nor his own
Persuasive lips, that emulate the strings
Of his own harp, himself in agony,
With wet and upturned eyes, upon his knees,
Pleading for life, could ever thus have turned me.
Let him bring David to me; I'll receive him.   [*Exit.*

END OF THE FIRST ACT.

ACT II.

SCENE I.

Gibeah. The Courtyard of the Palace.
Enter Two Officers *of the Royal household.*

FIRST OFFICER.

'Tis said that the Philistines,
Those restless dwellers near the salty main,
Again are pushing inland.   As the rain
From their own bounding ocean sweeps our plains,
So do their light troops recommence to shower
Over our border.

SECOND OFFICER.

　　　　　　　　David is departed,
To drive them back as quickly as they came.
David is to them as a mountain which
The clouds must clear ere they can feed old Jordan.
They break themselves against him, whilst he stands
Unbroken, and hurls their remnant home like scattered
Vapors, that, at a change of wind, return
To fall in drops again into the sea.

FIRST OFFICER.

They are a dangerous race, and sleep in armour.
One hand for lucre is, and for the sword
The other,—
　　　　　[*Enter a* COURIER *crossing the court-yard in haste.*
　　　　　What news?   Pray tell us in a breath.

COURIER.

David again hath overthrown the enemy.

SECOND OFFICER.
So soon?
FIRST OFFICER.
We dreamed not he had met them yet.
COURIER.
He fell upon them, and, through their own blood,
Drove them half drowned in slaughter.—Stay me not:
This news is for the hearing of the king;
And afterwards the town may with it ring. [*Exit* COURIER.

SECOND OFFICER.
Oh, David, valiant captain, wise and young!
FIRST OFFICER.
The king is swift, but David swifter still.
SECOND OFFICER.
He rises suddenly as doth the whirlwind,
And leaves us wondering at his prompt achievement;
Even as we wonder at the smoking ruin
The lightning has just made before our eyes.
Let's to the city, and there spread the news. [*Exeunt.*

SCENE II.

The Palace. A room commanding a view of the streets; SAUL, *pacing to and fro, and an* ATTENDANT *standing near a window. Acclamation without.*

SAUL.
What noise is that?
ATTENDANT.
                    It is a gathering crowd,
Shouting at the approach of David, who
Again victorious comes. They throw their turbans
Into the air until 'tis filled with them.
The streets are filling with the people, that
Thereinto flow like sea-waves into dykes
Whose sluices are drawn up; that soon they'll be
No more paved streets, but one hugh, head-paved sea.

SAUL.

Now get thee gone; I do no longer need thee.
            [Exit ATTENDANT.
I swear again that he shall die! Why did
I spare him when before I had so sworn?
Why have I sworn his life should be held sacred
To please that fool, his fond dupe, Jonathan?
I'll break all oaths
If they shall stand between me and my will.
Let Jonathan beware, or he may suffer
By standing between David and my fury.
    [Exit, and enter MALZAH *from the opposite side.*

MALZAH.

Now surely he'll kill David, and so end
My slavery; for I will enter him
On wings of blackest murder, and so fuse
With him in his infuriated mood,
That we will work together as one soul.
 [Exit, and enter DAVID *in armour in company with the* QUEEN.

QUEEN.

Oh, thou art welcomer than the tidings were
That told us of thy victory! Thou hast wings
Surely, and hastened to our nest, as though
Thou knewest the king would need thee. To him straight;
For he is tending towards his old distemper,
And in yon airy turret, like an eagle,
Now sits alone black-brooding.   *[Exeunt.*

SAUL.
Entering, having thrown a javelin at DAVID, *who has escaped as before.*

Now may a palsy light upon this arm,
For it has lost its skill!
He came unto his doom,—pshaw, pshaw, I've marred it!
But I will hound him out where'er he be.
       [Enter an OFFICER *and* SOLDIERS.
Go seize the avenues to David's house,
And slay him as he issues in the morning.
       [Exeunt OFFICER *and* SOLDIERS.

Now am I filled with malice to the crown;
'Till I've no room for pity, nor can enter
Thaw-wind at crack or cranny of my frame,
To melt my frozen heart into remorse.
All kindness' fire is out, all's dark i'th' house:
But I will grope unerring to my victim;
Toward whom I now will be as stern as are
The elements of nature, that ne'er swerve
From their fixed attributes for mortal thing.
How shall I wait till morn doth tidings bring!

MALZAH (*entering*).

Let me hide myself forever as a bungler!
I am ashamed, and Saul too is ashamed.

SAUL.

Why did my arm so shake?—it was not weak,
But as surcharged with strange, unnatural force.

MALZAH.

Ha, ha!
He herein not suspects me; I'm not blamed.
Let me not laugh;—indeed, I cannot laugh.
Ah, weary; I shall never more be cheerful.
I cannot laugh nor sing, and weep I will not;
Yet, had I the gift of rhythm and of rhyme,
Sighs should keep measure, and dropped tears beat time.
Oh, for an eye of water,—tongue of fire!
Go, go! go, go!
I cannot howl divinely, nor laugh uncouthly,
As some do in their agony; I cannot whine;
Nor will I rave as others: I am dumb,
Impatient waiting for the things to come.

SAUL.

Would I could sleep, or die, till it were done!
I'll get to bed.

[*Exit.*

MALZAH.

      Ay, prythee do, poor king.
Whither go I? shall I hang i'th' spider's web,

And therein sleep; or take the feline form,
And wink and doze upon the eaves i'th' moonlight?
Oh, to lie down on th' marge of fabulous Lethe!
Or with Peyona on a bank in hell,
Where fiery flowers bloom in unholy dell! [*Exit.*

SCENE III.

An upper room in DAVID'S *house. Time, night.*
A lamp burning.

MICHAL (*discovered seated*).

Cease, ye vile wars, ye perillers of his life.
Cease, ye fierce foes, or David cease to quell you.
Out of my sky, ye war-clouds, roll away,
That into night again have turned my day.
Ye purple-robed and rich inhabitants,
That populous make the margent of the sea,
Peace, and restore my husband unto me.

[*Enter* DAVID.

My prayer i'th' instant answered? It is he:—
Oh, David, do I clasp thee once again?
Let me look on thee: 'tis an apparition:—
Oh, 'tis the apparition that I love!
Yes, I now hold thee: art thou here unscathed?

DAVID.

The Lord in my last peril did stand by me.

MICHAL.

Oh, season of disquiet turned to joy!
This hour for days requites me: Sit, love, sit.
They tell me that I am too fond of thee.
Perhaps I am;—and yet not fond enough.
Oh, thou art dear unto me;—yet wert not
Dear, wert thou purchased with tenfold such fondness!
But let them talk, who know not what they say;
For what care I for prudes who never knew
Illapse into the lunacy of love.—

Oh, but you look most soberly to-night.
Come, get these soiled accoutrements from off thee;
Love will not dally in such horrid gear.
Let me unbind thy sandals: now I vow
That were it not for their dear wearer's sake,
I'd burn them for that they have borne thee so far from me.
Give me thy helmet;—I could burn it too,
But for the head 't has shielded. Fie on war:
It is the foulest pastime that you men
Delight in.—Ah, how easily I take
Thy casque from where it sits so seemingly.
I do remember when I had to climb
Ere I could take my father's from his brow.
Stay, let's dispose these war-disordered locks :—
Nay, do not think my lips shall challenge yours,
For 'twere a pity to disturb their silence.
Oh, but you'll talk when I have done, I know.
You are o'erspent by this last swoop; but thou
My eagle art in thy nest, nor shalt thou leave it
Till downiest embraces have repaid thee
For half the iron rigors of the war.

Enter a female SERVANT, *and stands by the door:* MICHAL *goes to her.*

SERVANT (*in an under-tone*).

Oh, my dear Princess!

MICHAL.

Well, what now?

SERVANT.

The king
Your father has beset the house with soldiers;
So that when out my master goes at morn,
They may at once arrest him.

MICHAL.

'Tis the old madding:
Get thee to bed.

SERVANT.

Pray let me watch with you:
They say the king projects our master's death.

MICHAL.

No; get to bed.

[*Exit* SERVANT.

[*Aside.*] Now what new demon's this?
'Tis the last spirit of ingratitude,
Come from the thawless region of the north.
What can be done in such dilemma? I know
'Tis dangerous to trifle with my father.
Oh, it is foul, 'tis foul of him, 'tis foul!—
And in this wild, desiring hour too;
Even in the white robe of my exultation,
To come and crape me over with black weeds;
Make me a widow in reality,
Which, all for him, I've half been since my nuptials.
My lord shall stay; my father dares not touch him:—
And yet I know not what he dares not do.
Miserable lunatic! [*Aloud.*] Oh, David, David,
I fear, I fear that thou, my own sweet singer,
My bird just to my bosom, must this night
Break from the cage and compass of my arms!

DAVID.

What hath she told thee? tell me what hath happened.

MICHAL.

Nay, nay, I cannot think but that thou knowest it.
'Tis but a little : save thyself to-night,
Or else to-morrow it may be too late.
My father's ta'en a fancy to thy death,
And round the house has posted guards to take thee
As thou goest out i'th' morning. I see thou knewest.
Well, get thee gone.

DAVID.

I was prepared for this.
Oh, Michal, I do fear that now no spirit,
Except his own, doth animate thy father.
We will not chide him; but thyself art witness
Whether I have ever breathed against him wrong.

He seeks my life for naught,—except, indeed,
I do offend him by exposing it
So much for him and his.   Weep not till I
Am gone.
MICHAL.
Thou shalt not go:—
No, let him come himself; I will withstand him.
DAVID.
He is thy father, and the Lord's anointed.
Let's pity and forgive him; but 'tis hard
For me to leave thee to the fury of
His disappointed malice, which, to-morrow,
Will break against thee in a storm of anger.
Now let us kiss and take our sudden farewell.
There, there; no more endearments: fare thee well.
The worst seems passed. Thy kiss thy love-pledge be,
And mine the sign thy sire's forgiven by me.
Now, let me down I pray thee, from the balcony,
That in the darkness I may 'scape in safety.
MICHAL.
Tarry yet.
DAVID.
I will, if thou desire it.
MICHAL.
Oh, no; go.
Thou art not safe a moment in this house;
For if my father should bethink him, he
Would come at once himself and seize upon thee.
Away!
DAVID.
[*They advance to the balcony.*
The heavens seem one archangel! the countless stars
Appear to me as many cherubs' eyes
That watch, love, for my safety. God is yonder,
Although I see him not, and looking down
Benignly; and where'er I go, be it
By night or day, in Canaan or beyond it,
He will watch o'er and keep me.
[MICHAL *lowers him from the balcony.*

MICHAL.

Oh, now come night indeed, and let hoarse thunders
Bellow and drown my cries. Ye lightnings, shoot;
Let, through the black waste of the frosty air,
Your flashes reach and blind this wicked father!
No tears;—I will not weep; but I will howl,
Ay, howl my fill, for vengeance and for David.
Covered with martial glory;—oh, let hell's smoke
Blacken it, rather than it gild my sire!—
Ere on my lips had died the congratulations;
While the hot kisses that he meeting gave me
Thereon yet live in feeling;—can it be?
I have been dreaming all this half hour, surely,
And am not yet awake: David, ho, David,—
Oh, let me now be stifled, or I shall
Awake the slumbering echoes of the night,
Till David's name shall ring 'midst Gibeah,
And he return to ask me why is this.
So little time! so much to have been done!
But now he went to meet the enemy;
But now he did pursue the flying foe:
He's now pursued himself. Oh, these but nows!
He's homeless now; his home hath cast him out.
Ingratitude! Nay, nay,
The wolves methinks thus drive not forth their cubs.
Oh, I could rend my insane father's form,
And let him see I too can play the fury.
Is he the king? Then am I not his daughter?
Is not my husband I? Oh, horrible
Dispatch!—No more, no more of that; I feel
I, too, have rising in me a foul spirit.
Silence, poor Michal; know thy proud reunion,
Thy sunrise of new nuptials, is bleak night,
Thy marriage black divorce. Saul, father, but
I will not curse thee;—no, but I will chide him,
And rate him, at my pleasure, with my tears.
Has he forgotten his partings with my mother?

And how he kissed me and my sister Merab,
Erst ere he went to battle? Has he forgot
All that? forgot his wife and children? all?
Has he forgot who charmed him from the demon?
                      [*After weeping in silence.*
I will deceive this madman parent now;
I shall be justified: I will deceive him,
And any whom he may hereto dispatch:
For in the stead of him whom I had thought
That I this night should shelter in my arms,
Yet now is lurking shelterless and cold,
I'll place a senseless image in the bed;
And when my father's messengers ask for him,
I'll say that he is sick, and so say truth;
For he is sick, and sick they'll see am I.
I'll do it, and so gain breathing for my husband.

SCENE IV.

A room in the Palace. Time, morning.

SAUL.

'Tis now past daybreak, and he rises early.
Hath he escaped them too? or does his fond
Wife Michal hold him thralled, to take her fill
Of his fair body after her brief fasting?
Poor child, she soon will have more fasting; for
I will not break my fast till it be done.
                [*Enter the* OFFICER *and* SOLDIERS.
How now? Where is he? Have you left him dead?

OFFICER.

Your majesty, he is sick, so Michal says,
And keeps his bed.

SAUL.

           Back with you instantly;
And bring him to us on his bed, that we

May do unto him what you should have done.—
You have not seen him, have you?

OFFICER.

Your majesty, no.

SAUL.

So thought we. Go; 'tis a convenient sickness:
But he shall yet be sicker. Away with you.

[*Exeunt* OFFICER *and* SOLDIERS.

Away, white thoughts! how can I let him live?
See how the sun comes up in fulgent red,
And shews what is my course's proper hue.
Now if they bring him not, I'll slay them also.

[*Enter a* SERVANT.

Is the Queen stirring?

SERVANT.

She is, your majesty.

SAUL.

Tell her that I am better: bid her keep
Her chamber. [*Exit* SERVANT.
'Tis not meet that she should witness
His death; for she would raise such stout resistance
That I might kill her too; and then,—why then
I should destroy myself, and all for nothing,
Except my own damnation: then I'd done
At least one murder,—for I will not count
The killing of mine enemy a murder;
But, oh, to kill her were to kill ten friends.
Shall I wait here and let him perhaps escape me?
No, to the fiends go all compunction; now
I go to seize him in his den, and send
His soul whereunto souls departed wend.

[*Exit.*

SCENE V.

A corridor and staircase in David's house.
MICHAL, *the* OFFICER *and* SOLDIERS, *near the door of David's bedchamber.*

MICHAL.

But that you stand as proxies of my father,
I, with these woman's hands, would hurl you down.
For shame, like brutal ruffians to attempt
To violate the chamber of the sick.—
Nay, if you will, you enter over me.

OFFICER.

Lady, refrain; because, e'en as you've said,
We represent the king; and dare not to him
Return unless we have your husband.

MICHAL.

Take him, then, if you find him.

[*The* OFFICER *and* SOLDIERS *enter the bedchamber.*

FIRST SOLDIER (*within*).

Here is no David, only an image, abed !
And far less fair than he too. He is gone.

SECOND SOLDIER.

Now there will be the king's best rage to do ;
And help him will his demon.

THIRD SOLDIER.

Oh, these women,
They are the very devil for cunning ! See you,
How she has helped the lame dog o'er the stile !
A bolster of goat's hair, and cloth o'er all !
We must not tell the king that he's escaped :
He'd javelin us.

[*Re-enter the* OFFICER *and* SOLDIERS.

OFFICER.

Good princess, tell us sooth ;
Where is your husband ? for the king will have him.

MICHAL.

Good! Should I now be good were I to tell you?
Let the king come himself and question me;
I'll answer you no farther.

[*A noise heard below.*

SECOND SOLDIER.
       He is here.

OFFICER.

Now pray, your highness, do not mock your father;
For he is in a very fatal humour.

[*Enter* SAUL.

SAUL.

How now, unduteous? let me see thy husband.
They tell me he is sick, and I've a cure for him.

MICHAL.

Ah, little care you for him, sick or cured;
He who has cured you ere now in your sickness.
He is not here.

SAUL.
    Minion, what hast thou done?

MICHAL.

My duty unto him who claims it foremost.

SAUL.

That is myself; that is thy father, Michal;
That is thy sovereign. Tell me where he is.

MICHAL.

I know not where he is; I know not you,
I know no father, and I know no sovereign,
Who would compel me not to know my husband:
For to reveal him now were to forget him.
But go, O man, and let me see no more
Those horrid looks. I know not where he is,
For you have driven him from me; and may he
Never return to do you further service,
Ungrateful man!—Nay, I can bear thy frown;

For I've beheld this moment on thy face
My husband's murder. Ah, I know your heart;
I know what your intent was;—but he's gone;
So do your worst on me, for I am bold
As you this hour are barbarous.

SAUL.

      Spoiled child,
Be not too bold, nor trust the o'erstrained tie
Of consanguinity. I find thou art bad
As he: take in thy sail in time, sweet craft.
You are two vessels pressed on by one storm:
And though he has slipped his cable and is scudding
Before the wind, dream thou not tempt the sea;
For I, his storm, at anchor will retain thee,
And may too blow upon thee to thy hurt,—
Yea, for aught I know, sink thee. Whither hath
He fled, girl?

MICHAL.

    No where. He would scorn to flee;
He left this at his leisure.

SAUL.

     Oh, thou viper!
      [*Attempts to seize her.*

OFFICER, *rushing between them and holding* SAUL.

Your majesty, be calmed.—Oh, now between you
I, a poor soldier, stand, and in this breach,
Here in this royal and unnatural quarrel,
Perhaps may fall:—e'en let me fall; but, oh,
Israel, lead not thus to the assault
On that fair citadel your august self;
Nor us command who now would follow you,
Against our enemies, on any hope,
Howe'er forlorn.

SAUL.

   She is mine enemy!

OFFICER.

Oh no, my liege; but now be calm. Remember
Whilst you thus wrangle David is escaping.
Oh, king, be calmed. I dare not liberate you,
Although I know this all a mockery;
That in your grasp myself would be a sparrow
Within the clutching talons of an eagle.
Forgive me, oh, forgive this sacrilege,
In having laid hands on the Lord's Anointed!
But 'tis to hinder you from desecrating
That graceful wing of your own hallowed temple:
I but restrain you from yourself. See how
She weeps. Oh, there is much excuse for her:
All creatures madden when they are bereaved.
She is your daughter, and this hardy spirit
Of hers is but a fragment from the rock
Of your own steadfast soul, that hath withstood
Both foes from desert and from salty flood.

SAUL.

Unhand me now; I'm calmed.
These women are the marplots of our lives,
For when we will they will not. Are all wives
Of such a kidney?

OFFICER.

      My liege knows, and others
Know, that her mother is gentle as the dove;
And that herself is playful as the lamb
When sunshine's on her pasture. If she bleats now,
Why 'tis her nature, and the gift of women;
Whose tongues, amidst the sweet strains of their music,
Will sound sometimes a flat or a harsh discord.

SAUL.

Tell me, thou false one, whither has fled thy husband.

MICHAL.

He did not tell me where he meant to go.
I cannot tell; and if I could I would not:

So there are double bars upon my lips.
And should you kill me and take out my heart,
That you might look into its closet, you'll
Not find him in it, though he will be there.

SAUL.

Now, by the furnace of mine anger's fires,
To which thou addest fuel, speak not thus,
For fear I take thy life instead of his;—
Yea, having, impious, tasted of such blood,
I then, from very piety, pursue him,
And, having overta'en him, take his life
As an atonement for thy illtimed death.
Whither hath thy husband fled to? say.

MICHAL.
        Would you
Have me to drag my husband forth to slaughter?

SAUL.

Tell me, or yet I'll yield thee to my vengeance;
That, when he comes to find thee, it shall be
With him as even now with me, he'll find
The one he seeks for missing.

MICHAL.
        Thus he said,
When I would have restrained him, (thus you place me
Between two meeting perils of fire and water,)
He said unto me fiercely, " Let me go ;
For wherefore should I kill thee ?"

SAUL.
        This is falshoood;
For thou wouldst harness for him the untamed winds,
And yoke them to the chariot of the night,
For his escape, so much thou dost affect him.
Avaunt! I'll watch; and if thou succour him,
I will not say to thee what I will do,
But my frame shudders at the unuttered deed.
Come on! he shall be hunted.
    [*Exeunt* SAUL, OFFICER, *and* SOLDIERS.

MICHAL.

Oh, hard to bear! a husband's mortal hazard;
A father darkly threatening me with murder,
For what else could he hint at? Oh, too much
To have to bear this sudden load of suffering!
Yet not enough to bear for thee, my David;
My David laden by my ingrate father.
Oh, David, loved more by me than's my father:
Oh, altered father; oh, now lawless man!
Yes, yes, let Saul return, let Saul return,
And rage against me like the storm 'gainst Carmel,
Yea, seize me by the hair and drag me to his feet,—
As the grim tempest might the battlements
Of his own palace, and dash them in the dust,—
I would not tell him of one rood (did I know it)
Of the way, David, that thou wentest. [*Exit.*

END OF THE SECOND ACT.

ACT III.

SCENE I.

Gibeah. A Room in the Palace.
SAUL *and a* COURTIER.

SAUL.

Why lingerest thou, if business be done?
Why must I bid thee go? I've little taste
Now left for gossip when affairs are ended.
What hast thou on thy tongue, that thus thou standest
With parted lips yet silent?

COURTIER.

Your majesty,
David now dwells with Samuel in Naioth.

SAUL.

Ah, he crops out at last! Go thou, and take
Soldiers along with thee, and bring him hither.
If thou but render him to me, alive or dead,
I'll put live honors blooming on thy head.
[*Exit* COURTIER.
I'll follow him unto the utmost corner
O'th' earth, but I will have him in my power;
And when that is, he troubles me no more.
I know this parasite will hold him hard;
For what will not men do for a reward!
[*Exit.*

SCENE II.

The borders of a grove at Naioth. Samuel and a company of young prophets chaunting.

Enter the COURTIER *and* SOLDIERS *with* MALZAH *in the midst of them.*

MALZAH.

I'm now become the veriest drudge,
From Gibeah to Naioth made to trudge:
And all to be a pitchpipe to these fellows.
Oh, to be leader unto such a choir!
Why brought they not with them the town-crier?
This seems a very mockery of my woes.—
But what needs must be must be, so here goes.

Air by MALZAH, *the* COURTIER, *and* SOLDIERS.

In this retreat doth Levi dwell,
And welcomes him who came distressed;
Amidst these sacred scenes, awhile
The fugitive doth safely rest.
Here we would rest and praise the Lord,
At ordered hour, with sweet accord!

MALZAH (*aside*).

Never greater lie was spoken by me and you,
Ye fag-end and subservient crew,
That will to aught your voices screw!

SAMUEL.

Who and whence are you, that, conspiring, come
To these sequestered and religious shades,
Intent to mock our rites?

MALZAH (*aside*).

                I mock not them
Nor thee, prophetic, hoar, and reverend being,
Who, in the majesty of virtue, standest,
Here in this still recess and wooded vale,
Serenely girt by thy young ministering band;

Even as the midnight moon, when it, full orbed,
Hangs in the heaven's blue hall, what time the night,
Along with it and some selectest stars,
Holds court unseen by the dull, slumbering world;—
But I am wrath, and will sweep through these men
Like lightning, so that they not breathe again.

[MALZAH *vanishes, and the* COURTIER *and* SOLDIERS *drop to the ground.*

MALZAH (*again visible*).

I have not power their life to spill:
I hear them loudly breathing still.
And, lo, Zelehtha through the air
To Gibeah warns me to repair:—
Oh, to be dragged against my will,
To be her moping vassal there!
[*Exit.*

SAMUEL.

The Lord hath visited them: they are from Saul,
And for his sake thus wrought on: let them lie.
[*Exeunt* SAMUEL *and the young prophets.*

SCENE III.

Gibeah. A room in the Palace.
Enter SAUL *and the* COURTIER.

SAUL.

You fell to prophesying? then take others.

COURTIER.

Your majesty, we lay upon the ground
A long hour senseless.

SAUL.
　　　　　　Take ten chosen men,
Or twenty if thou wilt, that fear no mortal;
(For there are such;) choose such as do respect
Nor God nor prophets; twenty take of such,
And haste thee bring here David.　　[*Exit* COURTIER.

                              I will send—
If these should fall like to the former ones—
Unto that treason-hatching den of Naioth,
Till all my army lie entranced around
Its circling woods, as rank as soon the leaves
Will lie around them, spread by biting gales.
                                                   [*Exit.*

    MALZAH (*entering*).
 Again to Naioth I crawl,
 To teach a score of knaves to drawl!
 But whether holy psalm it be,
 Or a chant of irony,
 Hangs on chance or change of wind,
 Or humour of Jehovah's mind.
 I hear the crew!
 I must pursue;—
 Ah, something tragic yet I'll do.
                                                   [*Exit.*

SCENE IV.

The same. Time, the following day.
Enter SAUL *and the* COURTIER.

    SAUL.
Sayest thou these latter also prophesied,
And sunk even as the others to the ground,
After a sudden rhapsody?

    COURTIER.
                              I do, O king.
Though of them and affected like unto them,
I saw them with these eyes, and with these ears
Heard their hard breathings and their broken mutterings.
Except those heavy and uneasy signs,
A day and night we lay there as if dead;
Cold 'midst the fervour of the noontide sun,
And 'neath the pinching of the freezing moon
No colder, but a frost like that of death
Suffering while yet we lived,—for sure we lived.

SAUL.

Did you not wish to die then?—but you live.
Go back and lead on fifty. Pick thy men
Of various spirit; so that naught there be
Of sympathy between their fears or wills,
Whereby they feel as one though they be many.
Now hasten with thy mongrel band away,
And better luck than with the former stay.
                                              [*Exit* COURTIER.
This is the very workmanship of fear.
They carry thither a bugbear in their souls,
And fall, at length, before it. Yet how know I
But that some evil spirit may be busy
With them as still with me? I'll strive to sleep:—
Strive, did I say? There was a time when sleep
Was wont to approach me with her soundless feet,
And take me by surprise. I called her not,
And yet she'd come; but now I even woo her,
And court her by the cunning use of drugs,
But still she will not turn to me her steps;
Not even to approach, and, looking down,
Drop on these temples one oblivious tear.
I that am called a king, whose word is law,—
Awake I lie and toss, while the poor slave,
Whom I have taken prisoner in my wars,
Sleeps soundly; and he who hath sold himself to service,
Although his cabin rock beneath the gale,
Hears not the uproar of the night, but, smiling,
Dreams of the year of jubilee. I would that I
Could sleep at night; for then I should not hear
Ahinoam, poor grieved one, sighing near.   [*Exit.*

SCENE V.

The same.

MALZAH, *entering and crossing the room.*
Now here's the king in a pretty rage,
And something rich I do presage;

For his fifty fools I felled like trees,
Fools of various degrees.
Fifty fools with fifty fears,
May they lie there fifty years,
Night and day in groans and tears.

SAUL (*entering*).

These last too have succumbed! Three several bands!
What can be in the world, that the tough sinews
Of stubborn men should slacken, till their owners
Sink to the earth, and, grovelling, lie thereon,
Like trees, that, rotten at the core, have fallen,
Even in the prime and stiffness of their years,
To slander the whole forest? Why stay I here?
I'll face this mystic influence myself,
And dare it to o'erthrow me.

MALZAH.

Well, I'll be there, although thou shalt not know me.
[*Exeunt severally.*

SCENE VI.

The Border of the grove at Naioth. SAMUEL *and the Sons of the Prophets.*
Enter SAUL, *followed by some Attendants.*

SAUL.

Vile man, once more see Saul amongst the prophets!
Am I, like others, come to be demented?
Come hither, Samuel. Now, by my sword,
Which I throw from me, and which thou may'st take
Up, and on me, on Saul, play Agag with it,
What wouldst thou do? Down thou too, shield. Ay, bellow;—
I dash down thee. Off, helmet, off! Ay, crack
And roll away, and take the king's head in thee.
Now in the air I stand uncovered, doffed
Before thee and thy disappointed Levites!—

What, am I not yet naked? yet more skins?
Off, off, ye comfortable robes! off, off!
Why should I lie 'neath you and have your shelter,
When all the flowers o'th' forest can lie bare?
Rust there, my armour, ye my garments, rot;
For Saul himself is, yet himself is not.
　　　　　　　　　　[*Sinks on the ground senseless.*
　　　　　　　SAMUEL.
Now take him up, and watch him till he wake.
He suffers this for his rebellion's sake.
Exeunt the Attendants, carrying SAUL, *and the Prophets, softly chanting a solemn strain; then* MALZAH *enters and crosses the stage.*
　　　　　　　MALZAH.
　'Twas featly done!
　And more adroit than I is none.—
　Ha, ha! ha, ha! let them begone.

END OF THE THIRD ACT.

ACT IV.

SCENE I.

Gibeah. An apartment in the house of JONATHAN. *Time, dusk.*
Enter JONATHAN *and* DAVID.

DAVID.

What have I done, what fault have I committed,
Wherein have I offended 'gainst thy father,
That he doth thus persist against my life?

JONATHAN.

No, not in peril is thy life, dear friend.
I know my father will do nothing, David,
Or great or small, without my knowledge; hence
I know he would reveal to me this purpose,
If he did entertain it.

DAVID.
      Jonathan,
As I now swear to thee that it is true,
So hath thy father sworn to take my life;
But being aware that I have thy good will,
He hath not told thee, knowing how 'twould grieve thee:
Yet, certainly as the Almighty liveth,
And as thyself dost living stand before me,
There is but one poor step 'twixt me and death.

JONATHAN.

Oh, David, thine's a hard, unhappy case,
Exposed unto the jealousy of a madman,
Who, 'twixt the demon and the changing moon,
Veers like a creaking vane from side to side.

And still, although he thrice hath sought thy life,
I deem not that 'tis now imperilled: yet
Tell me how I can help thee, for whatever
Thou'dst have me now to do for thee I will.

DAVID.

Then hear me, and perform for me this favor.
To-morrow 'tis new moon, and I should eat
At table with the king; but let me go,
And in the environs conceal myself,
Until the third day's evening. If his majesty
Miss me, then to him say, " David most earnestly
Sought leave of me to hie to Beth-lehem,
Where now is due an annual sacrifice
For all his family." Now, if he shall say
"'Tis well," then am I safe; but if he's angry,
Thou shalt be sure he means to do me evil.
But, Jonathan, act thou with candour towards me,
For sake of that high compact which we made
At Ephis-dammim: still, if I deserve it,
Slay me thyself; betray me not to the king.

JONATHAN.

And am I then so black? Ah, thought unkind!
Dost thou, then, think that I could prove so faithless?
No, far from me be that.—Oh, David, David,
Was I not first to warn thee heretofore?
And if I knew for certain that my father
Now meant thee malice, should I hide it from thee?

DAVID.

Forgive me, Jonathan, what I have uttered
In the forgetfulness of my spirit's sorrow:—
But who shall tell me if it be not so?
And what if Saul should yield thee a rough answer?

JONATHAN.

Listen:
When I to-morrow, or 'tween then and the third day,

Shall have my father sounded touching thee,
If I should find he means towards thee no ill,
And tell thee not, may God in kind requite me;
But if I find that he still bears thee malice,
I'll send thee safely hence,—and may the Lord
Be with thee as He once was with my father.
But let us go abroad, and, in the twilight's
Cool, tranquillizing air, discuss this matter.

[*Exeunt.*

SCENE II.

The Armoury in the Palace. Time, immediately succeding that of the last scene.

Enter SAUL *in haste, seeking to escape from* MALZAH, *who enters close behind him.*

MALZAH.

Here's a dead calm and blank now in our being.
I will have entertainment; sing or wail!
Give voice now, else I'll rack thee to a pitch,
And screw thy nerves and tendons to a height
Beyond all human gamut save thine own;
Then fret and play upon thee till thou sweatest,
And screamest hatefuller than the peacock doth,
And uglier growest before my cruel eyes
Than is the gray rat or the pimpled toad.
Sing, or I straight will enter thee perforce,
And squeal myself, not solely through thy mouth,
But also through thy nostrils, eyes, and ears;
Yea, rant and bellow out at every pore.

SAUL.

Now, desperation, aid me! Monster, hence!
Or, for that thin and incorporeal form,
Be solid man, and so, grown vulnerable,
Forth challenge me to the wood; or, in this paved,
Resounding hall, come on with arms and armour,
And he who fails shall be the other's slave.

MALZAH (*going*).
Ho, ho! ho, ho! was ever such a Saul!

SAUL.
Stay, stay, I bid thee; let this commerce end.
Tarry, bad Apparition; linger.—Ah,
Like to a star that fades away at morn,
Out at the gate it glimmers:—it yet looms:—
'T has vanished.
How long shall this strange creature persecute me!
Perhaps I'm a sinner in some other sort
Than yet I have suspected.
[*Re-enter* MALZAH.
Monster, hence;
Begone, Infernal Shadow, to Gehenna,
Or take thy winging way beyond the desert,
Or sink into the centre of the earth,
If thou have any right to inhabit longer
A world that's walked by man.

MALZAH.
Ha, ha! ha, ha! ha, ha!
[*Exeunt severally.*

SCENE III.

The apartment in the house of JONATHAN. *Time, immediately succeeding that of the last scene.*

JONATHAN.
Come in, for the chill zephyrs fan me sadder.
Come in; and do not doubt my faithfulness,
Although I be thine enemy's son. Be cheered,
For thou in turn must now cheer me. David,
I could now prophesy, but let me not
Anticipate a melancholy doom.—
Answer me not, but now let me bemoan me;
Grant me the privilege of sorrow; for I

Feel that the fortune of our house is cast,
And that I never can be king in Israel.
And as I know not whether I again
Shall view thee, but in this dim instant see
Distinct the vision of thy future greatness,
Not during my day only shalt thou shew
Forbearance, and my life consider sacred,
But thy regard shall cease not towards my family
When I lie rotting in the sepulchre,
And when in Israel thou hast no foe
Unconquered, uncut off.   Swear that unto me.

DAVID.

I swear it, Jonathan.   But why ?

JONATHAN.

Oh, ask not.
Dread hath this moment hold upon me, David,
And horror rounds me like a dismal night,
Till I am even timorous as a child.
Yea, for my children am I timorous ;
'Tis for my offspring that I now feel dread :
For thou at length, like all, must be no more ;
And then thy children will be found with mine,
Saul's hate remembered but my love forgotten.
Hence blame me not for sore anxiety ;
But swear, in the strange name of the unborn,
Hereditary friendship ; swear to me again,
For, not for mine own sake but my dear children's,
I'd bind thee to me doubly in oaths' bonds.

DAVID.

Ah, why require now oaths like these from me,
As if I were a formidable thing ?
I who, ere long, in likelihood shall be
An exile ; and this very moment stand,
Beneath thy friendly roof, in jeopardy,
Knowing not but fatal hands shall shortly grasp me.

JONATHAN.
Swear to me nevertheless.
DAVID.
Yea, so I do;
And now i'th' name of my posterity,
Whom God requite if they shall injure thine.

JONATHAN.
My sorrow's tumult now is half allayed,
And its red tide beneath this moon goes down;
For thou art like the moon, and thy young horns
Are filling fast, even in this very hour,
When thou believest that my father seeks
To drain thy beam and break thy shining crescent,
E'er it shall grow into the perfect orb,
That shall illume this night of Israel,—
This night of the Lord's frown upon our house.
From thee shall come our country's proper dawning;
For Saul has only been a meteor
That crossed the welkin ere the break of day,
And then went out for ever. But no more:
I will no longer chant the doleful truth.
To-morrow is new moon, and thou'lt be missed
When 'tis thy duty with the king to dine.
Three days conceal thyself; then straight come down
And take thy station by the rock of Ezel;
And I will come and shoot three arrows near it,—
As though I shot them at a mark,—and send
A boy them to recover. And now listen:
If I expressly say unto the lad,
"The arrows are on this side; quickly bring them,"
Then come thou: there is peace for thee, not danger.
But if I say unto him thus: "Boy, see,
The arrows are beyond thee," prompt depart,
For 'tis the Lord that bids thee. And as touching
The other matter whereof I have spoken,
Be He between us a continual witness.
And now farewell a while.

DAVID.
                       Farewell a while.
                                        [*Exit* JONATHAN.
Did e'er despair and resignation sit
Before on one so worthy? His farewell
How sad and solemn! Tears, flow for Jonathan.
He seems as gifted with divining sorrow,
And to have more fear than hope even for the morrow.
Oh, morrow, come; elapse, three pregnant days.
Lord, come what will, thy servant thee obeys.
                                                            [*Exit.*

SCENE IV.

A dining-hall in the palace. Time, second day of the moon.
SAUL, JONATHAN, ABNER, PUBLIC OFFICERS, *and* COURTIERS, *dining.*

JONATHAN, *aside.*
This is the second day o'th' moon, and he
Hath no inquiry made, as yet, for David.
Still must I not infer too much from that:
Silence hath oft most meaning; and deep malice
Brawls not, no more than does the deep, slow current,
That, imperceptible, attracts the vessel
Unto the gulfing whirlpool: yet I wish
That some enquiry he would make of me
Concerning David's absence, so that I
Might better know his thoughts toward my dear friend.

SAUL, *gruffly.*
Why comes not Jesse's son to eat with us,
Nor yesterday nor to-day?

JONATHAN.
                              Most pressingly
David sought leave of me to go to Beth-lehem,
Where there is yearly made a sacrifice
For all his family. So earnestly
He begged of me, that I permitted him
To let his seat be vacant this new moon.

SAUL.

And by what right hast dared give him furlough?
His place is here, and not at Beth-lehem,—
To eat with me, and not to sacrifice.
By hell, I'll sacrifice him now! Speak not:—
I will allow no answer. Knave,
Thou canst no more deceive me. Knave!—nay, fool!
Oh, to have thrown such base fool from my loins!
Thou froward fool,
Thou son of the perverse, rebellious woman,
Do I not know thou hast chosen Jesse's son
To thy disgrace and unto her dishonor?
Thou fool begotten of a wicked woman,
Have I not told thee, heretofore, that neither
Thy person nor thy power can be in safety
So long as Jesse's son still walks the earth?
Instantly send and fetch him;—send and fetch him,
For now I am resolved that he shall die.

JONATHAN.

Now, by the Great Eternal that's in heaven,
I will bear this no longer! Asperse, Sir, me,
But not my mother, neither my dear friend
David, my brother, and thy too-good son.
Oh, father, shame! how hast thou done him shame,
Even in his absence and before these Peers!
Go fetch him! Shall I be commanded, like
A butcher's boy to fetch a calf or sheep,
That his bloat master may it stick and flay?
Shall I hale David to you to be slaughtered?
What hath he done? Say wherefore he should die.

SAUL casts a javelin at JONATHAN, who leaves the hall in great anger, and convinced that his father is determined on DAVID's death.

AN OFFICER.

My liege, forbear.

ABNER.

Cousin, what would you do!

SAUL.

I'll kill both the traitor and yon traitorous son!
I will pursue him to the ends o'th' earth!

    [*The company all rise in confusion and leave the hall.*

Yet I repent me that I threw that dart;
And fear that I am growing weak and wild,
To have in fury thus assailed my child.

    [*Exit, and enter* MALZAH *at the other side.*

MALZAH.

I've had no part in this. I'm sorry too
(Like thee, king) that I ever came unto thee.
Zounds! why I ought to have strong penance set me,
Or else be branded with some sign of shame,
For having volunteered for his undoing.—
There's no essential honor nor good i'th' world;
But a pure selfishness is all in all.—
Nay, I could curse my demonhood, and wish
Myself to be thrice lost for that behaviour.—
But I believe I am a very mean spirit.

    [*Exit.*

SCENE V.

Near the rock Ezel. Enter JONATHAN *and a lad.*

JONATHAN.

Run now and find the arrows I shall shoot.

    [*As the lad goes forward,* JONATHAN *shoots an arrow past him.*

The arrow is beyond thee: quick, stay not.

    [*The lad having found the arrow, returns with it to* JONATHAN.

I find I am not in the vein this morning:
Return with my artillery to the city.

The lad departs, and DAVID *comes from concealment, and, with signs of great respect and emotion, approaches* JONATHAN, *who embraces him, and they weep upon each other's neck in silence,* DAVID *most passionately.*

JONATHAN.

Oh, cease, dear friend, these bosom-rifting sighs,
These horrible convulsions that so shake thee:
I cannot loose, yet cannot bear to feel thee
Thus sob and agonise on me like a woman.

DAVID.

Oh, for a woman's shriek, to cut the cord
That binds my woe down on my swelling heart
Until I suffocate! Oh, let me weep!

JONATHAN.

I could myself pour all my soul in tears,
'Till we both stood in a hot pool of grief.

DAVID.

Jonathan, my heart will break.
    [*They again weep in silence:* JONATHAN *at length speaks.*

JONATHAN.

How long shall these dull-spelling tears postpone
The syllables I must at length pronounce?
David, my father hates thee.

DAVID.

                      Without a cause:
'Tis that makes this so bitter.—Crack, heart, crack;
Spill all this dreadful agony at once!

JONATHAN.

Check this salt inundation, and each speak
As man to man his sorrow.

DAVID.

                    Water flees
From fire; so now, perforce, gush forth my tears
Out of my heart fierce burning. Jonathan,
I have heard say that there are boiling springs,
Heated by secret fires within the earth;
So at my eyes gush forth these scalding tears,
Boiled by the bosomed furnace of my anguish.

I have heard tell of hollow mountains too,
Belching out flames that thaw their summit snows:
I am a mountain whose head Saul hath lifted,
By unsought benefits, and, as with snow,
O'erspread with flakes of unenduring honors.
Chide, if thou wilt; say ought that may congeal me:
For I am snow, and this event is fire;—
I thaw beneath Saul's hot, unnatural rage.

JONATHAN.

Against its zenith-blaze and noonday fierceness,
We must be obdurate as unsunned ice;
And a cold, March-like blast of speech, and frown
Worse than November's on the brow, must cow him.
Kindness but irritates him, and thy wrongs
Too great already are to be forgotten.

DAVID.

Oh, could I find out some sweet dissolution,
Some friendly, cheating, false oblivion,
Would cause me to forget what he hath done!
Oh, would the king himself forget his errors,
And be unto me as in days long past;
Or that it had not been my lot to know him!

JONATHAN.

It is too late: and I have chidden him,
More than becomes me towards a madman father.
He's mad, he's mad, cast off of Heaven; and now
Doth, in his hell-inspired fatuity,
Cast from him thee, his last, his only angel.
But let us dry these ineffectual tears,
And, with such truce to sorrow as we may,
Wend each from each his sad and several road.
Now go in peace; remembering that the Lord
Is always witness to the covenant
That late we made beneath mine own rooftree,
Both for ourselves and our posterity.
Farewell.

DAVID.

Farewell; perhaps farewell for ever.
[Exit, still weeping.

JONATHAN.

He is o'erwhelmed by bodeful clouds of gloom.
And now this world seems unto me a tomb.
Methinks 'twere better I should with him flee;
For court nor city can again charm me.
[Exit.

SCENE VI.

Nob. Interior of a small sanctuary with an altar at one end. A lamp burning. Time, night.

Present AHIMELECH, *an aged Priest, and* DOEG, *an Edomite and principal herdsman of* SAUL; *the former officiating at the altar, the latter reclining at a distance. A knocking heard.*

AHIMELECH.

Who's knocking there so softly?
[Takes the lamp and opens the door.
Who art thou?
*[*DAVID *enters.*

David?

DAVID.

The same. Speak low.

AHIMELECH.

What is the matter?
At this strange hour, my son, and unattended!

DAVID.

The king hath charged me with a special business,
And I have left my followers o'er the hill.
Say, what provision hast thou? Give me five loaves,
Or what else thou hast ready.

AHIMELECH.

Hallowed bread
Is all I have at present; but if thou

And all thy servants have, at least, abstained
From women, thou mayest have it.

    DAVID.
          For three days,
(The time since first we started,) certainly
Women have been kept from us; and our vessels
Are holy; and the bread, too, in a manner,
Is common, even supposing that it had
This day lain sanctified within the vessels.

  AHIMELECH (*having fetched the bread from the altar*).
Here take this from the altar: and if I
Do wrong in giving thee, let not the error
Fall on my soul; for 'tis the king's command
That to the action prompts my doubtful hand.

    DOEG (*aside*).
'Tis well that I am here to have beheld this.
He is a fugitive, and, when I home
(Which I shall towards so soon as liberated)
Am come, I'll turn this scene to my account:
For tidings brought of him will please the king;
And I do hate these Israelitish priests,
Though with my offerings I am here to feed them.

    DAVID.
Hast thou got neither sword nor other weapon?
For there are vagabonds about these parts;
And I have come unarmed, so suddenly
Was I dispatched.
    AHIMELECH.
       There is Goliah's sword,
Wrapped in a cloth and placed behind the ephod.
But 'twere a load for thee to bear it: yet
If thou wilt take it, I will give it to thee:—
Indeed it unto thee belongs:—moreover,
Here is no other.
    DAVID.
      Father, give it me:
There is none like it.

AHIMELECH.
Here it is.

DAVID.
Thanks, thanks;
'Twas the grim giant's.—Now I'll hurry on;
And of this visit see thou tell to none.
[*Exit* DAVID.

DOEG (*aside*).
I will feign sleep; and the old, stupid priest
Make think I have not seen this.

AHIMELECH.
Sir, awake:
The night apace is wearing. I knew not
You slept.

DOEG.
Nor I;—but sleep's a treacherous thing,
And steals upon us. I am somewhat chilly.—
Beshrew me, but I could have sworn most roundly—
But for your word—I'd not been sleeping soundly.

AHIMELECH (*aside*).
Perhaps 'tis well he has not seen our motions.
Son, it was wrong to sleep at your devotions. [*To* DOEG.

DOEG.
Forgive me.—But how goes the hour? All's silent.

AHIMELECH.
We've climbed almost unto the ridge of night.
'Tis very dark, for not a star is out;
And, I believe, 'tis raining. God help all
Who are unhoused now, for it blows a squall.
Listen! Now come within and take thy rest:
I have performed the rites thou didst request.

DOEG.
Father, lead on. [*Aside.*] Now evil me befall,
If round thy head I do not raise a squall.
[*Exeunt.*

SCENE VII.

The environs of Nob. Time, immediately following that of the last scene: dark and stormy.

DAVID.

Whither should I proceed? In my own country
There is no safety for me; for the foot
Of Saul will follow me where'er I go.
A foreign land must shelter me; yet which?
For Israel's neighbours are but neighbouring foes.
Egypt and Edom hate us, Ammon and Moab:
And proud Philistia hath too rudely felt
Lately our ire; and who as much as I
To them obnoxious? Yet thither shall I go:
The brave are always generous, and the treachery
Of all besides around, deters my seeking
To cross their borders. Lord, direct my path.—
I'll shelter seek of Achish, King of Gath.

SCENE VIII.

The royal court at Gath. ACHISH, LORDS, CAPTAINS, ATTENDANTS, *&c., and* DAVID.

DAVID.

Behold me, king, a Hebrew fugitive,
Who comes to thee for shelter from oppression.
Graciously let me, with my services,
Buy thy protection, and the right to live
Molestless 'neath thy sway.

ACHISH.

      Thou'rt safe a while,
Whoe'er thou art, or whatsoever wind
Of fault or fortune may have blown thee hither.

A CAPTAIN *to another, and in an undertone, but overheard by* DAVID.

Is not this David, worshipped by his countrymen?
Whose king, 'tis said, he shall be; and of whom

The Hebrew maidens chanted in these words:
"Saul hath his thousands slain, but David tens
Of thousands," over our defeat rejoicing
In their hilarious dances?

SECOND CAPTAIN.

          So I deem it.

DAVID (*aside*).

Oh, it is hard to hide the shining truth!
'Tis as the sun's ray fighting through the clouds
Its way to men: yet guile must serve me now;
For I discover that they do suspect
Who 'tis I am. How must I cheat them? I
Will straight feign madness.

DAVID *begins to let his spittle fall upon his beard, and scrabbles on the door-post. The* FIRST CAPTAIN *whispers to* ACHISH.

ACHISH.

'Tis David, sayest thou? 'tis a madman. See,
The man is mad: why did they let him enter?
 [*Exeunt except the* FIRST *and* SECOND CAPTAINS *and* DAVID.

FIRST CAPTAIN.

No man than he was saner even now.
He overheard us, doubtless; and now merely
Assumes this changed and rabid-like demeanour.

SECOND CAPTAIN.

He hath discovered our suspicion, and
His madness is as opportune as sudden.
          [*Exeunt* CAPTAINS.

DAVID.

Where should I fly to next? I am as one
'Twixt fire and water, either fatal to him.
I've heard there is a cave, Adullum called,
Which lies not far from here. I'll strive to find it;
For I in safety cannot house with men.
'Tis in a barren wild, yet God can there
Preserve me still, and hearken to my prayer.
            [*Exit.*

SCENE IX.

Ramah, not far from Gibeah.

SAUL *seated beneath the shade of a tree, and with a spear in his hand;*
DOEG, *courtiers, soldiers, and servants (chiefly Benjamites),*
disposed around him.

A COURTIER.

My liege, I've news meet for the royal ear.
From Naioth David did escape to Gath;
But it being there suspected who he was,
He thence fled to the cavern of Adullum;
And there drew men to him even as amber straws,—
They that were in distress, youths hopelessly
In the entanglements of love, and they whom debt
Had gripped, and was fast holding to deliver
Over in bondage to the creditor;
And malcontents of all kinds daily joined him;
But, at the instance of the prophet Gad,
He left the cave, and lurks in Hareth's wood.

SAUL.

Ye've long known this. [*Aside.*] Bear it, my sore-strained heart.
Yet hard to bear, as is the unfaithfulness
And disobedience of false wife and children,
Is this defection and foul lack of duty.
Of Judah and of Levi I could well
Have this expected. [*Aloud.*] Ye unfaithful Benjamites,
Think ye that Jesse's son will give you all
Vineyards and farms, and make you every one
Captains, and dub you all of high degree,
That ye have every one conspired against me,
And none inform me that mine own son Jonathan
Is in collusion with the son of Jesse?
Yet so it is, and with your knowledge, yet
Not one among you is at all concerned,—
Not one amongst you all is sorry for me;
Nor tells me that my son hath stimulated
A subject thus against me to rebel.

[Aside.
None answer me, none answer;—treason, treason
So fills the air that all have grown infected.
Oh, treachery, oh treason, hollowness;—
I'm sick, I'm sick to death with hollowness;
I'm pierced all over by these ingrates' arrows.
How many of these men have I made great!
Yet of them all on this not one breaks silence.
I am alone, I am alone 'midst numbers.
I am a lone house 'midst a populous city
Whose tenants are abroad, where thieves have entered,
And there is none about to cry out "Robber!"
I am deserted; all do now desert me;
And, in the middle of this grove of men,
I'm bare and barren, waste and bitter hungry;
Yea, hungry and no one will help to feed me,—
Will help to feed my gnawing, just revenge.
[Aloud.
Are you all silent yet? Will none inform me
Of all he knows of David's evil-doings?

DOEG (*aside*).

Now is my moment, and I'll make the best on't!
[Aloud.
Pardon me, but I thought naught of it at the time;—
Pardon me, king, but, being there myself,
Detained before the Lord in holy rites,
I saw the son of Jesse come to Nob,
To Ahimelech, who sought for him the Lord,
And gave him victuals and Goliah's sword.

SAUL.

Ah, worse than Naioth this! Go fetch
Ahimelech, and all related to him;
Bring every priest that you shall find in Nob.
Away, and fetch the traitors; swift, away.
If they be guilty, they shall dearly pay.
[Exeunt all save the King.

At last I'm getting on a beaten track
O'er which to move in certainty, in place
Of floundering in quagmires of suspicion ;
Or, half bewildered 'twixt my rage and fear,
Deviously wandering in dim surmise.
I'm dawning now ; and still, amidst my night,
This danger, like a lurid polestar, pointed
Ever toward the priestly north.—Out, out ! All night
My soul hath watched them like a pacing sentry ;
My spirit has been like a couchant mastiff,
Winking with eyes directed on the robber,
And now shall spring upon them.—Gad, in Hareth !
The priests are at the bottom of it all ;
But heavily shall vengeance on them fall.

[Exit.

SCENE X.

The same. Enter Two Soldiers, *meeting.*

FIRST SOLDIER.

Woe, woe !—Now will a curse light on him !
Ahimelech and all the priests of Nob,
Are, by the orders of the king, just slain.

SECOND SOLDIER.

Take back thy words, thou impious jester ! Slain ?

FIRST SOLDIER.

Slain ;—nay, believe, for soon the thunder of heaver
Will peal it o'er the world.

SECOND SOLDIER.

Oh, horrible !
But who in Israel were found so vile ?—
Who did the deed ?

FIRST SOLDIER.

None, none of Israel,—
All ours refused ; but that damned Edomite,

Doeg, who for our priests no reverence knows,
Fell on them with a double-handed sword,
Like a strong thresher on a heap of corn,
And cut them up in pieces. Here he comes.
Oh, the blood-streaked and impious human tiger!
The sacrilegeous demon!—Let's not stay.
His hands are reeking;—yea, his breath is bloody.
See, with a ruddy lustre yet his eye-balls glare.
Surely from hell hath been cast up that monster!
   [Exeunt, and enter DOEG *with a huge sword.*

DOEG.

Fourscore and five of the perpetuators
Of hate against my nation have I silenced:
But am not yet contented; for my rage
Rose, as a tempest might, at its own sound;
Rose as I wreaked it, and I thirstier grew,
As, with the broad lips of this heavy blade,
I tasted of each sacerdotal beaker.
But I have shed and shattered them all now;—
And 'tis the king's work, who, with his own hands,
Might have killed me had not I straight obeyed him.
       [Enter SAUL.

SAUL.

Thou art the noblest butcher in the land.
Now go to Nob; first having gathered men
Who, like thyself, having heard the royal hest,
Incontinently do it. Wash thyself;
For so transformed by thine ensanguined favors,
Thou 'dst raise but few recruits.
Raze Nob to the ground; and every living thing,
Human or bestial, do thou cause to perish.
Let none escape old memories to cherish.
       [Exit.

DOEG.

O king, the first of vinters, I will tread
This wine-press for thee; but first these grim stains
Deterge, that come from Edom-hater's veins.

Having tasted of the cup, I'd broach the tun,
And with my fellows drink till it be done;
Then, rubicund, return, and thee before
Stand proudly heady, and encrust with gore.

[Exit.

SCENE XI.

The forest of Hareth.

DAVID.

Who hither comes with such dishevelled hair
And garments torn? Despair and woe appear
To urge him toward me, e'en as if he meant
To cast his sorrows' weight down at my feet.
I know him now: 'tis Abiather, son
Of good Ahimelech, the priest who lately
Did, at his peril, give me friendly succour.
Some evil hath befallen Ahimelech!

[Enter ABIATHER, *the Son of Ahimelech.*

Welcome, my benefactor's son. How is
Thy father?

ABIATHER.

Well.

DAVID.

Thy kindred?

ABIATHER.

Well.

DAVID.

And Nob?

ABIATHER.

No more; for, with a ruthless butchery,
Saul hath it visited with such horrid war
Of fiends in human shape, that I alone
Live to remember its past days of peace.

DAVID.

Now help me, God, to disbelieve thy servant!

ABIATHER.

Believe my story for its very truth's sake;
Revenge it for mine own, my sire's, and God's.

DAVID.

Oh, horrible!—And did your sacred order
Avail you naught? Whence did he gather monsters
That dared to do this sacrilegeous deed?

ABIATHER.

That treacherous Edomite, Doeg, whom thou
Didst see at thy brief calling, led them on.
They did surround us, and, with uncouth yells,
Fell on us, sparing none.

DAVID.

Hush, heart;—
But I must speak or burst. Oh, awful Judge,—
I have no words to clothe my indignation;
And oh, what phrase would fit this hideous theme!
Oh, let me weep, weep, weep! heart, break to shivers!
Yet must I speak, yet must I groan a curse
On Doeg and his crew. May they all perish!
May they go down alive to hell for ever!
Why wert thou slack then, hell, nor didst engulf them?
And why was Heaven slack too?—Peace, lips, oh, peace;
For ye too are grown impious.—But did Heaven
Behold these monsters and not rain down fire,
As erst it did on Sodom and Gomorrah?
Shall there not be another dark Dead Sea
Where'er they shall be buried? The sacred Nob,—
God's holy priests,—thine unoffending father,
Good, charitable man,—nay, now shall mortals
Shoot at the stars, and seek to mar the mansion
Where angels do inhabit. Oh, what will
This raging king do next? He will o'erthrow
All altars; snatch therefrom the sacrifices.—
E'en that were little after this great horror.

ABIATHER.

Bate not as yet your words: pour out the torrent.

DAVID.

All perished, said'st thou?

ABIATHER.
All.

DAVID.
Age was no shield?

ABIATHER.

No more than is its ripeness to the corn
Against the sickle.

DAVID.
And the sword devoured
Your children?

ABIATHER.
On them they rushed, as on young lambs
Rush the remorseless wolves: but it was Saul
Who set them on;—Saul, Saul destroyed our fold.

DAVID.

Oh, 'twas his demon, 'twas his demon working;
It was his demon in the form of Doeg!
Ah, Abiather; I knew when I saw Doeg
That night at Nob, he would inform the king.
I have myself caused this catastrophe.

ABIATHER.

'Tis thou who must avenge it.

DAVID.
So I will,
On Doeg and on Edom, to my fill.
Come with me further into this dim wood,
Where I abide with many brave and good.
Never, although poor Nob now razèd be,
Shall't be erasèd from my memory.

[*Exeunt, going further into the forest.*

END OF THE FOURTH ACT.

ACT V.

SCENE I.

Gibeah. A room in the Palace.

SAUL.

Now lively action breaks up stagnant death;
For, lo, that outlaw David's in a snare,
Having entered wall-girt Keilah. I shall crush him
Now; since I will beseige him with a host
That shall stop up each avenue of escape
So thickly, that if he but sally forth,
'Twill only be to render up his life.

[*Enter an* OFFICER.

How now?

OFFICER.
My liege,
David hath passed from Keilah.

SAUL.
'Tis not so!
How came the news?—Speak; tell me quickly.

OFFICER.

By one who Keilah left at David's heels;
And says the town's inhabitants had meant
To have delivered him to your majesty.

SAUL.

And which way went the traitor, says he?

OFFICER.
Toward
The wilderness of Ziph.

SAUL.
Thither will we steer.
Go get thee ready.
[*Exit* OFFICER.
Every day shall see
An active search made for our enemy,
Until we take him; and, he being dead,
Subsides our danger of him and our dread.
[*Exit.*

SCENE II.

Border of the wilderness of Ziph.
SAUL *and his army in pursuit of* DAVID.

SAUL.

Now, being upon the margin of his haunt,
Put on your vigilance; outspread yourselves,
And, marching, sweep the region clean before you.
[*The army having passed.*
Ye savage and dark-wooded wilds, disclose
The traitor to me: rocks, if ye do hide him
(As it is said you do) behind your doors,
Reveal him: wind, blow towards him, so that I
May follow thee as a vane; or if thou'rt from him,
Whisper into mine ear where 'tis he lurks;
Or you, ye penetrating sunbeams, play
For me the spy.
[*Exit.*

SCENE III.

The skirts of a wood in the wilderness of Ziph. Time, twilight.
Enter JONATHAN.

JONATHAN.

How silent all is here! Here is, at least,
Peace; and methinks that peace is likest heaven.

Now could I, too, become a fugitive,
Ne'er to review the turmoil of the city,
The court's intrigue, and distuned passion's jar
That frets so this sweet world; for I am ill
Composed for earth. Methinks the radiant ether
Should be my world; and all my intercourse
Should be with heroes that resemble David.
Where art thou, David, much-abusèd brother?
Thou art not far from me, methinks:—how far, then?
If thou beest here, nor like to the shy beasts
That rise at night and seek therein their prey,
Approach to me behind night's shady shield;
Come catch me in thine arms thy prisoner.—
How gain with him but one hour's intercourse?
I will invade these boughs, and, in the glades
O'th' forest standing, woo him with my voice.
He hath not yet forgot the air I'll warble.

      [*Enters the forest and sings.*

 Come to me, love, come to me, love.
 Lo, the moon gaily climbs up heaven;
 And stars appear to twinkle clear,
 And Hesper, queen o'th' seven.

 For the gentle, nameless hour is come,
 The hour 'tween day and night;
 When feeble Age takes rest at home,
 And abroad young Love delight.

    DAVID (*rushing in*).

Jonathan, it is thy voice!
    JONATHAN.
     Oh, David, David,
Thine should I know out of all Israel's.
How hast thou fared since last we said adieu?

    DAVID.

A tale too long to tell, by far too sad:—
Yet not all sad; for in this uncouth exile
The Lord is with me, even as He was
Within the polished city.

JONATHAN.

       Still thy trust
Put in him,—He will not fail thee; and fear not
My father, who hunts after thee in vain.
I know thou wilt be king of Israel yet,
And that I shall be next to thee in power;
Which well my father too in secret knows.
But let's not speak of this, for I am glad;
So truce to thoughts that cannot but be sad.

DAVID.

So be it, my dear prince, and fastest friend:
Forget that now; for joy breaks in myself,
Like sudden morning, at your highness' presence.
Angels of old have visited mankind;
And now your highness' visit unto me
Seems even as one from heaven's hierarchy.

JONATHAN.

As the maid longs for tryste, I've longed for this!
But deeper tempt this thick, involving shade,
And there, in brief, recount thy late adventures;
For should this night my jealous father miss me,
It might detain him here: 'tis understood
That this will be the last watch on this wood;
But he is fierce at the sore disappointment.

DAVID.

Alas, poor king!

JONATHAN.

      Yea, David, pity Saul;
For as thou risest, 'tis his doom to fall:
But let Heaven's will be done, that orders all.

            [*Exeunt.*

SCENE IV.

A room in the Palace at Gibeah.

SAUL.

We are returned unto our den more fierce
Than we rushed out of it; we're coiled again,
After a snake-like spring. But we'll abide
And watch with patience, as the spider doth
For the entangling of the distant fly.
As it, 'neath pressing hunger, quiet sits
Within its lonely aperture, until
It sees or feels far off its fated prey,
We will in Gibeah bide to wait for David.
I must remove that fascinating serpent,
Before it shall have grown a mighty dragon,
To wear my crown. But that he is encouraged
By my besotted and unnatural son,
I had him crushed ere now. Beware, beware,
Jonathan, thou mother-counselled weakling, lest
I trample thee to death in killing him.

[Enter an OFFICER.

What now?—Are the Philistines coming?

OFFICER.

         No,
My liege: they know too well who'd meet them. No;
But up from the wild wilderness of Ziph,
Which we have left so lately, men are come
With tidings for you.

SAUL.

      Bid them straight come hither.

[Exit OFFICER.

Now I'll be slow and cautious, and look deep
Into each villain's eyes; for how know I
But that they come to cheat me, and to draw,
Out of the sudden treasure of my joy,

Unto themselves some gain. I do believe
That every Ziphite is a friend to the rebel.
But I'll detain the knaves, if knaves they be,
As hostages for th' truth of their own tale.
                                    [*Enter* ZIPHITES.
They look like honest men;—and yet but little
Can be inferred from looks. The crafty soul
Can clothe itself according to its pleasure,
And at the oriels of the eyes stand, shewing
In guise of saint, when 'tis, indeed, a devil.
You are from Ziph?

              FIRST ZIPHITE.
We are, your majesty.

                   SAUL.

We were ourselves there lately. 'Twas a pity
You were not saved this journey, by delivering
Your news at home.

              FIRST ZIPHITE.
                        Your majesty, when you
Were with us, we had nothing to deliver;
Except it were (which we, indeed, did do)
To offer you our services, to aid
In capturing him you sought for : but you scarcely
Had left us, when, emboldened by your absence,
He and his followers exposed themselves,
Pale, lean, and hungry, and entreating food.

                   SAUL.
And did you give it to them?

              FIRST ZIPHITE.
                        What they would
They from us took; then straight with it retired
Unto another forest, the one that covers the hill
Of Hachilah, which has many secret caves;
And overtopples so with loosened rocks,
That they who enter first into the forest,
Might send them lumbering on all later comers.
The hill is south of Jeshmon.

SAUL.
> Is it so?
> Sirs, you shall lead me thither: and the head
> Of David shall be yours, if you do find him;
> But if you do not, your heads shall be mine.
> Is it well?

SECOND ZIPHITE.
> Alas, your majesty, the eagle
> May fly away before we reach his eyrie.
> But if you find that he was not on Hachilah
> When we left Ziph, take not alone our heads,
> But let our innocent babes meet the desert
> Of those who'd dare to trifle with the king.

SAUL.
> Ye trifle now, believe me, with your souls,
> If you do sport with me in any way;
> Either by foul collusion with my foe,
> To draw on me some loss by stratagem,
> Or for yourselves an undeserved reward.
> Then give to me at once some evidence
> That I may know that what you say is true,
> And that yourselves are not the emissaries
> Of this ill wanderer. Shew the mean snare,
> If you have purposed one; or, once I've found it,
> It shall yourselves clasp, and not you alone,
> But the whole treacherous wilderness of Ziph.

FIRST ZIPHITE.
> So be it done, and more, if Heaven's judgments
> May second thine. Let the earth open and swallow
> All souls up, true with false, if we deceive thee.

SAUL.
> Amen. As Dathan and Abiram perished,
> And went down live to hell, so may go all
> Who shall (through you) tempt me to scale the top
> Of heaven-touching, perilous Hachilah.

THIRD ZIPHITE.

More than thine imprecation be upon us,
And upon all our country, if we're false !
But come down quickly, and thy forces hold
Ready to seize him, whilst our part shall be
To lead him unawares into thy power.

SAUL.

God's blessing be upon you, Ziphites; for
Ye have compassion on me ! Go and spy,
And ascertain his most familiar haunts.
Learn who hath seen him there: for we are told
He is most wary; therefore be exact.
Find out beforehand all his lurking places,
And come to me with safest certainty:
Then I'll go with you; and, if in the land
He be, will capture him, though I should have
To search throughout all Israel.

FIRST ZIPHITE.

          We obey,
O king.

SAUL.

Go secretly to work.

SECOND ZIPHITE.

          We will.

SAUL.

Yet diligently too; and your reward
Is sure. Return to me with all prepared.

          [*Exeunt* ZIPHITES.

What were another journey thither ! Far better
A hundred toilsome marches there and back,
Than thus to live misgiving. Were he dead,
There were an end, save in his recollection:—
Ay, there is what restrains me,—yet restrains
Me not; for I will hunt him to the death,
Though it make sick myself: I'll be assured;
I will endure much smarting to be cured.

          [*Exit.*

SCENE V.

The wilderness of Ziph.
The same ZIPHITES *as in the preceding scene.*

SECOND ZIPHITE.

'Tis as I ventured to forewarn the king:
The bird has flown to the bare plain of Jeshmon.

FIRST ZIPHITE.

So much the worse for the bird then: for the king
Is at our heels with twice his former numbers;
And stealthily he marches without sound
Of clarions blowing, nor has banners cast
Unto the wind; but, wisely now discarding
Slow military pomp, comes, like a falcon, swooping
Back on the quarry that it lately missed.

SECOND ZIPHITE.

But David hath been warned of his approach,
And is among the crags of Maon gotten.
In Ziph, too, more are for him than against him;
And some have run before the whispering wind
To warn him of his peril. Bad is brewing:
What we have done, others have been undoing.

[*Enter* SAUL *and some military.*

SAUL.

Where is he?

FIRST ZIPHITE.

Pardon us, your majesty,
He has just fled from Hachilah; but the desert,
Which he hath crossed, exposed him, even as winter,
Leafless, shews the lean moorfowl; and bare rocks
Now shelter him, only, with treacherous turn,
To raise against him the gaunt arm of Famine,
Who ever dwells there, and will him compel
At length into your power.

SAUL (*aside*).
                    The ostrich hides
Its head, and thinks that all is hid; so he:
But I will track him to the mountain crag,
Swifter than Ishmael's horsemen o'er the sands
Chase that dull bird.   [*Aloud.*] Go ye before me swiftly.
Let no one think of halting all this day.—
                [*Aside.*
Methinks I have him now a certain prey.
                                [*Exeunt omnes.*

SCENE VI.

DAVID *and his Company on the side of a mountain.*

DAVID.

Hasten, or we shall be surrounded; for
The king is near, with doubled numbers, striving
To hem us in, and to possess the gorge
Ere we can pass it.   Let your arms be covered,
Lest that they, tell-tale, glitter in the sun;
For we will not uplift them 'gainst our nation,
Nor its anointed king.   Let God be judge
'Twixt him and us, and be our Succourer.
        [*Exeunt, and enter* SAUL, ZIPHITES, *and* SOLDIERS.

SAUL.

Angels or demons,
Which of you is it that delivers him?
Again the eel has glided from my grasp.
                        [*Enter a* MESSENGER.

MESSENGER.

Is the king here?

SAUL.
            He is.   Hast thou seen David?

MESSENGER.

No; but the Philistines ravaging the land.
Haste back, O king; for Jonathan bade me tell you

He doubts his power to hold the foes in check,
So quickly swarm they on him.

     SAUL *(aside)*.
          Curses light
Now on this twice foul fortune! [*Aloud.*] This is false
Jonathan sent thee not hither.

     MESSENGER.
        Yea, your majesty;
And with stern words of hastening, which he bade me
Repeat to you, and bid you to yourself
Apply them thrice repeated.

     SAUL *(aside)*.
Surely there is a Power that stands between
My purpose and its crowning! [*Aloud.*] I will follow thee;
For thou must back with diligence to the prince,
And tell him that I come.
         [*Exit* MESSENGER.
      The scene of sport
Hath changed, brave soldiers: we must hasten back;
For out, full-mouthed, are the Philistine pack.
Hence are we bootless bound to leave this place,
And start forthwith upon a nobler chase.
           [*Exeunt.*

SCENE VII.

Gibeah. A hall in the Palace.

    MALZAH *(entering)*.
Heydey, I've oft heard say
That when God naps, the demons play.
Why am I here retained? why must I still
With this untoward, gloomy king abide
Ever alone, nor know embrace seraphic?
I'll hither summon Peyona.—What, so ho!
Prythee come up, my consort, from below!

PEYONA (*rising*).

Malzah, what hath made thee call me?

MALZAH.

Dost come unwillingly?

PEYONA.

Why, no.

MALZAH.

'Tis well, or—oh, immense distraction!—
But put thyself in capering action.
Come: I am in a moving mood.
Last time we danced was at the flood.

PEYONA.

Oh, is this falsehood or forgetfulness?—
But thou mayest well forget, so long it is
Since thou forgot to play with me the gallant.

MALZAH.

Why, madam, how is this? Have you forgot that
When I would dance, you always thus would preach?
And even now you fall to contradiction.—
But dance, not talk; for, just now, speech
Would give each carcass too much friction.

PEYONA.

I cannot dance to-day.

MALZAH.

Then I will make you.—Music, ho! I pray.

[*Music heard, and they dance together.*

PEYONA.

I'll dance no longer: let me from thee go.

MALZAH.

You have no urgent, pressing task below.
Slut, why request, then, to return so soon?

PEYONA.

I must return, for I am called.

MALZAH.

Who calls thee?

PEYONA.

I know not.

[PEYONA *begins to descend.*

MALZAH.

Liar! Oh, soft, deceptive eyes,—
Out, coals of hell, or I will tear you out.

[PEYONA *disappears.*

Disclose yourselves, ye dark and terrible gulfs,
That, in immensity and eternal night,
Have to this hour in sullen silence yawned,
And swallow her up!—I'll follow her to hell.

ZELEHTHA (*entering*).

Whither art thou bound?

MALZAH.

To Acheron.

ZELEHTHA.

Stay here
'Till I dismiss thee.

[*Exit.*

MALZAH.

I will stay no longer.
Grieve Saul thyself; kill David; ay, kill me:
For to live thus is worse than Tophet's torment.

SAUL (*entering*).

Now from one tumult pass I to another.
From David 'scaped, I turned to the Philistines;
From the Philistines quelled, I turn to David,
Who, on the stony mountains of En-gedi,
At present roams. Shall he elude me thrice?
Three thousand chosen men I'll lead against him,
And end him now with all his band of outlaws. [*Exit.*

MALZAH.

I will end thee,—I'll tear thee yet to pieces;
Kill or be killed, or die as other men:
Then will my liberty be mine again.
I do begin to find this task beneath me,
And hate thee even as I hate Zelehtha. [*Exit.*

SCENE VIII.

A wild, hilly district, with the Mountains of En-gedi seen beyond, and the mouth of a Cave in the foreground.
Enter TWO SOLDIERS *of* SAUL'S *advance-guard.*

FIRST SOLDIER.

Wilder and barrener this region grows;
Till naught but sheep, and they of smallest size,
Draw from it sustenance. No fields of corn
Are here, nor rye nor barley; neither roots
To fare the frugal shepherds, who appear
Dwelling within the doors of blank starvation:
A rising, melancholy moorland, that
Ascending keeps, until the sterile hills
Seem to be hanging in the sombre clouds.
What that hath life can harbour there?

SECOND SOLDIER.

There lives
The wild goat only, and with snow still cools
His hot and lecherous blood. Nor bear nor fox
There dwelleth, neither wolf,—naught but the goat
And the heaven-searching eagle; whilst the tempest,
Sullen, within the towering fastnesses,
Mustering its strength, sweeps thence far o'er the plain.

FIRST SOLDIER.

How awful doth it seem to pass a life,
Though but an animal's, amidst such horror
And constant solitude! I almost shudder,
Though with a host, at thought of entering
Such a bewildering, wild world of crags.—
What were we smitten by a waterspout?
Or in a narrow gully (and we might be)
Caught by a torrent sweeping from the peaks,
That had ripped up the clouds? Or what if blown
Down from some scarpy side into the yawn,

That lies a thousand fathoms down below,
To batten there the vultures; or perchance
Rolled down into some deep-worn channel stream,
To be by its fierce billows onward swept,
And buried in the ocean?

SECOND SOLDIER.

      Cease, I pray thee:
Thou dost infect me with an idle terror.
What! do not David and his men live there?

FIRST SOLDIER.

'Tis said they do, and yet I know not how;
For though they may in caves find shelter, yet
They cannot eat the rock: nor herb that feeds
The barbed and shaggy denizens of those heights,
Is sustenance for them: and the shy lords,
The goats, whose rule begins where man's must end,
How shall the swiftest hunter overtake,
Or his ascending arrow, when they spring
Up the jagged precipice, as sweeps the shadow
Of the swift cloudlet?

SECOND SOLDIER.

     I am told they span
As with a bridge, in their arched leap, a chasm;
From whose sloped verge the hardiest shrink in horror,
Riding, as if with sudden gift of flight,
Its overhanging air. 'Tis also said
That they upon their horns can safely drop
From crag to crag,—upon their crowns' strength proving
Themselves true kings.

FIRST SOLDIER

     Lo, where our own crowned king
Prepares to halt; and our old general, Abner,
Makes wave the signal for our bands to rest.
Let us along, nor bivouac too near them.
    [*Exeunt, and enter* SAUL *and* ABNER

SAUL.

Ere we commence this last and wildest stage,
Let the men take some rest. When once up yonder,
No rest is ours; and the now travelled foot
Must with its soreness cope the untrodden way,
If way to yonder rugged realm can be;
For nature in such hideous confusion
Was never seen before.

ABNER.

It were a mercy
To take the offender thence; for there to dwell
Is surely lingering death.

SAUL.

To shorten pain
Is charity in whomsoever doth it.
The man who hath to die, had best die soon.
What is there in this life, that men so love it?
What afterwards, that men should so fear death;
For we have conscience here, and what can we
Have worse hereafter? A foe is but a foe,
Whether he be before us or behind us;
And, granting death is but unconsciousness,
Then all are dead when sleeping, and all sleep;
So all do die, and often, that do live.
I in this cave will strive to sleep a little,
Dying a while that I may longer live;
Live, as I hope, to yet see die mine enemy.
Let me be roused if I repose too long.

[*Exit* ABNER, *and* SAUL *enters the cave.*

Interior of the cave. SAUL *lies down and falls asleep; then* DAVID, ABIA-
THER, *and* ABISHAI *advance from amongst their men, who are in the
sides of the cave.*

ABIATHER.

Now, now the opportunity is come
To cut him off. Now wherefore shouldst thou scruple?
Would he spare thee now, wert thou in his power?—
Nay, I will not hear even thee plead for him!

Did he himself once listen unto pleadings,
Vented with agony and wringing hands,
For me and my dear father and my kindred?
Oh, end him now; talk not of his anointing:
For he, in our so impiously shed blood,
Himself hath washed the anointing from his heart.

ABISHAI.

Yes, end him; for behold the hour is come
Of which God spake when He said unto thee,
" I will deliver thy foe into thy power,
That thou shalt use him as thou may'st think fit."

DAVID.

I will not listen to his taking off.

ABISHAI.

He will take thee off perhaps this very day.

DAVID.

The Lord defends me. I will not harm Saul.

ABIATHER.

Is, then, my story naught? Hast thou forgot
The story of the day when all my kindred
Perished before his bidding? As the leaves,
Green and all juicy, and the boughs, still waxing
Lustier, of some brave tree, on sudden smitten,
Even in the verdant summer of its glory,
By the red bolt of heaven, their massacre.
Oh, David, think it was at his fell order
That Doeg, the Edomitish infidel,
Set on my kindred, and the gory soil
Strewed with the carnage of a sacred race.
Think on the horrible destruction whence
I rushed, like splinter 'fore the woodman's axe;—
Think on the day when thou didst see approaching
My wounded self to thee.

DAVID.

I do remember;
Oh, Abiather, yea I do remember:
But cease thy wild appeals to me, nor ask
Me, parricidal, to destroy the fount
And spring of Michal's and of Jonathan's life;
Requiting his foul sacrilege, committed
On thee and on thy consecrated line,
By one upon himself. Remember Saul
Is still the Lord's Anointed.

ABIATHER.

No; not now.—
Retire: thou shalt not see what I will do.

ABISHAI.

Leave it to us. Away!

ABIATHER.

Stand back: I'll kill him.

DAVID.

Defile not thou thy sacerdotal hand,
Though I should let thee, which I do not mean.

ABIATHER.

Howl! howl! for now there is no Blood-Avenger
Dare follow this vile king, whose 'circling crown
Is to him e'en a city of refuge' walls.
Ah, I perceive my words are all in vain!

ABISHAI.

Cousin, I pray you take his life at once;
And in the taking of it, keep your own.

[DAVID *advances to* SAUL *and cuts off the skirt of his robe.*

DAVID.

I will take this, but not his life. In person
He is too near, if not too dear, to me.
For Michal's sake and Jonathan's, and more
Because he is indeed the Lord's Anointed,
I will not touch him vengefully.

[*To his companions in the sides of the cave, having approached them.*

            God forbid
That I should break yon consecrated vessel,
Although, its hallowed wine being spilled and drained,
It now stands foul and empty. Friends, beseech not:
I dare not hold him common, and life's flame
Quench in yon lamp by Samuel once made sacred.

The BAND *murmur; and* SAUL, *having awoke, rises and leaves the cave,*
  DAVID *and his men coming forth into the midst of it.*

Remain you here: let no one follow me.

DAVID *goes to the mouth of the cave, and, seeing* SAUL, *at a little distance,*
      departing, calls after him.

Stay, stay, injurious king; oh, father stay,
If I may yet so style you. Why dost thou
Listen to those who say I am disloyal?
Lo, in this hour, and in this very cave,
How easily could I not have ta'en your life;
As some did bid me do, but I refrained.
"I will not harm," I said, "the Lord's Anointed."
In proof of which behold here your robe's skirt,
Which sole I took, yet could as easily
Have ta'en your life as it. Yes, look on this
Upbraiding proof; yes, look on this dumb witness,
Then stand convicted of injustice toward me.
Believe, oh, cruel and suspicious king,
That since I took but this and spared your life,—
At last, believe me honest. Oh, my father,
Why hast thou ever deemed that I was other?
Why dost thou hunt me like a beast o'th' forest?
Let the Lord judge between us; let the Lord
Be mine Avenger: for I will not harm you.
Oh, that your majesty should have dread of me!—
Have dread of one so poor and weak as I!
For what could I do (even were I so minded)
Against your majesty? But I will nothing:
Let the Lord judge between us; let Him enquire;
Yes, let Him plead my cause still with your anger;
Let Him from it, at length, deliver me.

SAUL *(without and aside)*.

Is this an Ekron apparition! Nay:
It is the very form and voice of David,
Whom witchcraft saves, for I can never kill him.
Fie, to be conquered thus! With this strange fence,
Magnanimous, he doth disarm my hand;
And now compels my tongue to speak the words,
No more its own, than erst were Balaam's beast's
Those of the mouth that spoke them. I must speak,
And not in anger. [*Aloud.*] David, is that thou?—
Is that indeed thy voice, my lost son David?
Nay, I confess that thou art better than I;
Because I have requited thee with evil,
Whereas thou hast requited me with good.
Thou hast now proved thy past fidelity
And present friendship, by thus sparing me
When in thy power; for when foes come on foes,
They do not let them thus escape unhurt.
May God reward thee, then, for this forbearance!
And now I am convinced thou shalt be king,
And give a dynasty to Israel:
Then swear unto me by the Lord, that thou,
When thy strong hour of sovereignty is come,
Wilt not extirpate my posterity.

DAVID.

I swear it. [*Re-enters the cave.*

SAUL.

It is well,—and yet not well.
Still I'll no more pursue him; for I am
Now as a country that has long been harried
By predatory hordes, and that, decayed
By its own follies, vices, feuds, and factions,
Hath more to suffer yet from the barbarian,
Who shall at last possess it and o'errule.

[*Exit.*

SCENE IX.

Gibeah. An apartment in the Palace.
SAUL *and* JONATHAN.

JONATHAN.

I say your majesty has not the right
To take again thus that which once you've given:—
Nay, have not given; for he bought my sister,—
Bought her of you with peril of his life.

SAUL.

Hast thou forgot that, by our holy law,
Parents may stone a disobedient child?
They can retake the life which they have given:
How much more then may I, both king and parent,
Withdraw my child from an approvèd traitor?—
Traitor thyself; for well I know thou lov'st him,
Better than thou dost me, or mother or sister.
Peace; for thy sister is his wife no longer:
She shall be given to Phalti.

JONATHAN.

        Rather say,
She shall be stolen from David.

SAUL.

        She is childless
Yet;. and I'll see there shall not be a creature
Evoked from her's and David's elements:
Though thou, I know, would'st gladly see a cub
Made up of Saul and David; so that I
Could not destroy the one without the other.

JONATHAN.

Am I myself not next unto the throne,
In the due order of inheritance?

SAUL.

Thou art; but wouldst vacate and place him on it,
Didst thou possess it, and had I, being dead,
For abdication lost the power to punish thee,

And him for usurpation. He shall lose
Not merely wife but life :—yes, he shall die
Whilst I yet live; for whilst he lives, I cannot
Or live or die in peace.
JONATHAN.

         'Tis many a day
Since you were ruled by reason. Yet some freak
We had allowèd you; but this last folly
Crowns David's wrongs, and heaps your deeds unholy.
               [*Exit.*
SAUL.

Never will I consent to see the throne,
And all its regal honors, alienate
From me and mine! That may arrive indeed,
When the clear eye of manhood has assumed
The dull, cold stare of dotage : but ere then
I will pursue him to a mortal end;
Will, with soul set upon a tragic issue,
Hunt him into the cold, still shades of death,
Since only by his death my line may live.
           [*Enter the* ZIPHITES.
Ah, my old friends! What news ?
     [*The* ZIPHITES *whisper to* SAUL, *and then depart.*
            Ha, ha! ha, ha!
In his old haunt on Hachilah of the wild,
And doubtless thereon his old treason hatching!
            [*Enter an* OFFICER.
Three thousand men, with Abner to command them.
Well chosen let them be; and ready at nightfall,
To march where I shall wish them. [*Exit* OFFICER.
        Prompt my deeds
Shall be henceforth, and close on the conception;
Between which and the nimble execution
No space shall be wherein a doubt may lodge,
Like moisture within walls, to freeze my will,
'Midst a cold winter of anxiety,
Into irresolution, and, therewith,
At last o'erthrow my firm-built purpose' frame.
                [*Exit.*

SCENE X.

Near the wooded hill of Hachilah. SAUL *and his staff.*
Enter an OFFICER.

OFFICER.

Your majesty, your enemy has fled
Out of the covert fastness of the hill,
On to the savage plain.

SAUL.

              On after him.
Bid Abner to advance his force with speed.
                                    [*Exit* OFFICER.
Straight all assist to get our men in motion:
The soldier rests no more than doth the ocean.
                                    [*Exeunt Staff.*
Wherever he shall flee to, I will chase him,
Though it be down to hell! Now come, kind Fate:
If ever I have well deserved of thee,
Now will I. All corporeal vigor, and
The higher and stronger ministry of the mind,
I'll task unsparingly, and be prodigal
Of present pains; that I may spare pains when
The future comes,—may sit and play the fool
When pilfering years have made me weak and cool.
                                              [*Exit.*

SCENE XI.

The Wilderness. Time, evening.

DAVID (*alone*).

Saul comes again to seize me, treacherous man!
Ungrateful monarch, when will he forbear?
Arise to my relief, oh, Lord, rise quickly; for
My spies inform me that, in very deed,
He yonder comes.
                [*Enter* AHIMELECH *the Hittite and* ABISHAI.
                      Good friends, what news?

AHIMELECH.

        The king
And all his force, compelled by weariness,
(For such unparalleled exertions, both
In speed and width of range of his advance,
Which, like the month of March astride the wind,
Driving before it winter's gloomy reign,
Were surely never made beforetime,) have
Encamped ; but, to their weariness adding wariness,
Have round them dug a trench, to make secure
Their snatch of sleep.

DAVID.

      So be it; for the Lord
Surrounds us stronger than their trench can them,
Nor ever sleeps. Who will accompany me
Their camp to reconnoitre?

ABISHAI.
        I.

DAVID.
         'Tis well.
When night hath doubled her down-falling vail,
We toward them steal. 'Tis favorable that
The moon is mobbled up in thick-woven clouds.

ABISHAI.

The firmament is blank, and black as is
A yet unlighted hall: nor will the stars,
Methinks, at any time to-night find favor
To hold their tiny tapers in the air,
And shed down light to expose us; for the clouds
Grow heavier, and more vapor cometh up
From seaward.

DAVID.
    Even so : let's start at once.
           [*Exeunt.*

SCENE XII.

The Camp of Saul. Time, night.
SAUL *sleeping in the trench, his spear stuck in the ground near to his head.*
ABNER *and the rest lying around him.*
Enter DAVID *and* ABISHAI *and approach to* SAUL.

DAVID.

The king was wont to have his watch kept strictly.
Step softly now. How odd is it, to be
Walking by night a narrow plank of hazard,
Over a gulf of foes, with whom as friends
We once trod life's broad road in day's broad beam!
I know the most of these who come to take me.
See yonder, Abner in the darkness lying;
And there see Gad and Dan; and there lies Zohab;
And here, close at our very feet, behold
The form to be distinguished 'midst ten thousand,—
The king, my most unreasonable foe,
My royal, wretched, raging persecutor.

ABISHAI.

Twice God hath given him to thee. Stand away,
And let me strike him;—let him not escape.
Prythee let me now;—nay, hinder not. I'll pin him
With his own spear to the earth, and with one blow,
That there shall need no second.

DAVID.
      Thou wilt wake him.

ABISHAI.

Ay, that I will. Release me; for, by heaven,
I'll send his soul this instant down to hell.

DAVID.

Thou shalt not harm him.

ABISHAI.
     I'll not break his nap.
So quick and clean I'll send his spirit forth,
That it shall seem still sleeping in his frame.

DAVID.

I will not let thee do it; kill him not:
For who can take the life of God's Anointed,
And yet be guiltless? There requires no haste:
For, sure as God rules kings, who rule the world,
God's self shall visit him; or else his time
Shall come that he must die like other men;
Or his gigantic figure shall descend
And perish, yet, in battle. God forbid
That I should lift my hand against the Lord's
Anointed, and to-night, unbidden,
Finish his reign! No; but now take his spear
There at his bolster, and the water-cruse,
And let us quick begone.

ABISHAI.

     And leave him scathless?
Let me impale him with the spear. I'll pin him
Down with it, as with a pin would lad a fly.—
Nay this were foolisher than the cutting off
Of his robe's skirt!

DAVID.

     I will not let thee hurt him.
Obey at once: take them and let us go.

   [*Exeunt,* ABISHAI *taking the spear and cruse.*

SCENE XIII.

The top of a hill at a distance from the camp.
Time, immediately succeeding that of the last scene.

DAVID (*shouting*)

Awake, awake, ye mockery of soldiers!
What, ho! awake, awake! oh, Saul, awake!
Abner, awake! Why answerest thou not, Abner?

ABNER (*from the camp*).

Who calls thus on the king?

DAVID.

Art thou not, Abner,
Chief in command? Then whence this negligence?
For, on a stealthy and unnoticed foot,
One has been 'midst you seeking the king's life.
As the Lord liveth, ye deserve to die
For having failed to guard His own Anointed.
Was this the discipline when I was with you?
Could this thing have been done when I commanded?
For look ye where the king's spear is, and cruse
Of water, that was standing at his bolster.

SAUL (*from the camp*).

Now may this night hang over us for ever,
Concealing this disgrace! Bring hither the sentries.
I'll be their Nahash: they shall lose their eyes!—
Yea and their ears, who have forgot to use them.
Can that again thy voice be, my son David?

DAVID.

It is my voice.—Oh, if your majesty
But knew my heart well as you know my voice,
You would not, cruelly, thus persecute me!
Tell me, my liege, yea, tell me, Israel,
What have I done that I am hunted thus?
What ill intention do I harbour 'gainst thee,
That thou dost thus persist to seek my life?
If it be God inciteth thee against me,
Let me appease Him by an offering:
But if, instead, it be but wicked men,
Be they accurst in his most holy sight;
For they at length have forced me into exile,
Saying, Worship false gods, in false temples bow.
Cease longer seeking, then, to spill my blood
Before God's face; for I will go from Israel.

SAUL.

Where'er thou go, may thou be blest for this!
David, I am convinced I have done wrong;

For since thou hast again respected me,
I am persuaded thou dost deem me sacred.
And now let Heaven do what it hath ordained:
My hand shall never with thy blood be stained.
I've played the fool; I've grievously outráged thee.

DAVID.

Behold your majesty's spear! Send one to fetch it.
And may God render unto all of us
According to our justice and forbearance.
How I have twice forborne to take thy life,
When it before me lay, like a lost jewel,
He, who beholds all deeds, knows even as thou.
Let Him judge now between us: and since I
Continued to regard your life, so may He mine
Continue to preserve, and save me from you.

SAUL.

Fear me no longer!
My malice toward thee's dead: for thou hast killed it
This night by not killing me, but fearing God;
Whose blessing be upon thee, my son David,
For thou art destined yet to do great things,
And shalt still over all thy foes prevail.
I swear that I will never more molest thee.
Now go thy way in peace.

DAVID.

Peace to your Majesty.—
Despite his oaths, I know that by his hand
I yet shall perish, should I stay in Israel.
Naught better is there left for me, than that
I should escape at once into Philistia;
So that he shall despair to find me more.

[*Exit.*

END OF THE FIFTH ACT.

ACT VI.

SCENE I.

Gibeah. An apartment in the Palace.
SAUL *and an* OFFICER *of the royal household*

OFFICER.

Your majesty, David hath shelter sought
With Achish, king of Gath.

SAUL.

There let him stay,
And never be his name more mentioned here.
Leave me, and see my latest orders done.
    [*Exit* OFFICER.

Samuel is dead, and I prize life no longer;
My children hate me, or, at best, despise me;
Ahinoam is mouldering in the grave.
I am forsaken now of God and man;
For though no one dare openly rebel,
No more exists that fond alacrity,
Shewn to my hests when first proclaimed my reign.
Now all are slow, and must be bidden loudly;
Or if there be in some a show of zeal,
'Tis but eye-service.
    [*Enter a* COURIER.
Well, what is thy news?

COURIER.

My liege, of the Philistines, who have crossed
Once more our border, and encamp at Shunem.

SAUL.

Before I bid them welcome, say their numbers.

COURIER.

In truth, 'twas hard to count; but they are greater
Than e'er before were brought against your arms.

SAUL (*aside*).

At length I feel that I am growing loth
To meet them, hazarding my life for others.
And yet why cherish 't, since I prize it not?
How sayest, sirrah, thou knowest not their numbers,
But knowest they are more than former hosts?
"The more the merrier," is the word at revels;
And more their numbers, more our sword shall revel
Up to its neck in blood, and, as a drunkard
Over his cups is loth to journey home,
So shall it grieve to return unto its scabbard.
Go get thee some good cheer, for thou look'st weary.

[*Exit* COURIER.

Now come, thou butcher Saul, thou man of blood,
Rise up and kill; rise up within thyself.
What matters what thine enemy's numbers are,
If thou and thine be yet as once they were?

[*Exit.*

SCENE II.

Another apartment in the Palace.

MALZAH (*slowly pacing to and fro*).

Alas, alas!
If I were mortal I should now expire,
From rumination and forced solitude.
To be restricted to these palace walls,
Is nearly as intolerably dull
As to lie hutched i'th' compass of Saul's skull,
(As late I did,) like chicks within their eggs:—
'Tis more; for 'tween each moon's new birth and full,
I could abandon it to stretch my legs.
Why am I still retained by Heaven's warden,

Who no more urges me to enter Saul?
Yet sure I feel her influence slackening;
And Saul's gone to the wars, and (strange for him)
Loth and despairing: all which seems to tell
That I, full soon, shall bid to him farewell.
Poor, wretched monarch, he is ever gloomy:
And though at times he strives to shake off sorrow
As I have seen an old and half-blind eagle
Shake out its haggard pinions o'er its eyrie,
Then wind with youthful speed into the skies,
True cheerfulness of heart is from him gone.
Why did I ever, thoughtlessly, engage
To make his soul more wretched than mine own!
I have my moments of insane delight,
But he is never pleasant.—
'Twas in an evil hour I came to tempt him:
For this most vile transaction ends not here;
But I shall ever self-upbraidings know
Oft as I meet him in the realms below.
                                        [*Exit.*

SCENE III.

Gilboa. The Hebrew camp.
Enter SAUL *and a Hebrew* GENERAL.

SAUL.

The foe hath marched on Aphek: we must wheel,
And plant our answering standards on Jezreel.
                                    [*Exit* GENERAL.
With Gilgal in my memory, and all
The evil done and suffered by me since,
I fear to fight this last and greatest host,
Without some sacred sanction; and repent
Now, more than with my old and fixed remorse,
The slaughtering of Nob's prophets, though they were
Fomenters of rebellion to a man.

And well I know that I was then possessed;
I know that I was then beneath the demon:
Therefore Jehovah may be merciful,
And, not imputing it to me, yet answer;
For I will order that His priests forthwith
Assemble on this hill and seek Him for me.

[Enter ABNER.

Abner, how seem our men?

ABNER.
      They seem to think
Defeat and death are surely waiting for them.
To take them to the assault, or with them hope
To bear the brunt of battle when it comes,
'Twere fond as hope to stop an avalanche
With yielding air, or falling rocks with water.

SAUL.
I know that they, as once they did at Gilgal,
Increase each other's bodings by communion.
But hear it, and then wonder at it, Abner:
I have resolved on what may give them courage;—
I have resolved again to seek the Lord:
His priests shall seek for me his Oracle.

ABNER.
'Tis joy to hear you uttering such words:
And not a soldier but will swear new fealty
To you and yours, when hearing of such purpose.

SAUL.
I know not that.—However, gather thou
The priests, to ask the Lord what He doth wait
For me to do, me whom they still must hate.

ABNER.
Be this but the beginning of fair days!

[Exit ABNER.

SAUL.
I feel that I, at last, am come unto
The crisis and the pivot of my fortunes.

Long lost amongst dark mounts and crags, at length
I stand upon a pointed pinnacle,
From which I shall ascend into the sky,
Or topple to the abyss.

[*Exit.*

SCENE IV.

Aphek. The Philistine army deploying. At length appear ACHISH,
King of Gath, and his force, in the rear, followed by DAVID *and his six hundred men.*
The Philistine PRINCES *observing.*

FIRST PRINCE.

Now, by great Dagon, why are these found here?
Shall we bring danger to our midst, and hug it
As though it did not bare its bristling teeth,
And snarl and scowl upon us, from Jezreel?
By Baal, 'tis the maddest thing I've known,
To press a proven enemy to our bosom.—
'Tis well we've seen this, ere too late perceived
In the dim midst of battle's storm and struggle.

SECOND PRINCE.

Well said, my gallant Lord. Shall we by day
Receive the accomplice of a band of thieves
Into our house, so that he may have power
T' open its doors at midnight to the burglars?
Gath, wherefore hast thou hither brought these fellow
Who in the battle must perforce be traitors,
Or unto us or to their king and country?

THIRD PRINCE.

Nay, in the name of safety, this is seeking
To perish by the alien hands that hate us

FOURTH PRINCE.

Oh, lower than the lowest leap of folly,
Achish, to trust Philistia shall find
Faithful auxiliaries in yon Hebrew band!

ACHISH.
Peace, angry cousins: he who at their head,
Tallest, comes like a galley's prow, is David,
Deep implicated enemy of Saul.

THIRD PRINCE.
Do we not know him, even to our cost?
Be not your grace deceived.   Let him withdraw;
Lest he, betraying, should upon us turn,
E'en in the midst and imminence of the strife.

FIRST PRINCE.
He shall not mingle with us in the fight.—
What, shall we take a headsman to the field,
Whose practised arm shall toward us fatal wield!

FOURTH PRINCE.
Too-generous Gath, imagine not for that
He feeds now at thy hand, that thou hast tamed him.
As the wild beast borne to its native woods
Forgets his keeper and attempts to tear him,
So shall thy client, found among his nation,
Regain towards us his old injurious bent.

FIRST PRINCE.
Hath not the beast oft tasted of our blood?
Did he not buy—plebeian that he is!—
Saul's daughter, his so lately royal wife,
With—oh, dishonor, shall I name it!—with
Twice told a hundred foreskins;—and what better
Shaggy peace-offering could he take to Saul
Than were our heads?

SEVERAL PRINCES.
                        Slay him

SECOND PRINCE.
                 Hadst not thou sworn,
He and his band should now be cut to pieces.
Let them begone; for fear they die before thee,
To appease vexed Dagon and the grieving manes
Of the Philistine legions he hath slaughtered.

ACHISH.
Chide me no longer; for he shall begone,—
Though better or more faithful have I none.

FIRST PRINCE.
My Lord of Gath, see to it.

THIRD PRINCE.
Do so, my Lord;
For tis not well this recreant stay here,
To rouse our wrath or put our souls in fear.
[Exeunt the PRINCES.

ACHISH (*to* DAVID, *who has now approached him*).
David, those Lords, my princely Peers, mistrust thee.
Thou must return, for their displeasure's high.
Yet do I find thee unimpeachable,
And grieve to lose the service of thine arm.

DAVID.
My kind Protector, say what have I done,
Since I have found asylum in Philistia,
That now I am suspected?

ACHISH.
Ask me not.
Thou art as faultless now in my esteem
As were a ministering angel of thy God
Faultless in his great service; yet our princes
Have, with bad unanimity, declared
Thou shalt not with them play thy part i'th' field:
Hence, soon as dawns to-morrow's streaking light,
Haste back to Ziklag; lest the Amalekite
Ravage the south, and, on the wings of ire,
Consume thy substance with swift sword and fire.
[Exit ACHISH.

DAVID.
They do mistrust me with a grounded dread.
To Ziklag let me go, nor wish to stay
And, perhaps, see issue of disastrous day;
For howsoever the event may fall,
It must be hurtful or to me or Saul.
[Exit.

SCENE V.

Jezreel. Time, the morrow. Enter SAUL *and* ABNER.

SAUL.

Rapid this march hath been;—but oh, I'm sad.
The prophets have not honestly enquired!—
No wonder;—neither wonder what I'll do.
I will have knowledge of a kind beyond
That of my present insight. In dark hour
I persecuted those who dealt with spirits.
Why did I it with o'er-officious zeal,
To please Jehovah, who now leaves me darkling?
Nay, look not grave, Abner; rebuke me not:
My mind is bent unto my altered lot.
Find for me now, I charge thee by our kinship,
One that hath gotten a familiar spirit.

ABNER.

Good cousin, pray have not recourse to witchcraft!

SAUL.

It is the best craft going: for since Samuel
Died, priests are all imposters; and the line
Of Aaron, long imagined half omniscient,
Are blank as other men.

ABNER.

This is the very moving of despair:
And never did despair yet win a field,
Or sable doubt yet yean white victory!

SAUL.

I can no longer live, coz, thus! Oh, I
Could live on hope, as the camelion
Is said to live on air! but faith has ceased
To animate me in these latter years;
And what there is hereafter, I have lately
Forgot to fear, as long since ceased to hope for.

ABNER.

Nay, cousin, cease; or I indeed must leave you.

SAUL.

Even strife and change can now but feebly stir me.
I feel I'm growing old; and creep along
The remnant of my shortened days of age,
Indifferent, toward where looms desolate,
Death's sullen land. As a tired traveller
Crosses a dull, monotonous, windy common,
Beyond which lies his goal, some smoky town,
Like him, I journey to some foul obscure.
Oh, I am sick to th' bottom of my being!
And there is no physician; no going back
To youth, and health, and herd-keeping in Gibeah.
They say that beggars may not choosers be;
And I have knocked at heaven's door in vain,
So I will e'en betake me to another.
For some superior guidance to mine own
Mere veteran skill and courage, have I will.

ABNER.

But it is said that all familiar spirits
Are spirits of evil.

SAUL.

     Than myself, there'll be
More evil none, not one more desperate.
I will enquire myself, for I am set.

              [*Exit.*

ABNER.

I tremble: for I fear the hand of doom
Is on him, since no good may come from such
Dark consultation; and it hath been said
None seek such, save they from whom God has fled.
I'll after him; for once this purpose known,
'Twill soon be bruited over all the army.

    [*Re-enter* SAUL *and a* SOLDIER *with him.*

SAUL.

The devil's found much sooner than the Lord,
By those who dare to seek him.   This man says
There is a woman now near Endor living
That speaks by help of a familiar spirit.
[*To the* SOLDIER
Thou shalt go with me to her.—Ah, thou palest!

SOLDIER.

Your majesty, I have two comrades who
Would dare the very devil in his den.

SAUL.

Go fetch them me : they are the very men.
I will to-night be with the witch at Endor,
Put her in peril and from it defend her;
For that great oath which I 'gainst such have sworn,
I break myself in my estate forlorn.
How art thou, Abner ?   Come, good mate, be cheery,
Although this season is but dark and dreary.
I prythee, cousin, do not let us quarrel.
I go disguise me in some plain apparel
See that it is not known where I am gone;
And be my absence hid from Jonathan :
And may the powers that rule within the air
Hold all until to-morrow in their care.

ABNER.

I dare not say Amen to that.—But go ;—
And may your errand work you little woe.

SAUL.

Whate'er it work, my will shall not abate
To know the best or know the worst of fate.
But principally to the witch I go
To be informed what 'tis that I should do.
Alas, that I should to such strait be driven
By an old quarrel with resentful Heaven;
Or, as I doubt, mere priest-fomented feud,

Inveterate, being mixed with their own blood.
On Samuel may the feud's accountment fall,
And th' blood be on the fiend that stirred my gall.
He goes as gay, but sad at heart is Saul.—
Abner, wilt with me to my toilet come?

ABNER.

Lead on, I'll follow; but with dread I'm dumb.
[*Exeunt.*

SCENE VI.

Gibeah. The Courtyard of the Palace. Time immediately after that of the last scene.

MALZAH (*running in wildly*).

Oh joy! How sweet is liberty regained!
I feel that I am free; I cannot doubt it.
Let me begone from these abhorrèd precincts:
I cannot curse them in this happy mood,
So happy is it, that I'm growing good.
Prosperity would renew in me the angel!—
Nay, the wide world will now seem new to me,
And as romantic as at first did heaven.
[*A female servant crosses the court.*
Ah,
There's the sly slut that rated me so often
For entering her master. Shall I tease her
With swelling 'neath the waist, thick ancles, fleas, or
Black nipples, pimples, or the like; or even
Give her the erysipelas in the face,
That she may seem a young and fiery drunkard?
Shall I so blight her now that none will woo her?
Oh no: I cannot harm her in this vein,
For joy has drawn from me my sting of mischief.
I will believe in goodness from this hour.

But how I talk! Now let me fly,
On legs of love and wings of joy;

And peep into each crystal glass
Of fountain, as I by it pass,
To see if from my visage go
The traces of my recent woe:
Then blithely let me journey on
To meet Great Zaph ere sets the sun,—
Before the sun sets 'neath the sea,
Again to Zaph re-render me.

[*Exit.*

SCENE VII.

A forest near the sea. Time, evening.
ZAPH *seated, and* ZEPHO *standing near him.*

ZEPHO (*aside*).

At eve
How happy in these upland shades,
To mark the sun through vista glades!—
To mark the sun set o'er the sea,
While slumber comes o'er Zaph and me!—
My master is about to speak.

ZAPH.

Zepho, the sun's descended beam
Hath laid his rod on th' ocean stream;
And this o'erhanging wood-top nods
Like golden helms of drowsy gods.
Methinks that now I'll stretch for rest,
With eyelids sloping toward the west;
That, through their half transparencies,
The rosy radiance passed and strained,
Of mote and vapor duly drained,
I may believe, in hollow bliss,
My rest in the empyrean is.
Watch thou; and when upcomes the moon,
A-towards her turn me; and, then, boon,
Thyself compose, 'neath wavering leaves,

That hang these branched, majestic eaves:
That so, with self-imposed deceit,
Both, in this halcyon retreat,
By trance possessed, imagine may
We couch in heaven's night-argent ray:
For fond 't were not to make this earth
All that to us it can be worth;
Which is (from out the major driven)
To appear to us a minor heaven.
But few things are what they appear,—
The smoothest 'neath the face are riven;
And 'tis as safe to slumber here
As, Zepho, erst it was in heaven:
So here I lie, since it doth seem
I soon shall sleep, perchance shall dream.

   A VOICE (*trolling merrily*).
I'm coming, I'm coming along in my glee:
I'm in the odour of sanctity;
And to stay therein I've sought each bloom
Whose saintly mouth doth vomit perfume.
A holy, holy, holy rent
Mine own mouth is, that thus gives vent:
I'm purged with sun and washed with dew,
And girt with woodbine, coming to you;
Coming to you,
Coming to you,
Ha, ha! ha, ha! I'm coming to you.

    ZAPH.
What cawing rook is that?
    ZEPHO.
     I'll look, sir. Oh,
It is a spirit that you know,—
Malzah.
    ZAPH.
  Malzah? Why, then, there's news.
      [*Enter* MALZAH.

My long lost Malzah, is it thou!
Thou wert indeed most jovial now.

MALZAH.

I've long been sad : 'tis time a cock should crow
When morning breaks.

ZAPH.

Rich through the evening air we heard thy voice
Borne nearer, vassal.   Thou hast escaped from Saul;—
But how ?

MALZAH.

       I felt that I was liberated :
So straight came hither, past the Hebrew camp;
Whence Saul this day unto a witch hath gone
To seek advice, since God to him gives none.

ZAPH.

What is his present and particular plight ?

MALZAH.

A piteous one : composed of doleful cheer,—
That last, worst state, despair combined with fear.
For the Philistines have invaded Israel,
In greater multitude than heretofore ;
And conscience, for the slaughter of Nob's priests,
Now on him presses with forebodings sore.
I fear his course is drawing to an end.

ZAPH.

I thought these witches were beneath his outlawing.

MALZAH.

They were ;—but who on prey hath never pounced,
Which once, to others, dirty he pronounced ?
The Israelite is famishing for knowledge.

ZAPH.

His host encamps on Gilboa?

MALZAH.

       No, not now ;
But in the fruitful valley of Jezreel.

ZAPH.

At once from land and sea my spirits I'll call.
My flighty Zepho, for them posting go.

ZEPHO.

I'll bring them to you in a trice or so.
[Vanishes.

ZAPH.

Samuel is dead; but my revenge survives,
And will while Gloriel in triumph thrives.
So let me all my energies arouse
To thwart the side that Gloriel shall espouse;
Whether it be the huge, Philistine host,
Or Saul to drive them homeward from his coast.
Zepho hath found my vassals easily!
They're nearing; for I hear their roar,
Like billows tumbling to the shore.
[Enter ZEPHO and the demons.
This is done well. None can more prompt than you,
When you desire your discipline to shew.
Now take with me, in circles high, your flight,
To drop upon Jezreel when drops the night;
There to avenge (if may) the wrong that fell
On us at Michmash from proud Gloriel;
When, to assist the valiant son of Saul,
Beneath the ground he made us shake and crawl.
[Exeunt, soaring through the top of the forest.

SCENE VIII.

Endor. Outside of the WITCH'S *house. Time, night.*
Enter SAUL *in plain garments, and two* SOLDIERS *attending him, but disguised as his companions.*

SAUL.

By the description, this must be the dwelling.
It stands alone, is ample, yet a hovel;
With only one small window, that can scarcely

Admit sufficient light, even at noonday,
To chase thence darkness.   Doubtless 'tis the place:
It seems fit habitation for dark rites.
Decay eems to possess it, and around
Mute in the dimness looms dilapidation.
Knock thou, and make inquiry of who comes.
                    [*The first* ATTENDANT *knocks gently.*
She comes not.   Knock again ; and louder this time.
                    [*The* ATTENDANT *knocks a second time.*
                    [*Aside.*
Danger hath made the creature cautious ; and as I
Seek, in the darkness of my present plight,
To peer through her skill's medium, and learn
What were the best that I should do, so she,
Perchance, is, from the darkness of her dwelling,
Noting us through the casement, so that she
May know if to admit us.   Some one comes.

The door is slowly and partially opened by the WITCH, *who stands timorously within, with her hand upon the latch.*

FIRST ATTENDANT.

Lives here the Wisewoman ?

WITCH.

                    What Wisewoman, stranger ?
There lives a woman here both poor and lonely.

FIRST ATTENDANT.

And is she now alone, and art thou she?

WITCH.

I am the only woman dwelling here.—
You surely have not hither come to rob me !
Alas, what is there in this place forlorn ?

FIRST ATTENDANT.

Art thou the Witch and art thou now alone?
Tell us, for we are seeking to consult her.

WITCH.

And were I both, pray what would you want with me?
To inquire of such were now a misdemeanour,

Did any such survive beneath Saul's rigor.
Witches are none in Israel now thou knowest.

SECOND ATTENDANT.

Fear not: we are honest men. Art thou the witch?
For we are told that hereabouts there dwells one.

WITCH.

Art thou not mad to ask me such a question,
When such are now not to be found in Israel?
Then how darest use that dangerous name towards me?
Why come ye laying snares for a lone woman?

SECOND ATTENDANT.

We lay no snares; but art thou not the witch?

WITCH.

What, I?

SECOND ATTENDANT.

Yes thou thyself. Do not to thee
The love-crossed wights and pining maids repair,
To learn their fate, or purchase from thee charms?
Canst thou not tell where missing treasure is?
Dost thou not prophesy who shall grow rich,
Who shall have fruitful wives, who disobedient
Children; who early die, who live to see
Four generations and be called great-grandsire?

SAUL.

Speak fearlessly. Art thou not one of those,
Who, in the weird sagacity of their art,
Foretell which course shall prosper and which not;
What critical and pregnant enterprise
Succeed, and what result in black disaster?
Art thou not one of those proud sorceresses
Who have prevision, and the power to summon
Back to the world the spirits of the dead?

WITCH.

The wind blows cool: come in.

[*They go in, and the* WITCH *closes the door.*

WITCH.

Enter this inner room ; for I to none
Give entertainment in the outer one,
That the rude winds do enter, and, for aught
I know, where stands now at the door a wolf,
Which may to-morrow howl among the hills
That I to-night was hospitable to you.
How know I you're sincere ! How do I know
But that you come to pry, and see if I
Be she who here (as goes, you say, report)
Follows the witch's now illegal art !
Ah, I suspect you ; strongly I suspect you !
I like not thee, tall stranger :—thou'rt a spy,
And these men are thy witnesses. Ah, base
And cruel witnesses; for ye know well,
Full well ye know all three, what Saul hath done,—
How he hath put to death all female kind
Who had familiar spirits, also male
That dared commune with goblin, or foul fiend,
Spirit, or power of the invisible world,
'Till not a wizard is left in all the land !
Then wherefore come ye three men unto me,
As though I were to conjurations given ?
Why lay a snare for me, that ye may hale
Me hence to execution ?

SAUL.
     Peace. I swear—

WITCH.

What dost thou swear by ?

SAUL.
     By whate'er thou wilt :—
By hell, for thou'st no interest in heaven.

WITCH.

How much hast thou ? Swear to me by the moon,
That is the witch's workshop and arcanum,
From whence they cast on those who persecute them
All woes that body and that mind can bear,
Pain, horror. Swear, then, to me by the moon.

SAUL.

I will not swear unto thee by the moon,
But by the moon's Creator. As God lives,
There shall no mischief unto thee occur
For doing what I bid thee.

WITCH.
            Thou hast sworn.

SAUL.
And I will keep mine oath.

WITCH.
            I tell thee, stranger,
That thou hadst better; for I shall have given
To me thy soul in endless slavery,
If thou prove treacherous. Remember: and
Now say what I must do.

SAUL.
            Divine to me
By thy familiar spirit, since thou hast one,
And bring up him whom I shall name to thee.
Begin thine incantations; for the moments
Fly, and I've far to go and much to do
Or ere the dawn.

WITCH.
            Whom wouldst thou I should shew thee?

SAUL.
Shew to me Samuel.

WITCH.
            Samuel! Thinkest thou
That he'd appear for such as thou art? No,
He would not come for any less than Saul:—
No, nor for him; for he is now abandoned,
And we whom he tormented are revenged.
Long have they said that God has left him.—Well
Others have lost their souls beyond redemption.
They say he has a demon—so have others—
But come, I'll disappoint thee; for, remember,
Samuel will not be roused for thee, although
I'll knock with thunder at his resting-place,

w

And send my piercing spirit (who, like frost,
Can penetrate a rocky sepulchre)
To próject molten lightning through his bones.
Prostrate yourselves; nor, till I bid you, look
At what shall lie before you soon agape,
The yawn of hades, the dark mouth of hell.
[SAUL *and his companions fall prostrate.*
Ha hee! ha hee! ho! Adramuel,
Adramuel, Adramuel, thee shew,
From sunny height or gloom below!
Adramuel, why is it so?
Dost thou not thy mistress know?
[*A strange sound heard. Appear* ADRAMUEL.
Oh, my sweet slave, oh, my dear friend and master,
Still, still so faithful to me! Now go faster
Than do the fabulous coursers of the wind,
To Ramah, or to Hades, and bring Samuel.
[ADRAMUEL *vanishes.*
[*Aside.*
Whither would not Adramuel go? Brave spirit!
If I command him, he would wind his way
Into the presence of the sons of God,
And there, although in vain, demand the prophet.
It cannot be; for Samuel may not come
From Abraham's arms. I mock my mighty demon.
But whence this tremor creeping through my frame?
Ah, I am strangely warped! I have a loom
That he I've sent for, will arise and come.
Be still, ye tottering limbs. Adramuel hastes;—
[*Listening.*
Adramuel nearer comes. I hear a mourning,
As if he bore within his arms
A soul that came unwillingly to my charms.
[*Bending forward as if to see something.*
Roll, roll away, thou stygian smoke,
And let me into the abysm look. [*Shrieks.*
[*Crying with a loud voice.*
Ah, why hast thou deceived me?—Thou art Saul.

SAUL.

Calm thee. What hast thou seen?

WITCH.
        Oh, gods ascending.
Angels I saw or gods—I know not which—
Out of the earth ascending, and another
Borne up amidst them careful.

SAUL.
      Of what form?

WITCH.
An old man, and upcovered with a mantle.

SAUL (*aside*).
'Tis Samuel here again!
 [SAUL *bows his face to the ground, and the ghost of* SAMUEL *rises.*

GHOST (*inaudible except to* SAUL).
Unhappy king, why hast thou summoned me,
Out of the tranquil ecstacy of death?—
Why hast thou troubled me to bring me hither?

SAUL.
I am in great distress, for the Philistines
Again are making war against me, and
Invade my kingdom; whilst the Lord hath left me,
And answers me no more by dreams or prophets,
Neither by Urim's light nor kindling Thummim's:
Therefore I've called on thee that thou mayest shew me
What I shall do.

GHOST.
      Forsaken by Jehovah,
Why hast thou thus resorted unto me?
God now performs that which, by me, He promised
To David, and now finally ends thy reign;
The kingdom being no longer thine but David's,
Because thou hast been disobedient,
Nor didst God's vengeance upon Amalek.
Therefore God leaveth thee this hour in darkness.
Yet, not obedient to charm or spell,

Which thou hast wickedly employed, I come
Declare, He will thee and thy host surrender
Into the power of the Philistines; tell thee
Thou and thy sons shall be with me to-morrow.

SAUL *faints away, and the* GHOST *and all supernatural phenomena disappear with a dull sound.*

SECOND ATTENDANT.

'Tis thunder, and it shakes to its foundations
This crazy dwelling. Lo, the witch's form
Trembles like it, and is as pale as moonlight,
As, like to a detected culprit, she
Stands with clasped hands, aghast at her own doing.

FIRST ATTENDANT.

Now may I ne'er again assist at magic!

SECOND ATTENDANT.

This has surpassed my dreadest anticipations.
The king has swooned.

FIRST ATTENDANT.

      Quick; let us take him up.
          [*They raise* SAUL.
This was an impious act! What hast thou done, hag?

WITCH.

That which his majesty bade me do. See to him.

FIRST ATTENDANT.

Although I apprehend not all he knows,
I know it must be awful; since the flash
Of that pale witch's shriek appalled me, and
The crack of her few words: oh, then, what must
Unto his heart have been the perfect peal!
He seems as dying: set him on the bed.

SECOND ATTENDANT.

What hath the vision told him, for thou knowest?

WITCH.

Ask not, but help to raise him. This I know,
That he will not die here: he'll rally yet.

SECOND ATTENDANT.

How knowest thou that?

FIRST ATTENDANT.

Mark him!—I do believe
That he will not go hence a living man.
Oh, I am sick myself,—and so art thou;—
I shudder even to the very marrow!

SECOND ATTENDANT.

He lives; but, oh, how corpse-like!

FIRST ATTENDANT.

We are all four
As pale as winding-sheets: my own voice sounds,
Methinks, sepulchral.—Man, express thy horror.
Thou seest not thyself: thine eyeballs roll,
As if from some great under-agitation,
Which yet sends no true billow-swell of phrase
Up to thy white-shore lips.—Mine own feel stiffening,
As if with mortal chillness.—See that creature,
How her teeth chatter! Witch, use thy croaking tongue,
And tell the worst that thou hast seen and heard.

WITCH.

Peace; for the king returns unto himself.

[*Casting herself at* SAUL'S *feet.*

Hear me, your majesty. I have obeyed you,
And at your instance put my life in peril;
Then do not punish me for what you've seen.
Forgive my lying boast against you; and
Permit me (in the safety of your oath,
Wherein you said no harm should happen to me)
To set some food before your majesty,
That you may gather vigor to depart,
Since you declared that you had far to go
And much to do before the morrow dawned.

SECOND ATTENDANT.

Ay, thou hast done thy mischief, witch; and now—

FIRST ATTENDANT.
Hist, hist!
SAUL.
What hour is it? Have I slept long? No, no,
I cannot eat; why should I? I'll take nothing.
FIRST ATTENDANT.
We pray you do. Your majesty cannot return
Still fasting; and there is no time for rest
If you would reach Jezreel before the morning.
SAUL.
I cannot eat: I loathe both food and life.

[*To the* WITCH.

He came up like an old man, didst thou say?
WITCH.
I did, oh king;—but bid me cook some food.
SAUL.
Wouldst cook food for the dead?—
What were they broiling in that hideous smoke?
SECOND ATTENDANT (*aside*).
He is the semblance of despair and horror!
He has seen more than we, or than we dream of.
Urge him to eat, or he will never rise
Up living.
FIRST ATTENDANT.
Take some food, my liege;
Your majesty, be persuaded. We oft put
Things disagreeable unto our mouths,
Which things we do call medicines, as they are;
So be your majesty persuaded to take food,
However much in taking you may loathe it,
And think 'tis medicine, for 'twill so prove to you.
SAUL.
I will not: I'm past cure.
SECOND ATTENDANT.
His majesty
Knows that the army will require his presence.

SAUL.

Bring me some food, woman, quickly.
                                    [*Exit* WITCH.
                    Ere the morn
Shall tint the orient with the soldier's color,
We must be at the camp.   What watch is it?—
Bring the food hither quickly.   Hath the moon
Yet risen?   Look out and tell me; look out at th' window.
          [*The* FIRST ATTENDANT *looks out at the window.*
                    [*Aside.*
The last outlook has come, and drear it is!
                    [*Aloud.*
Well, what's the moon a-doing?

FIRST ATTENDANT.
                                    Your majesty,
With visionary dawn she is advancing
Unto the whitening frontier of the east.

SAUL.

And yet she rises late to-night: she's old.
We must begone, we must begone.   Poor moon,
She is old, and so am I!—Is the food coming?
Bring food here with dispatch; or th' moon up heaven,
Will, with her ancient, silver feet, be treading
Ere we upon our road.—How old is the
Moon now?

SECOND ATTENDANT.
        She is in her last quarter.

SAUL.
                                    Then
I shall behold her this last time when she's
An emblem of myself.   Yet she'll return
And rule the night; but I shall from my shade
Come up no more!—Say, is the food a-coming?
I have heard tell of culprits who have ravened
Upon the margin of their execution, and myself
Begin to feel an hungered.—Comrades, comrades,
You'll butchers be to-morrow, and can fatten you.
To-morrow—oh, come thou dreadful morrow!

FIRST ATTENDANT (*to his companion*).
                                        Mark.
            SECOND ATTENDANT.
His mind is wandering.
            FIRST ATTENDANT.
                              I know not that.
He has been warned of some dire mischief coming.
            SECOND ATTENDANT.
And yet I'm sure he wanders.—Oh, see, see,
How thought-fixed are his eyes, rigid his muscles!
His soul is toward the camp: it is not here.
He wanders homeward, like to a lost creature
That through foul roads still drags its mirèd limbs.
Your majesty, lie down, and rest whilst waiting.
The witch is making haste: I hear her busy.
            SAUL.
No no, not yet: there'll be a long lie down
Anon. Yes, presently there'll be a sleep
With time enough to dream in. [*Aside.*] Oh, how all
Like to a dream seems my career now closing!
How like a troubled April day it seems!
How like a famine-smit, disastrous year!—
Will that foul witch be long?
            SECOND ATTENDANT.
                              Your majesty, no.
            SAUL.
'Tis well. [*Aside.*] As round some spent, delirious one,
Fallen, at last, asleep, the hand of friendship
Draws the thin curtains, who shall draw around
My memory apologetic shade?
For Ahinoam is dead; and Jonathan,
And Melchi-shuah, and Abinadab,
Shall go to morrow with me, and the rest
Are all too young.—Yet Abner may remain
And vindicate me somewhat. But if he,
Too, die, (for David will not curb the priesthood,)

Then I must leave a blotted name behind me,
And enemies whose pens shall slander me
On biding parchment. No, not slander, surely:
I would not abdicate. Oh, love of rule,
For thee I may have damned my soul to hell,
Murdering for thee the sacred priests of heaven!
It was the fiend,—yet will the fiend for 't suffer?
Shall I not be beneath with him to-morrow?—
How now? The food, the food!

[*Enter the* WITCH *with viands.*
Thou'rt here. Woman,
Are these your sorcerer's victuals?

WITCH.
Your majesty,
Although these hands of mine prepared them, they
Are pure as any that, by hands of priests,
E'er did on altar smoke in holy rites.

SAUL (*aside*).
The priests! the priests!—'twas Doeg's hands, not mine:
Mine are not red with Aaron's blood.—Oh, but
My heart is black with blood that rage then caused
To overflow it, and which still it wears;
Even as earth is covered to this hour
With relics of the angry Deluge' wave.
The priests! the priests! the priests! [*Aloud.*] Why eat ye not?
Fall on: from ceremony I absolve you.
Nay, nay: no more request me to partake.

[*The men begin to eat.*
[*Aside.*
Why should a dead man eat!—Oh, that the dead
Could come again and live!—that Aaron's sons,
While I in death put off my royal robes,
Revived, could fill again their sacred vestments!
Cannot the spirit live again in clay,
E'en as old tenants to old homes return?—
Return to life, ye murdered priestly shades;
Live in the sanctuaries of your ancient forms!
Oh, Life, how delicate a thing thou art,

Crushed with the feathery edge of a thin blade!
Frail!—why wert thou not made inviolable?
Why art thou irrecoverable as frail?
Thou, noblest guest, art all as much exposed
To foul ejectment from the flesh, as is
The spider from its web by maiden's broom.
Yea, with a little wielded iron, any
Can drive thee forth from thy recesses' walls,
Which thou wilt not repair; for thou, weak fool,
At voice of death, from thine old banquet-room
Start'st like a haughty noble that, in huff,
Leaves his convives, and will return no more.—
Why should I cherish thee, why feed thee now!
Yet I, a breathing corse, must mumble,—I,
A shadow, raise my sunken, phantom maw
With the refection of this solid world.
      [*Rising, after having eaten a little.*
Now let us go. Here take these shekels, woman:
I pay thee for the evil thou hast shewn me.
Live and repent of thy black arts, ere death
Shall send thee where there may not be a whitening.
      [*Aside.*
She may still live and bleach by pious sighs,
And showers of tears, and dews of holy deeds;
But I must due, with foul sins on my head,
Betake me to the region of the dead.
      [*Aloud.*
Lead, and unbar the door;—and see thou sellest
Amulets no more while on the earth thou dwellest.
What I have given thee will thy wants supply.
Amend thy life; for thou, too, shalt soon die.
           [*Exeunt.*

SCENE IX.

Amidst the Hebrew Camp. Time, night.

    JONATHAN (*coming out of a tent*).
Why should I wake within my tent? for darkness
Is on my soul as well as on the soil.

I cannot sleep; and both my brothers toss
Upon their truckle-beds, and moan and mutter.
There's evil near us; either of defeat,
Or death to one or more of mine own race.
Strange, that my father should be absent now!

[Enter ABNER.

Who's there?

ABNER.

A friend.

JONATHAN.

'Tis like the voice of Abner.

ABNER.

Not like it, but the same. Thou'rt Jonathan,
And like me wanderest, ghostlike, ill at ease.

JONATHAN.

Abner, there lies across my path a shade
That I must pass to-morrow; let it be
Even the billows black of death's deep gulf,
Or a mere frowning shallow of a hazard.

ABNER.

To-morrow seems a space that I must clear,
Swept by a thick, continual shower of darts,
And which I shall not cross without many wounds.

JONATHAN.

But that my father hath forbidden thee,
I would command thee to inform me where
He is this hour.

ABNER.

Let us his narrow gap
Of absence fill with our sufficient presence.
Back to our tents. Good night.

[Exit.

JONATHAN.

Through this thick gloom,
And th' mask of my brave kinsman's countenance,
I saw a lurking grief. Where is my sire?

Where he is flies despair. Saul, father, come!
Why art thou absent on the eve of battle?
Come, sire, come, morrow, though thou dark dost loom!
Whate'er it be, 'tis Heaven shall send the doom.
  [*Disappears among the tents.*

SCENE X.

The Hebrew Camp in the valley of Jezreel. Time, morning.
Enter SAUL *and* ABNER, *followed by* JONATHAN, ABINADAB, *and* MELCHI-SHUAH.

SAUL.

Ask me no more to tell thee what the witch said.
  [*Aside.*
I'll hide it to the last; and none shall learn,
Out of my mouth, that I am dead while living.
  [*Aloud.*
Come hither, sons. [*Aside.*] Oh, now what shall I say?
  [*Aloud.*
This is our latest field; and should it prove
Our last one also, (and you know such might be,)
Then let it be our noblest. Go, dear sons,
And in this dark hour shine forth in new deeds,
Striking, from th' flinty courage of your foes,
Out bright, enduring honor. Jonathan,
Forget not what thou heretofore hast done,
And let thy star this day become a sun.
Away now to your posts.
  [*Exeunt* JONATHAN, ABINADAB, *and* MELCHI-SHUAH.
  [*Aside.*] Darkness and death!—
But go, ye lights of Saul; be quenched, be quenched!
Oh, my poor sons, my sons, ye die for me!
'Tis for your father's follies that you perish!
  [*A trumpet sounds.*
Now, like a charger at the trumpet's voice,
Now let me rush into this forlorn field,
And struggle till I perish.—Oh, but ye,

My sons, shall ye go too? Oh, horror!—No,
I will not send my children to their death!
I will recall them.—Has not Samuel said,
To-day they march with me unto the dead?
Oh, thither march, then, sons.—Oh, sons, forgive me,
Who utter toward you such unnatural words!—
Not mine but heaven's. Oh, hell, upbraid me not,
Nor, loathing, spit upon me thy fierce scorn,
When, like a triple-offspring murderer,
I enter thee. I come, I come:
I feel the dreadful drawing of my doom.
How am I changed!—how am I turned, at last,
Into a monster at itself aghast!
Oh, wretched children, oh, more wretched sire!—
Oh, that I might this moment here expire!

ABNER (*aside*).

What can this strange commotion in him mean?

SAUL (*aside*).

        See there how Abner stands
With wondering visage and with slackening hands!
        [*Aloud.*
Abner, farewell.—But understand me right:
Do thou fare well, coz, in the coming fight.—
Go, go, dear cousin; go.

ABNER (*aside*).

            I'm loth to leave him;
For never, since I knew him, have I seen
Him wearing such a strange, distracted mien.
        [*Exit.*

SAUL.

All have gone from me now except despair;
And my last, lingering relics of affection,—
And now let them go too. Oh, break, my heart!
It is not those who shall die with me, but
Those whom I leave, shall shake my manhood most,—
My orphaned daughters, and my youngest born,

Poor crippled Mephibosheth. For the rest,
We are about to pass to one dark goal.
                              [*After weeping a while in silence.*
Now, let me scorn all further tenderness;
And keep my heart as obdurate as the hills,
That have endured the assault of every tempest
Poured on them from the founding of the world.
                                    [*Another trumpet sounds.*
Ay, blow thy fill, thou martial trumpet breath.
Come on now, war! come on, disaster, death!
                                                   [*Exit.*

SCENE XI.

Between Jezreel and Gilboa. A great noise and uproar of the battle.
Enter ZAPH *and his band of demons, including* MALZAH.

ZAPH.

It is in vain; for Gloriel and his troop,
Where'er we move, impenetrably standing
Between ourselves and the Philistine host,
Hinder our succouring of the Hebrew king.
Wheel off, then; though our reasonable hate
Shall yet be glutted, in the teeth of fate.
           [*Exeunt, and the Hebrew army pass retreating. Enter* SAUL.

SAUL.

Drive back our flying cowards on the foe!—
But will the blast be stayed by its own howls?
The doom that's on me weighs too on mine army,
Which, even whilst it combats, flees before
The slaughtering Philistines. But Gilboa
Again shall see me on it standing firm;
For they shall not hereafter say of me,
That I was slain in ignominious flight.
Oh, had I been allowed to win this field,
Though, by its last expended arrow, doomed
To fall and finish thereon my career,
I had died happy! for I'm old though strong,
Wearied although not spent. But this may not;
And I must hence, since the pursuit grows hot.   [*Exit.*

SCENE XII.

Gilboa. The sound of the battle heard faintly. Enter ABNER *and some* SOLDIERS *in haste and disorder.*

ABNER.
Where is the king?
Go urge him from the field, that fast is clearing;
But tell him not that his three sons are killed.
                              [*Exeunt* SOLDIERS.
Alas, alas, now do I think that he
Foreknew their fate at parting! Oh, the knell
Appears now sounded over Israel!
   [*Exit, and* SAUL *enters mortally wounded and sinks upon the ground.*

SAUL.
Now let me die, for I indeed was slain
With my three sons. Where are ye, sons? Oh, let me
Find ye, that I may perish with you; dying,
Cover you with my form, as doth the fowl
Cover her chickens! Oh, Philistia,
Thou now art compensated,—now art getting
Rich with this crimson, hot, and molten tide;
That waits not patient to be coined in drops,
But rushes, in an ingot-forming stream,
Out of the mine and mintage of my heart!
Oh, my three poor dead sons, where are you? Ye
Have gone before me into the hereafter
Upon such innocency-flighted steps,
That I, with feet cumberèd with clots of blood,
Shall lose of you all glimpse, and then my soul
Shall drop to the abyss. Gush faster, blood,
And gallop with my soul towards Hades,
That yawns obscure.
   A dull sound arises from the distance. SAUL *rises somewhat, but falls again upon the ground.*
               It is the enemy's horse!
                    [*Enter* SAUL'S ARMOUR-BEARER.

ARMOUR-BEARER.

Rise, or the foe will be upon my liege!

SAUL.

I cannot, boy; for I am dying fast:—
And yet not fast enough, it seems; so draw
Forthwith thy sword and with it run me through,
Lest those uncircumcised arrive and do it,
And afterwards abuse me.

ARMOUR-BEARER.

Oh, no, no:
I dare not take away your royal life!

SAUL.

Why shouldst thou fear to take what I would give thee?
Quick, run me through: the enemy are here.

ARMOUR-BEARER.

I dare not take away your majesty's life.
I cannot do it; indeed, I cannot do it.

SAUL.

Failed by a friend at last!
    [*Taking a sword that lies on the ground near him.*
Ah, here is one
Of that stern sort that never yet hath failed me.
    [*Having risen with a great effort.*
Sword, enter and drive out of this my spirit!
    [*Falls on the sword and expires.*

ARMOUR-BEARER.

Now what remains for me except to follow!
    [*Also falls on his sword.*

The Philistine cavalry sweep across the scene, and carry off the corpse of Saul.

END OF SAUL.

Jephthah's Daughter (excerpts)

JEPHTHAH'S ACCOUNT OF THE
EVENTS LEADING TO HIS RASH VOW

Who shall go scatheless and not suffer loss
That dare attempt to stipulate with Heaven,
And bribe Jehovah to bestow success?
Punish me, people, in my passing pride;
Fling me for food to vultures and to eagles;
Give me to wolves, or offer me to lions;
For I have given my daughter up to death; —
Myself, who gave her her beginning, have
Pronounced the fatal fiat of her end.
Oh, friends, despise me not that thus I weep!
Oh, wonder not that I before you rage!
Behold a rash, a wretched, ruined man!
Hear me, for I must speak, though you should curse me;
Listen, though, hearing, you should learn to loathe me.
Close were the armies gathered: Israel here,
There Ammon, bold embattled; insolent,
And claiming Gilead as his own, of old.
Dark were the heavens, and lowered upon our lines
(Oh, darker still was my fatuity!),
And much I feared, yet much I longed, to know
The issue of the pained and pregnant hour,
That, in the dim, cloud-curtained firmament,
With gusty throes and sullen thunders moaned,
And seemed to writhe as on a bed of travail,
And, with huge, globy drops, enormous weep,

And yearn to be delivered; whilst I stood —
Near me no priest, to shed from his gemmed breastplate
Prophetic light of Urim and of Thummim.
What could I do? What did I do? I cried,
'Lord God of Israel, the tribes' defence,
Their hope in peace, their help when waging war;
Jehovah, hear me, hear thy servant, Lord:
If, without fail, thou shalt this day deliver
Into my hands the Ammonitish host,
Then shall it be, that whatsoever thing
Shall issue first from out my doors to meet me,
When I return, victorious and in peace,
Shall be thine own, and, slain upon thine altar,
As a burnt-offering, be there consumed.'
Oh, rashly, rashly for my peace, I vowed!
Oh, dearly, dearly was the victory bought!
Its price, your ransom, my dear daughter — she,
Compared (oh, foolish, vain comparison!)
With whom the glory of this victory
Seems utter darkness, misery, and shame.
Shorten this shameful spectacle; withhold
The rest of what now seems mere mockery.
What am I midst these honours but a wretch?
I nothing have therein, now nothing prize:
Strip me of all, now that my child is gone;
Sword, shield, and judge's staff, all emblems take
That may betoken proud authority:
Take Gilead's chair, take all you promised me —
Alas! not Gilead's chair, with present power,
Nor future fame from this proud feat of arms,

Nor all the fulness of these fertile hills,
Were an equivalent for yon lone lamb,
That hither came, gay skipping from the fold.

JEPHTHAH'S DAUGHTER AMONG HER MAIDENS

And, while the wheels whirred like the hum of bees,
The chant rose softly as flow summer winds
Over ambrosial downs, or through the copse
Where linnets sing, or woods where wild doves woo.
But she, for whose soul's weal the music rose,
Felt not its charm; unlulled, unsoothed; but sat,
Tossed on a sea of doubt and fear. As one
Who, in the cozy cabin, sits below,
And hears the moaning of the windy main,
Perchance forebodes, so she, the while they sung,
Revolving mournful with her wondering soul,
Secluded, silent, dim, sat desolate
Within the tent of her dishevelled hair.
A grief that comprehended not its cause
Consumed her; and, as passed the tints of day
Out at the windows of the west, the light
Ebbed from her eyes, the colour from her cheeks
And lower, and still lower yet, she drooped,
As droops a fair and stately household plant
That misses its accustomed watering;
And, still no tidings from the absent Jephthah,
At length around her sat her maidens mute,
And looked into each other's face, perplexed.

He, in a dark delirium of distress,
Had sought a neighbouring wooded glen, and there
With Heaven thus pleaded for his forfeit child:

'God, God, oh, God, demand not, stern, thy due!
If I have ever moved thee by my prayers,
If favour ever found before thine eyes,
If I am father to my daughter, she
The only heir to my affections, — if
I am an heir of Abraham, the sad sire
Who to Moriah went to slay his son,
But for whose need thou didst provide a ram,
Oh, hear me now, dispense, or else provide!
Behold, I am a rash, imperfect man,
With but one cherished child, a daughter, lamb,
Whose life I staked, not knowing what I did.
Forgive, forego; or say what ransom thou
Demand'st, what price. I give thee all I have
Save her: take all, take me; e'en take the mother.
Take my whole household, all that throng my fields;
Choose Tabor for thine altar; I will pile
It with the choice of Bashan's lusty herds,
And flocks of fatlings, and, for fuel, thither
Will bring umbrageous Lebanon to burn;
Whilst, in the stead of wine and oil, there shall
Pour over it the blood of heathen kings,
So her blood thou wilt spare, and, gracious, give
To me some token that my prayer is heard."

    He said, and stood awaiting for the sign,
And hears above the hoarse, bough-bending wind,
The hill-wolf howling on the neighbouring height,
And bittern booming in the pool below.
Some drops of rain fell from the passing cloud,
That sudden hides the wanly shining moon,
And from the scabbard instant dropped his sword,
And, with long, living leaps and rock-struck clang,
From side to side, and slope to sounding slope,
In gleaming whirls swept down the dim ravine
(Ill omen!): and, mute trembling, as he stood
Helmless (to his astonished view), his daughter,
All in sad disarray, appeared,

Jezebel: A Poem in Three Cantos

CANTO FIRST
    'No tidings yet from Ahab — yet no news
Heard from my summoned priests. Why were they summoned?
Unless with supplications to bring rain
Unto the burning bosom of the earth.
    Three mournful years, and still no rain, no dew;
But every herb scorched up; all living things
Dying of hunger and excessive drought!
Lo, I am blind with tears, am hoarse with cries,
Am weary with long watching for the clouds,
That come not, but, instead thereof, the sun
Hangs flaring in the fiery firmament.
Oh, Baal, blot the sun from out the heavens!
Hang all the heavens in black, the livery
Of death; since without death's lent livery,
Soon all that live must die.'

    So spake sad Jezebel, half pride, half grief;
Then, turning, listless gazed into the west;
Till, as on sudden rises at a gust
The idle awning of a milk-white tent,
Her bosom heaved, her gaze grew keen, her face
Beamed in its pallor like the great, full moon;
And with disparted lips she stood; and still
The westward scanning with deep-searching eyes,
Thus to herself enquiringly resumed: —

    'Surely the blue relents; the void is void
No longer, but a cloud — a little cloud —
Comes like a chariot driving from the sea; —

Or is it but a mote before mine eye,
A mocking mirage? No, it is, it is
A cloud, a little cloud: — Joy, joy! clouds come,
And with them welcome darkness hurrying on.
Baal hath conquered; Baal sendeth rain.
Hark, how the wind awakes; it bends the trees: —
Baal bends their stubborn, stately tops, and makes
Them do obeisance; Baal comes, he comes; —
Behold, the waters come, behold the clouds,
Fraught with the fulness of the outscooped sea!'

And round she looked exultant, radiant strode
Across the chamber, and, elate, exclaimed:

'Where now is Ahab? Let him quick return,
Or ere the rain arrest him. Ahab, come;
Come to my side, as son unto his mother's;
And let me point thine eye to yonder clouds,
That surge as may the coursers toss their manes,
As drag they here thy chariot: — Ahab, come!'

And even while she called her husband entered;
Her husband, Ahab, whom she thus salutes: —

'Oh, Ahab, welcome home! Our horror ends;
And famine flees like to a hovering wolf,
Scared from the fold. Observest thou yon sky?
With overwhelming brows of sable clouds,
Hung fold on fold, and slowly curtaining
The heavens with a canopy of darkness? —

But wherefore is thy countenance as dark
As is yon sky? Light up thy countenance,
O Israel: Lift up thine eyes, and see
How comely black-browed shadow may appear,
As to his father's eye, the Ethiop's son.
Oh, Ahab, look, behold, it blacker grows!
The billows of the darkness deepen till
Midnight dethrones mid-day. The pregnant vault
With fulness overfilled, is at the birth,
And, even now, with huge, presaging drops,
Makes good the skyey promise. Lo, the lightning
Thereunto sets its seal, and, for an oath,
Peals the reverberant thunder. I am drunk
Methinks with joy; and thou shalt drink ere long
Deep in the due delights of trouble passed,
And the drawn wine of ruddiest revenge
On lost Elijah: — we will find him yet,
The hoary traitor; he who swore that there
For years should be no rain to feed the springs;
Neither for years should be allowed to fall
Dew to anoint the ground: — but, soft, my love;
Where hast thou left my prophets?'

     'At the foot
Of Carmel,' answered Ahab.

      'Carmel!' she
Exclaimed, 'And wherefore do they there abide,
To bear the imminent tempest, that fast brews,
And will not wait their leisure? 'Tis at hand!

The abated blue is blotted from the sky;
For calm comes chaos, and loud grows in rage
The rattling thunder, while the lightning leaps,
And plays before us midst the firmament,
As plays the fiery-eyed Leviathan
Amidst the floods; the floods now swift descend,
And in their blest abundance soon shall turn
Samaria to a sea. Again, what do
My prophets?'
      'Sleep.'
         'How? Thou art pleasant. Sleep
They in such pleasant weather? They should play
Amidst this deluge, as do dolphins play
Amidst the sea: How sleep?'

         'Most soundly: they
Will wake no more;' ejaculated Ahab;
'Soundly they sleep, for they are dead — are slain.'
'Slain?' cried she, startled, and her eyes upflashed,
As from the flint should be outstricken fire.
'Slain?' echoed she; and, 'slain,' re-echoed Ahab;
Who, turning from her in mixed fear and shame,
Wept, and with wringing of his hands, exclaimed:
'Slain are thy prophets; slain, alas! all slain.
Oh, Jezebel, this dear, descending deluge
Is bought with deluge of thy priests' shed blood!'
And, as he sobbed in his outbursting grief,
She thus replied in deep, denouncing tones:
'Oh, bloody bargain, that in blood shall be
Full soon rebartered! Say, who slew them, thou?

Caitiff, cease trembling, and declare thy guilt:
None but thyself could do it; art thou not
The King of Israel? Ahab, try me not;
Speak, let thy words run rapid as yon rain;
Let blow thy story, as now blows the wind, —
Fool! — madman! — speak, — nay, jest not with me, love;
I was not tempered to be jested with,
No more than to be fondled was the serpent.
Slain! slain! oh, slaying word! thou liar, slain?
Who slew them? speak; who dare, save thou? and thou, —
Oh, horror! if thou hast, — but tell me swift.'
 'I will.'
 'Nay, nay; thou shalt, for, by great Baal,
I'll have it all, and quickly, — and as quick
When thou hast told me will I launch revenge.'
 'Calm thee,' responded Ahab.
     'And is this
A theme for calmness?' cried the crazéd queen:
'No, I will rage like yonder crashing thunder,
And my red wrath shall fall like yon bright bolt. —
All slain! my priests! linger no longer, weakling;
Disclose thy secret; man, unlock thy lips,
And let thy story rush out like the rain,
That now comes headlong from the bursting skies.'
 So spake these two; she frowning; whilst he cowered,
And deprecatingly and hoarse responds:
'Nay, urge me not: — Oh, Jezebel, yon lightnings
Do scare me less than do thy scornful eyes.'
 'Proceed,' said she, 'for I am mute: thou wentst
From here to seek for herbage. What didst find?'

  'Elijah.'
  'Ah! returned? that traitorous viper,
That ancient, haughty troubler of the land.
Where is he?' she demanded; and she panted,
Like to a tigress at the smell of blood;
While Ahab, quailing:
      'He did gird his loins,
And ran before my chariot.'
      'With its wheels
Thou shouldst have crushed him to the earth!' she shrieked: —
'But soft; he is thy prisoner, so mine; —
Mine to be tortured.'
      'Nay.'
      'Say me not, nay:
I am not in the mood to be denied.
Ahab, where is he? I will have him rent
Piecemeal before me; and Samaria's dogs
Shall fill their slack and famine-wrinkled hides
With his torn carcass. Bring him forth to me;
For, by my gods, his hour at length has come.'

  'Oh, horrid woman! hungry tigress!' groaned
The stricken Ahab; whilst she at him shoots
Out arrows from her eyes, as doth the sun
Upon the festering carcass pour his beams;
And still she cried, 'Where is thy prisoner?
Where is Elijah? where my prophets? where?
Elijah, come; come hither, miscreant, come;
Come to thy speedy death.'
     'Aye, call on him;'

With sullen sadness Ahab slow replied;
'So called thy priests upon the sleeping Baal,
Who answered not, no more than will Elijah.'

'He shall reply; and thou shalt answer too,'
She said, and stamped her foot; and still she cried: —
'Where are my priests? Of thee will I require them;'
And still she cried with threatful iterance, —
Nor went without response, for Ahab, now
Made bitter, saucily thus answered: —
                              'Ask
Of Baal, him, thy father's faithless god,
Who did forsake them in their hour of need;
Although they prayed with frantic vehemence
From morn till noon, and leaped upon his altar;
And gashed themselves with knives, and still besought
The heedless god, and still upon themselves
In vain inflicted torment.'
                    'Tell me not,'
She interrupted, 'tell me not of this;
Nor taunt me with my father's god, but say
Who dared to slay my prophets? for as deep
As hell shall be my sought revenge, and high
As heaven will I soar, should there be need,
To reach the doomed Elijah: it was he,
'Twas he who slew my prophets.'
                          And she stood
Glaring upon her husband, who replied:
'Consume me not with thy grim, scorching looks.
Although thine eyes play on me burning brands,

As from the firmament the flames came down,
Thou dread diviner, I will tell thee all.
Thou guessest right, it was Elijah slew
Thy pampered priests; t'was he who challenged them,
That they should call on Baal, — they, four hundred;
He, only one, should call upon Jehovah;
And whoso answered from the heavens by fire,
Should be acknowledged God.'

                'And thou consentedst?
Oh, most ignoble truckler!' she exclaimed;
And cast again upon him withering eyes.

  'Nay, but the people did compel me to it,
Who were that hour as king; — what could I do?'
He urged upon her in appealing tones.

    And she, with scorn: 'What couldst thou do? Is this
The language for a king, who can do all
Things that his aggregated realm can do: —
Who can condemn or pardon, as he lists;
Say, "live," or, "be cut off." Thou didst discrown
Thyself. Unmonarched man! But tell thy tale.
What next?'

          'Baal answered not' —
                  'Why should he answer?
By Baal's self, this thing will drive me mad!
Why should he answer?' she infuriate cried;

And he responded:
    'Not by fire —'

              'Fire! no,
Declaimed she, looking wickedly and wild;
Jehovah hath sent fire for these three years, —
And with it famine: Baal now sends rain.
Which is the better god? Baal sends rain,
In pity, but Jehovah fire, in fury.
Three years Jehovah gave us up — three years,
Three weary, wasted, melancholy years —
To the intolerable sun; — but give
Me up, thou baleful bringer of ill news,
The end of this interminable tale,
Whose telling seems to be a burthen to thee,
As hath Elijah long been unto me,
But shall be little longer.'

          'Lone he prayed,
At time of evening offering,' said Ahab,
'And while he lifted up his voice, fire fell
From heaven and consumed the sacrifice;
Devoured the altar, too, and at one gulp,
Licked up the water in the thirsty trench.'

  'Which thou didst fill with blood of my slain prophets;
The veins of my four hundred thou didst empty,'
Replied the savage queen, and thus pursued: —
'Now may the gods as much do unto me,

And give, like theirs, my body to the butchers,
If I allow this monstrous massacre
To go by me unpunished. Benoniah,
What, ho! come hither, Benoniah, ho!'
And Benoniah entered, and there stood
Obsequious.

        'Haste,' she said, 'make haste,
And know, thine utmost speed will lag behind
The spurred impatience whereon rides my soul
Before thee to my purpose; haste, I say;
Haste to Jezreel, and say unto Elijah: —
'Now all the gods of Zidon do to me,
As thou hast done to Baal's slaughtered prophets,
If by this time to-morrow I make not thee
As one of them whom thou hast basely murdered,'
Away now with thee.'

        And the servant sped
Out of her sight; and, turning to the king: —
'Now do I feel me better,' she exclaimed;
'Go to thy chamber, and therein seek rest;
But ask me not to follow. I will know
No rest until Elijah's hither brought,
Then shall my sight-soothed eyes, sleep-weary, wink;
And to my ears his distant groans shall come,
A lullaby to hush me on my pillow.'
    She said, and went, and Ahab sought his couch: —
Sought sleep, and found it, little troubled he

With dreams, at blood of Baal's prophets shed: —
Way-weary, soon he slept: and, all that night,
Fell over Israel abundant rain.

CANTO SECOND
    So on the morrow when he early rose,
And went into his garden, there to walk,
All nature smiled, refreshed; its drought forgot;
Nor he remembering the prophets slain,
But sauntered through his garden's pleasant walks,
Careless, till he approached unto their bounds,
And there, conveniently contiguous,
Saw Naboth's vineyard. Many a time had he
Beheld it, but now saw it with new eyes.
Fairer it looked, although its hue was brown,
From long-borne drought; and many a gaping mouth
Yet opened in the soil, that, thirsty still,
Still called for drink. But birds were in the boughs,
And butterflies and bees abroad for flowers.
And Naboth, too, with thankful heart was there,
Anticipating the returning day
When he again should train and prune his vines;
Long blighted they, and, what was of them left,
Beat down and draggling from the recent storm.
So looked the vineyard, and the pleasant prospect
Each, in his reigning mood of reverie,
Saw; the possessor sweetly satisfied;
But Ahab the fair field viewed coveting;
And of its owner thus at length demands:

'Yield me thy vineyard, prithee, for it is
Convenient unto mine, and I will give thee
Another for it, better than is this;
Or, if thou wilt, its value thou shalt have
In shining shekels, so that thou mayst buy
Whate'er thy heart is set on, as now mine
Is set on these few acres.'

                          Naboth heard,
And, hearing it, grew sad; for he was loth
To disappoint the king; yet still more loth
To part with that which his progenitors
Received when first was parcelled out the land;
Loth was, and thus, with faltering lips, and words
Firm, although few, the harsh request refused:

'Nay, king; request not what I cannot give:
I cannot yield thee that which is not mine,
But was my father's, and must be my son's.
Ask me not for it, then; yet beg aught else,
And I will give it thee; but God forbid
That I should yield thee mine inheritance.'

And Ahab turned away, and went within: —
Sullen he went, with Naboth much displeased;
And lay upon his bed, and hid his face,
And took no food. As one with hidden grief,
From loss of wife, or child, or friend, or field; —
Or one, at friend's offence; or one who, by

The world offended, from the world withdraws;
Or he who, loving, has been love denied,
Henceforward shrinks from converse with his kind:
So Ahab in his house, offended, dwelt,
Self-exiled to his room, and on his bed
For Naboth's vineyard pined. Yet pined not long;
For Jezebel came to him and enquired
Why he was sad, and wherefore took no food.
Then he rehearsed to her what Naboth said;
And how he would not yield to him the vineyard.
Whereat the queen did utter a short laugh,
And toss her head in scorn, as if it were
An easy thing to get the vineyard; flippant
She tossed her head, as scorning let, and thus
Ahab retorts:

 'Toss not thine head, thou proud one,
For he will not resign to me his birthright.'

 And now she did not laugh; but in her eyes
Upbeamed the lustre of an ill intent.
Within them seemed to burn, as beacon fires,
When on the summit of opposing hills
Flames glare, to summon the marauding tribes
To kill and plunder, and thuswise she spake: —
 'Art thou not governor in Israel?'
She said, demanding with a deep disdain,
'Arise from off thy bed, and eat, for I
Will give to thee the vineyard.'

                    Those her words:
And Ahab rose at once from off his bed;
And would have kissed her, but she turned away,
Rebukeful, and as if to punish him:
Forbidding him approach to her, as one
As yet not all deserving of her lips:
Lips to breed longing, — lips now shut as close,
In their red meeting, by her heart's resolve,
As dungeon doors; the light within her eyes
Like to the lamp that gleams behind those doors
Whereinto pity enters not, nor hope.

   So Ahab went his way, and ate and drank:
And she her thoughts set straightway unto work
To obtain for him the vineyard. Thus she did:
   Letters she wrote in Ahab's name, and sealed
Them with his seal; directed them to certain
Elders and nobles that near Naboth dwelt;
Their contents these: 'Proclaim a fast, and set
Naboth on high amongst the people. Also set
Two men of Bellal before him, two;
And let each swear they heard him late blaspheme
God and the king. Condemn him quickly; then
Let him be hurried forth into the field,
And there be stoned to death.' These letters she
Dispatched; the cruel queen! and, having thus
Dispatched them, kept herself from Ahab meaning
To give him, with possession of herself,
Possession of the vineyard: — half in pride,

And half in love she acted thus; for though
She much despised, yet more she loved the king.

   Not long she waited; — soon suborned were men
To swear — for few dared disobey the queen
(Whose word was law, even unto the king);
Two perjured witnesses proclaimed the late
So prosperous Naboth one who had blasphemed
God and the king; the doom for each crime, death;
And death soon fell upon him, for forthwith
With shower of stones they smote him till he died.

   Then, with consistent haste, to Jezebel
The news was sent, that Naboth lived no more.
When to her husband with the news she hies,
And, meeting him upon the lonely terrace,
She with a lofty and yet careless air,
As though she threw some slight gift at his feet;
Even as one who largess of vast worth
Giving, bestoweth it as if 'twere nought;
Or one should throw a bone unto a dog, —
So she, as though thus casting somewhat, said:

   'Begone, and take possession of the vineyard:
What was refused for money comes for nought.
Naboth is dead.'

                   And Ahab stood amazed.
And yet but briefly was his soul amazed;

He knew whatever Jezebel desired,
Unscrupulous, she compassed. Yet divined
He not the mode wherein his spouse had wrought,
To give to him the vineyard: — but 'twas his,
The vineyard his, a forfeit to the king.
And to the vineyard straightway he proceeds;
Soon 'midst it stood, and felt a feeble joy;
A joy diluted with remorse and pity
For the departed, foully dispossessed; —
A feeble joy he felt; — he felt no more.
Around he casts unsatisfied his eyes,
Like a starved gazer on a painted feast.
What he had coveted with strong desire,
Like that which future mothers ofttimes feel,
Now, when acquired, he only loathes, as oft
Loathes the sick man the dish which late he craved.
There while he stood, as if within a waste,
Wretched, and poor, and destitute, amidst
Bounty so ill-bestowed, so foully gained,
Sudden appears that which he fears and hates, —
Elijah's figure. At the sight he starts,
Then strove to frown. But the stern frown he gave
Met frown more stern, and eyes that, on him fixed,
Were filled with doom. He would have turned away,
But was unable, and he there stood dumb;
Held by the glamour from the prophet's eye.
As might a culprit, caught red-handed, stand
And hear his sentence, so now Ahab stood
And heard these words pronounced: —

               'Thus saith the Lord,
Hast thou then killed, and hast thou ta'en possession?
There, in the place where dogs licked Naboth's blood,
Shall dogs lick thy blood!'

                    And the caitiff king
Trembled, despite his pride; despite his rage;
Despite his sinking heart and quivering knee,
At length demanded:

               'Hast thou found me, O
Mine enemy?'
                    'I have,' replied Elijah:
'Behold, because thou hast resigned thyself
To working evil, evil shall befall
Thee and thy children; none of whom shall live:
For I will make thine house like Jeroboam's,
And Baasha's, will I make it in my wrath;
So much hast thou provoked me, and hast made
Israel to sin. Away, and tell thy wife:
The dogs shall eat the form of Jezebel
By Jezreel's wall; and whoso of thy sons
Within the city dies the dogs shall eat;
And those that perish on the open field,
The hovering, hungry vultures shall devour.'

And, lo! the prophet left him as he came,
And Ahab in the vineyard stood alone;
There stood, as might a scarecrow in a field:

Then ran unto his house, and in the hall
Met Jezebel, all unattended, sole.
As once Iscariot distracted rushed
Into the presence of the Sanhedrim,
And there threw down the dread, accursed price
For which he sold the Saviour of the world; —
So Ahab stood in presence of his wife,
And to her thus distractedly appealed,
With look of horror and extended palms: —

'Take back thy gift, take back thy bloody vineyard,
And give me Naboth as he stood in life.
What hast thou done? Woman, what hast thou done?
The blood of Naboth is demanded of us!
Give me back Naboth, living, every limb
Fair as each was before the cruel stones
Rained on him ruin. Woman, bring him back;
Heal all his bruises, bathe his hideous wounds;
Stanch, stanch the blood that trickles from his brows. —
Behold, it gushes still! the greedy dogs
Lick it lithe-tongued, — and with it mingles mine, —
Mine that the dogs shall lick; and thee, — oh, horror!
The dogs shall thee devour by Jezreel's wall,
The belly of the dogs shall be thy tomb!
Fetch Naboth back, then, from the stony tomb;
Bring back his soul, or may thine own soul sit
Sad, solitary, fainting, and forlorn,
Like to an owl upon his tomb, and there
Hoot at thine hideous self; — to death's domain
Fly, and return with him; — or stay and crouch

For ever down in Hades, like a dog,
And howl in horror at the grinning ghost
Of this black deed.'
                    Thus cried he to the queen;
Who coolly stood and answered half in scorn:

'What means this rage? what dog hath bitten you?
What tarantula that makes dance thy tongue?
Capricious man, was it for this I strove,
And compassed how to get for thee the vineyard?
Worse than the child! if thou dislikst the toy
That I have given thee, return it me:
Mine is the vineyard; mine, unmettled man.'

But while she spoke her husband paced the stones,
And wrung his hands, and called on Naboth's name;
And when she ceased, he still cried, 'Naboth, come;
Come back to life;' and still he wrung his hands;
And yet he cried, 'Come, Naboth, back to life;
Take back thy vineyard, — Ah, I would thou couldst!'

'Cease, coward; wouldst thou, then, alarm the house?'
She hoarsely asks; and reckless he replied:

'Oh, be the house alarmed; call here all souls,
To seek for Naboth's soul and bring it back:
Be all the household summoned to assist,
All summoned here to pray: — Oh God, oh God!
Why hast thou this permitted? Punish her: —
Punish the terrible Zidonian.

Murderess, avaunt! How canst thou stand unmoved;
Who shouldst make all the house resound with shrieks,
The welkin stand astonished at thy cries?

To which returned the self-collected Queen:
'Thou dost alarm thyself with thine own noise,
And thinkst thou hearst a ghost denouncing thee, —
The words from whose imaginary tongue
Are but the utterance of thy crazy thoughts.
Thou art the very idiot of the hour.
Thou dost astonish me, and I do scorn
To call thee husband, and to call thee King!
What hast thou done? Thou hast not murdered Naboth, —
Nor I, — what is the life of any man
Who calls himself our subject? If we rule
To keep him in possession, we for once
May rule to put him out of it; or even,
If needful, put him out o'th' world. Come on;
Come on;' she said: and took him by the arm,
And dragged him stoutly with her, but he still
Bemoaned himself, and called on Naboth's soul;
And thus she dragged, half bore, him up the stairs
Unto a turret high, and far removed
From ears of prying servants or courtiers; —
There left him to grow calm, and let time dull
His terror, and remorse, and scorching shame.

CANTO THIRD
So the sad king did penance, and the Lord,
Beholding it, thus to Elijah spake: —

'Seest thou how Ahab doth abase himself
Before me, and in sackcloth sits, and fasts,
And meekly bears him, dwelling with remorse
On Naboth's murder? Now, behold, because
He grieves, and thinks with pity upon Naboth,
In his time will I not bring punishment,
But in his sons' days desolate his house.'

So said the Lord; and Ahab's soul was healed
Of the dire wound received in Naboth's death:
And for three years there was no war between
Israel and its old enemy, the Syrian.
But, after that brief interval of peace,
Ahab bethought him how that Ramoth-Gilead
Belonged to Israel; though by Syria held;
And, so bethinking, to Jehoshaphat,
The King of Judah, guest and kinsman, spake:

'Brother, wilt thou go up with me to battle,
To Ramoth-Gilead, that was ours, and shall
Be Syria's no longer?'
     And the King
Of Judah gave consent; but, first, desired
Thereon consult the Prophets of the Lord.
And Israel and Judah sat on thrones; —
Enrobed they sat hard by Samaria's gate,
And all the prophets prophesied before them.
The Lord, too, in that hour sat on his throne,
And all the host of heaven were standing by:
And round He looked on all his ministers,

Mute flames of fire, and asked them: — 'Which of you
Will go from out our presence and persuade
Enquiring Ahab, so he may go up,
And fall at Ramoth-Gilead?'
       And one spake
In this wise, and another spake in that;
Until a wilier spirit, offering, said: —
'I will persuade him!'

     And the Lord said: 'How?'
And he replied: 'I will go forth, and be
A lying spirit in his prophets' mouths.'
So he went forth, descending in their midst,
And all the prophets prophesied, and said,
'Advance on Ramoth-Gilead, for the Lord
Shall yield it unto thee.'
      And this pleased Ahab,
Who thereon thus Jehoshaphat addressed: —
'Brother, behold, I will disguise myself,
And so go down into the battle, dressed
But plainly; but do thou put on thy robes.'

And once again Jehoshaphat consented,
And Ahab went disguised into the field.
But Syria had said unto his captains
Of chariots: — 'Combat not with small nor great;
Fight only with the King of Israel.'
So, when they saw Jehoshaphat, they cried,
'Here is the King of Israel!' and each
Charged on the royal chariot; the whole

With noise of gathering thunder at the wheels,
From the wide radius of the furious field,
Converging like a wedge, with seven-fold force,
Came towards him overwhelming; till he fled,
And, flying, cried in terror. Thereupon,
Pursuing him no further, they retired;
But, as they did so, far off in the field,
A certain bowman at a venture drew
His bow, and with a random arrow pierced
The recreant Ahab. Instantly he felt
His doom; and sinking in the chariot exclaimed: —
'Convey me from the battle: I am wounded!'
And, wrapped in horror, made the driver turn
The snorting steeds, and bear him swiftly forth
Unto the quiet borders of the fight.
There in his chariot, his dying bed,
He lay and watched the battle, watched the sun,
Each sink alike, as sank his fleeting soul,
While lapsed his senses towards forgetfulness; —
And still he swooned, as still the blood ran down
Into the filling chariot, till it grew
Ruddy as grew the sunset sky, that seemed
Gory, with streaks like blood, that wrapped themselves
Around about the forehead of the sun.
Thus while the sun went down, and seemed to quit
The world with wounds, did Ahab close his eyes
For ever. Darker and yet darker grew
The scene, and darker grew his soul, that then
Went down with Death to wander, and to meet
The ghost of Naboth, and the shades of priests

Whom Jezebel had murdered. But his corpse
They to Samaria brought, and buried there;
And washed the bloody chariot in the pool,
And therein washed his armor, while the dogs
Licked up the blood; for so had said the Lord
Who now began according to his word,
Delivered by Elijah's mouth, to judge
The wicked house of Ahab.
                                  Thus he, dying,
Left Jezebel a widow, and her son,
Weak as his father, and as wicked, reigned.
Two years he reigned in Israel, and then
Prone from a window of the palace fell
This two-year king; and for his death she mourned;
Nor less she mourned because her second son,
Jehoram, in despite of her, removed
Baal's image, by his father, Ahab, reared: —
And sorrows on her came; and age, that is
A sorrow in itself unto the proud.
These came, and beauty went; and sad she saw
Departing half the terror of her charms;
As might an archer see his arrows grow
Blunt in the quiver; or the lion feel
His claws no longer terrible to rend, —
His dreadful jaws, that once were gates of death,
Depopulated of the crooked fangs.

Then followed many years of various fate;
Until at length Jehoram warred against
Hazael, to recover Ramoth-Gilead,

As formerly against the Syrian
His father, Ahab, had vindictive fought;
And, as his father, did the Syrians wound him, —
Not mortally, yet wounded sore; and sick
He was, — so sick, his nephew, Ahaziah,
The son of Athaliah, Ahab's sister,
And grandson of Jehoshaphat, went down,
Leaving the siege of Ramoth-Gilead,
To see him at Jezreel, whereto retired,
He waited to recover from his wounds.

And now the end of Ahab's house had come;
For to the army now Elisha sent
One of the children of the prophets, charged
To find, and secretly anoint as king,
Jehu, a captain of Jehoram's host: —
To tell him, likewise that, by him, should all
The house of Ahab perish; for the Lord
Had chosen him to smite the house of Ahab,
His master; that He might avenge the death
Of prophets, and all servants of the Lord,
Whom Jezebel had murdered. Thither went he;
And, there arrived, the captains of the host
Saw sitting, and amongst them dark-browed Jehu,
And did to him as had Elisha bidden.
Back then he fled; and Jehu told the captains
All. And they straight with pomp of trumpets' sound,
Proclaimed him king; who, letting none depart
From Ramoth-Gilead to convey the news,
Swept towards Jezreel. With him a band of men

Went onward urging to the royal town,
Where sick Jehoram lay: — soon saw its walls,
Approaching them behind a cloud of dust,
As might an enemy by night approach
The city that he meant at morn to storm.
So storming, on they drove, till from a tower
A watchman saw them coming: — saw, surprised,
The driving was like Jehu's, furious.
Then was the feeble and affrighted king
Borne from his bed into his chariot;
Into it lifted; and his kinsman, sound, —
His visitor and nephew, Ahaziah,
Of Judah King, made haste into his own;
And both rode out beyond the walls, to meet
The rumbling wheels of Jehu. As dark clouds,
Surcharged with lightning, caught midst adverse winds,
Approach each other with o'erhanging brows;
And, ere they meet and mingle, from the one
Outsprings the lightning, and, at once, as from
The other seems to come the thunder's boom, —
So did these meet each other, and, full quick
Demands Jehoram: — 'Jehu, is it peace?'
And Jehu roared, 'What peace, then, can there be,
While whoredoms of thy mother, Jezebel,
And her enormous witchcrafts are so many?'
And now Jehoram saw his peril, saw
The face of Jehu clad in frown; and turned
His reins; and, fleeing, cried out, 'Treachery!'
Cried out too late; for Jehu, red with rage,
With all his strength his bow against him drew,

And with the arrow pierced him through the back,
The wingéd weapon leaving at his heart;
That down he sunk into the chariot,
And vanished from the view, as vanishes
A shadow from the wall.
      So died the king.
And Jehu bade his captain, Bidkar, take
The corpse, and cast it into Naboth's field;
Saying: — 'Dost thou not remember when we rode
Once with his father, Ahab, how the Lord
Laid on his seed this burden? Take him, then,
And throw him thither, as the Lord hath said.'

There was he cast, and, meantime, Ahaziah
Fled like a hare. But Jehu followed him
And bellowed for his death: 'Smite him,' he cried;
'Smite *him*, too, in his chariot:' and he still
After the homewards-rushing fugitive
Swept like the blast. But still as swiftly fled
The scared Judean King, that Jehu's self,
All furious driver though he was, was fain
To leave to others Ahaziah's doom;
And at the going up of Gur they smote him,
And having reached Megiddo, there he died.

Yet Jehu's labor was but now begun, —
A labor great as that of Hercules
Who cleansed the Augean stable: Jehu's task
To cleanse the deep-stained throne of Israel,
With blood of prophets and of Naboth soiled: —

To cleanse the throne so fearfully defiled;
And wash to sweetness in the blood of sons,
The land the father's folly had made foul; —
Nor to restrict purgation, but to take
The clotted caldron of long-seething crimes,
And as a scullion to scour it clean
In the hot gore of bloody Jezebel.
    She now of Jehu's coming having heard,
Betook herself unto her chamber, where,
Grown old and withered, she bepaints her face;
Upon her head puts sparkling coronel,
With bracelets bound her wrists, with pearls her hair
All richly twined.
      Her toilet done, behold!
Down in the courtyard, loud with iron noise,
Stern Jehu enters with a troop of horse:
When, as upon the huntsman with his gun,
Atowards her climbing, might the mother eagle
Look from her eyrie built upon the crag,
She looked down from her window to the court,
Filled with ferocious men and trampling steeds,
And saw grim Jehu riding through the gate.
Soon as she saw the slayer of her son
Rage rose within her, and, forgetting all
The stately, cold composure of a Queen,
She scowling cried: —
     'Out of my sight, fell hound!
Usurping dog, begone! By angry Baal,
Thou yet shalt feel a traitor's doom. Avaunt!
Rebellious wretch, King murderer, Avaunt!

Hast thou forgotten thee, to set thy foot,
Blood-steeped, to stain therewith these courts?
    Here I
Alone have warrant. Thirsty bloodhound, hence!
And know me now; thou, whom I long have known,
And fear me too. I fear not thee, nor these;
Nor all the recreant bands that thou canst bring,
Deserting Ramoth-Gilead. Traitor, fly!
Begone, base regicide, thou horrid bowman,
Who drew thy shaft against thy king; who slew
My boy, my son; my darling. Thou hast slain
Him. Scorpion, thou hast stung him to his death.
Infernal dragon, to thyself take wings,
And to the uttermost of the wide world
Begone, and Baal blast thee! May his sun
Dry up thy blood! May fever parch thee! Ah,
I see another murder in thy look!
Thou king assassin, hast thou come to do
To me as thou hast done unto my son?
Do not too much, thou overweening man,
Nor dream to exterminate the house of Ahab.
Fool, when did treason thrive: Beware, beware;
Jehu, remember; say, Had Zimri peace
Who slew *his* master?'
                    Jehu nought returned;
But, looking upwards to the window, called: —
'Who there is on my side?' And as if day
Should call on night, two coal-black eunuchs came
Forth to the window; and again he cried: —
'Quick, seize and throw her down!' And slave-like prompt

They strove to seize her and to throw her down;
But failed, for lo! full far aback she springs,
Like the pressed panther, nimble as the squirrel,
Into the chamber, and there stood in shade,
Glaring with cat-like eyes. But glared not long;
For to the window back they dragged, and launched her
Sheer from the sill into the pavéd court,
Whereto, like wounded sea-fowl from its cliff,
She headlong with wild shriek of horror fell.
Some of her blood outspurted on the wall,
And some upon the horses; and the hoofs
Of Jehu's charger trod her under foot.
Then when the sated crowd had left the court,
Jehu went up into the banquet-room;
There ate and drank, till, warm with wine, he said: —
'Go down, and bury yon accursed woman;
She is the daughter of a king.'
       And down they went,
But nothing of her found, except the skull,
And feet, and palms; the rest of her devoured
By dogs; torn piecemeal; by them borne away,
And eaten in the portion of Jezreel, —
Even in Naboth's vineyard; nothing left,
That one might say: — 'Lo! this was Jezebel.'

Sonnets Reprinted from the Selection
Contained in *Jephthah's Daughter*

VII
Open, my heart, thy ruddy valves;
It is thy master calls;
Let me go down, and, curious, trace
Thy labyrinthine halls.
Open, O heart, and let me view
The secrets of thy den;
Myself unto myself now show
With introspective ken.
Expose thyself, thou covered nest
Of passions, and be seen;
Stir up thy brood, that in unrest
Are ever piping keen.
Ah! what a motley multitude.
Magnanimous and mean!

XIV
The stars are glittering in the frosty sky,
Frequent as pebbles on a broad sea-coast;
And o'er the vault the cloud-like galaxy
Has marshalled its innumerable host.
Alive all heaven seems! with wondrous glow
Tenfold refulgent every star appears,
As if some wide, celestial gale did blow,
And thrice illume the ever-kindled spheres.
Orbs, with glad orbs rejoicing, burning, beam,
Ray-crowned, with lambent lustre in their zones,
Till o'er the blue, bespangled spaces seem
Angels and great archangels on their thrones;

A host divine, whose eyes are sparkling gems,
And forms more bright than diamond diadems.

XVIII
How great unto the living seem the dead!
How sacred, solemn; how heroic grown;
How vast and vague, as they obscurely tread
The shadowy confines of the dim unknown! —
For they have met the monster that we dread,
Have learned the secret not to mortal shown.
E'en as gigantic shadows on the wall
The spirit of the daunted child amaze,
So on us thoughts of the departed fall,
And with phantasma fill our gloomy gaze.
Awe and deep wonder lend the living lines,
And hope and ecstasy the borrowed beams;
While fitful fancy the full form divines,
And all is what imagination dreams.

XX
What of the Past remains to bless the Present?
The memory of good deeds.
But what of great ones? Ambition to ambition leads,
And, each step higher, but cries, 'Aspire,'
And restless step to restless step succeeds.
What is the boasted bubble, reputation?
To-day it is the world's loud cry,
Which may to-morrow die,
Or roll from generation unto generation,

And magnify, and grow to fame, —
That quenchless glory round a great man's name.
What is the good man's adequate reward?
Sense of his rectitude, and felt beatitude
Of God's regard.

LITERATURE OF CANADA
Poetry and Prose in Reprint
Douglas Lochhead, General Editor

1 *Collected Poems,* Isabella Valancy Crawford
  Introduction by James Reaney
2 *The St Lawrence and the Saguenay and Other Poems,*
  & Hesperus and Other Poems and Lyrics, Charles Sangster
  Introduction by Gordon Johnston
3 *Our Intellectual Strength and Weakness,* John George Bourinot
  'English-Canadian Literature,' Thomas Guthrie Marquis
  'French-Canadian Literature,' Camille Roy
  Introduction by Clara Thomas
4 *Selections from Canadian Poets,* Edward Hartley Dewart
  Introduction by Douglas Lochhead
5 *Poems and Essays,* Joseph Howe
  Introduction by Malcolm G. Parks
6 *Rockbound: A Novel,* Frank Parker Day
  Introduction by Allan Bevan
7 *The Homesteaders,* Robert J.C. Stead
  Introduction by Susan Wood Glicksohn
8 *The Measure of the Rule,* Robert Barr
  Introduction by Louis K. MacKendrick
9 *Selected Poetry and Critical Prose,* Charles G.D. Roberts
  Edited with an introduction and notes by W.J. Keith
10 *Old Man Savarin Stories: Tales of Canada and Canadians*
  E.W. Thomson
  Introduction by Linda Sheshko
11 *Dreamland and Other Poems & Tecumseh: A Drama,* Charles Mair
  Introduction by Norman Shrive

12 *The Poems of Archibald Lampman (including At the Long Sault)*
    Archibald Lampman
    Introduction by Margaret Coulby Whitridge
13 *The Poetical Works of Alexander McLachlan,* Alexander McLachlan
    Introduction by E. Margaret Fulton
14 *Angéline de Montbrun,* Laure Conan
    Translated and introduced by Yves Brunelle
15 *The White Savannahs,* W.E. Collin
    Introduction by Germaine Warkentin
16 *The Search for English-Canadian Literature: An Anthology of Critical Articles from the Nineteenth and Early Twentieth Centuries*
    Edited and introduced by Carl Ballstadt
17 *The First Day of Spring: Stories and Other Prose,*
    Raymond Knister
    Selected and introduced by Peter Stevens
18 *The Canadian Brothers; or, The Prophecy Fulfilled: A Tale of the Late American War,* John Richardson
    Introduction by Carl F. Klinck

www.ingramcontent.com/pod-product-compliance
Lightning Source LLC
Chambersburg PA
CBHW071851290426
44110CB00013B/1102